THE ULTIMATE OXBRIDGE

INTERVIEW GUIDE: ECONOMICS

UniAdmissions

Published by *RAR Medical Services Limited*
www.uniadmissions.co.uk
info@uniadmissions.co.uk
Tel: +44 (0) 208 068 0438

THE ULTIMATE OXBRIDGE INTERVIEW GUIDE

ECONOMICS

BEN GREGORY

CHLOE BOWMAN

GRACE DAVIS

DR. ROHAN AGARWAL

UniAdmissions

ABOUT THE AUTHORS

Ben is an economist, currently studying for a masters degree in economics at **LSE**. He completed his undergraduate degree in PPE at the **University of Oxford**. His academic interests are in environmental economics and ethical investment. In addition to his economics research, he works closely with JP Morgan, and enjoys playing football with his local club in his spare time.

Chloe graduated with an **MEng in Engineering Science** from **Keble College, Oxford** in 2019. During her time at Oxford she researched the use of Carbon Nano Tubes

in a joint project with a team at the Large Hadron Collider at CERN. She was also awarded several national engineering scholarships sponsored by the Institute of Mechanical Engineers, Institute of Engineering Technology, and Jaguar Land Rover among others.

Chloe has since begun to study for a second Master's degree in Managing Technological Development, as well as having articles published in national and online press such as The Huffington Post. Since university, Chloe works as a tutor and educational consultant, specialising in supporting students applying to Science, Technology, Engineering, and Maths degrees at Oxford and Cambridge. Outside science and education, Chloe enjoys baking and tending to her aquaponics system!

Grace has recently completed her undergraduate in **PPE at Hertford College, Oxford**, and her masters in The History of Political Thought and Intellectual History at UCL/QMUL. She enjoys tutoring to teach more students about the intersection between Politics and Philosophy which she has found myself especially interested in over the course of her academic career. Having been the only person from her high school to have gone to Oxford, Grace has a particular interest in helping students to fulfil their potential and study at Oxbridge.

Rohan is the **Director of Operations** at *UniAdmissions* and is responsible for its technical and commercial arms. He graduated from Gonville and Caius College, Cambridge and is a fully qualified doctor. Over the last five years, he has tutored hundreds of successful Oxbridge and Medical applicants. He has also authored ten books on admissions tests and interviews.

Rohan has taught physiology to undergraduates and interviewed medical school applicants for Cambridge. He has published research on bone physiology and writes education articles for the Independent and Huffington Post. In his spare time, Rohan enjoys playing the piano and table tennis.

Contents

Preface

Oxbridge interviews are frequently the source of intriguing stories. You'll frequently hear tales of students who were asked seemingly obscure questions e.g. "Why do we have two nostrils but only one mouth?", or impossibly difficult ones e.g. "How many grains of sand are there in the world?"

If taken in context, both of these are very fair Oxbridge interview questions. The first would naturally lead to a discussion concerning the evolution of sensory organs and the pros/cons of having multiple mouths e.g. reduced risk of infections vs. inability to eat and speak simultaneously etc.

The latter question would test a candidate's ability to breakdown an initially very large problem into more bite-sized chunks in order to manage it e.g. surface area of the Earth, percentage of the Earth covered by land, percentage of land covered by sand, average depth of sand and so on.

Oxbridge interviews are not about testing your knowledge. Instead, they are about testing what you can do with the knowledge you already possess. Remember, once you're at university, you will rapidly assimilate a great deal of new information (so much so that you will start to wonder what all the fuss A-levels were about).

This is the main reason why it's not particularly useful for interviewers to ask purely knowledge based questions e.g. "What is the normal plasma concentration of magnesium?". Knowledge of isolated facts is neither necessary nor sufficient for a successful Oxbridge interview. Instead, it is the application of some basic facts to novel situation that is the hallmark of success.

One of the best ways to demonstrate this is to discuss my interview experiences at Cambridge when I applied to study Medicine several years ago.

Interview One:

This was my first science interview and the interviewer was delighted when he found out I studied physics at A2. His opening question was "What have you read recently?" I explained I'd been reading about the new drug Rosuvastatin – a statin that was being recommended for everyone above a certain age (regardless of their actual cholesterol levels). The follow-up questions were what you would expect e.g. "How do statins work?" (Ensure you know the basics of any topic that you voluntarily bring up), "What are the risks/benefits of giving them to everyone?"

This led to a discussion on how I would convince someone that this drug was useful for them, followed by how I would convince someone that blue light was more damaging than red. I struggled with this for a while, bouncing ideas back and forth (with each of them sequentially shot down) until I finally stumbled onto Einstein's $E=hf$. This led to a discussion about why the sky is blue and sunsets can be a myriad of colours. All of this culminated in the classic- "What colour is the Sun in reality?" (Hint: It's not yellow, orange or red!). This is the question that tabloids would take out of context to make the interview seem like an array of bizarre questions when in fact this was perfectly reasonable giving the preceding questions.

This interview serves as a perfect example of a non-scripted interview, i.e. one where the interviewer was happy to bounce ideas between us and forced me to think about concepts in ways I never had. I'm certain that if I had offered a different answer to the initial question about my reading, the discussion would have gone along a significantly different route.

Interview Two:

My second interview was more scripted — the interviewer had a pre-set agenda with corresponding questions that he wanted to discuss. Given that this person is known to ask the same interview questions annually, I've refrained from including specifics in order to not spoil the plot for everyone and to unfairly put future applicants at an advantage (or disadvantage!).

After going through my BMAT essay very briefly, he asked me to draw a graph on his whiteboard. This was no easy task. I spent fifteen minutes struggling with this graph due to its unusual axis. Like many candidates, I made the mistake of learning about excessively complex topics like the Complement Membrane attack complex and ignored much core A-level topics like human physiology. This meant that I wasn't completely sure about a basic fact that was required for the graph. This was a tough interview and at the end of it, I was certain I had flunked it. This was compounded by the fact that other candidates were bragging about how they had got the correct graph in only thirty seconds.

When you're in the waiting room with the other candidates, it may appear that many of them are far smarter than you and know a lot more. Again, remember that the entire point of an interview is to assess your ability to apply knowledge.

People get nervous and unconfident whilst waiting for interviews. One of the ways they try to feel more secure is by exerting their intellectual superiority. In this example (although there were some exceptions), the students who tended to arrive at the answer very quickly were unsuccessful. This is likely because they had previous knowledge of the question from their school/extra reading. Although this allowed them to get the correct answer quickly, they were unable to explain the intermediate steps that led them to it, i.e. they *knew* the topic but didn't *understand* it.

Learning Points:

As you can see, I made lots of errors in my interview preparation. Please learn from them. Good students learn from their mistakes but *great* students learn from others' mistakes.

1) **Don't be put off by what other candidates say** in the waiting room. Focus on yourself – you are all that matter. If you want to be in the zone, then I would recommend taking some headphones and your favourite music.

2) **Don't read up on multiple advanced topics in depth**. Choose one topic and know it well. Focus the rest of your time on your core A-level syllabus. You are not expected to know about the features of Transverse Myelitis, but you will be expected to be able to rattle off a list of 10 cellular organelles.

3) **Don't worry about being asked seemingly irrelevant questions** that you'll often hear in the media. These are taken out of context. Focus on being able to answer the common questions e.g. "Why this university?" etc.

4) **Don't lose heart** if your interviews appear to have gone poorly. If anything, this can actually be a good sign as it shows that the interviewer pushed you to your limits rather than giving up on you as you clearly weren't Oxbridge material.

5) **Don't give up.** When you're presented with complex scenarios, go back to the absolute basics and try to work things out using first principles. By doing this and thinking out loud, you allow the interviewer to see your logical train of thought so that they can help you when you become stuck.

Good Luck!

Dr Rohan Agarwal

THE BASICS

What is an Oxbridge Interview?

An interview is a personal 20-30 minute session with one or two members of academic staff from Oxford or Cambridge. The interviewers will ask questions and **guide the applicant to an answer**. The answers usually require a large degree of creative and critical thought, as well as a good attitude and a sound foundation of subject-specific knowledge.

Why is there an Interview?

Most of the applicants to Oxbridge will have outstanding grades, predicted exam results, sample course work and personal statements. Interviews are used to help **determine which applicants are best-suited** for Oxbridge. During the interview, each applicant has a unique chance to demonstrate their creativity and critical thinking abilities- skills that Oxford and Cambridge consider vital for successful students.

Who gets an Interview?

At Cambridge, any applicant who might have a chance at being accepted to study will be called for interview. This corresponds to approximately **90%** of applicants. At Oxford, a slightly smaller **40-80%** of applicants are interviewed (applicants are shortlisted based on their admissions test results and UCAS form). No one is offered a place to study without attending an interview.

Who are the interviewers?

The interviews are conducted by a senior member of staff for the subject you've applied to; usually this person is the **Director of Studies** for that subject. There may also be a second interviewer who takes notes on the applicant or also asks questions. Interviewers describe this experience as just as nerve-wracking for them as for the applicants, as they are responsible for choosing the right students for Oxford and Cambridge.

When is the Interview?

Interviews are held in the **beginning of December** and some applicants may be invited back in January for a second round of interviews at another college. There are usually multiple interviews on the same day, either for different subjects or at different colleges. You will normally be given 2 weeks' notice before your interview- so you should hear back by late November, but it is useful to **begin preparing for the interview before you're officially invited**.

Where is the Interview?

The interviews are held in Oxford and Cambridge **at the college you applied to**. Oxford applicants may have additional interviews at another college than the one applied to. Cambridge applicants may get 'pooled' – be required to have another set of interviews in January at a different college. If you are travelling from far away, most Oxbridge colleges will provide you free accommodation and food for the duration of your stay if you wish to arrive the night before your interview.

Very rarely, interviews can be held via Skype at an exam centre- this normally only applies to international students or for UK students in extreme circumstances.

How should I use this book?

The best way to gain the most from this book is to let it guide your independent learning.

1. Read through the **General Interview** section.
2. Read the **Subject Interview** chapter for your subject.
3. Read chapters on PPE & HSPS and Maths.

Finally, work your way through the past interview questions – remember, you are not expected to know the answers to them, and they have been included here so that you can start to appreciate the style of questions that you may get asked. **It is not a test of what you know – but what you can do with what you already know.**

Oxbridge Tutorials & Supervisions

Hopefully, by this point, you're familiar with the unique Oxbridge teaching system. Students on the same course will have lectures and practicals together. These are supplemented by college-based tutorials/supervisions. A tutorial/supervision is an **individual or small group session** with an academic to **discuss ideas, ask questions, and receive feedback** on your assignments. During the tutorial/supervision, you will be pushed to think critically about the material from the course in novel and innovative ways. To get the most out of Oxbridge, you need to be able to work in this setting and take criticism with a positive and constructive attitude.

The **interviews are made to be model tutorials/supervisions**, with an academic questioning an applicant and seeing if they can learn, problem-solve, demonstrate motivation for their subject. It is by considering this ultimate goal of the interview that you can start to understand how to present and prepare yourself for the Oxbridge interview process.

What Are Interviewers Looking for?

There are several qualities an interviewer is looking for the applicant to demonstrate during the interview. While an applicant may think the most 'obvious' thing interviewers are looking for is excellent factual knowledge, this is already displayed through exam results. Whilst having an excellent depth of knowledge may help you perform better during an interview, **you're unlikely to be chosen based solely on your knowledge**. The main thing an interviewer is looking for is for the applicant to demonstrate critical thought, excellent problem-solving skills and intellectual flexibility, as well as **motivation for the subject and suitability for small group teaching**. It is also important for them to see that the applicant is willing to persevere with a challenging problem even if the answer is not immediately apparent.

How to Communicate Answers

The most important thing to do when communicating your answers is to **think out loud**. This will allow the interviewer to understand your thought processes. They will then be able to help you out if you get stuck. You should never give up on a question; show that you won't be perturbed at the first sign of hardship as a student, and remain positive and **demonstrate your engagement with the material**. Interviewers enjoy teaching and working with students who are as enthusiastic about their subject as they are.

Try to **keep the flow of conversation going** between you and your interviewer so that you can engage with each other throughout the entire interview. The best way to do this is to just keep talking about what you are thinking. It is okay to take a moment when confronted with a difficult question or plan your approach, but ensure you let the interviewer know this by saying, *"I'm going to think about this for a moment"*. Don't take too long- if you are finding the problems difficult, the **interviewers will guide and prompt you** to keep you moving forward. They can only do this if they know you're stuck!

The questions that you'll be asked are designed to be difficult, so don't panic up when you don't immediately know the answer. Tell the interviewer what you do know, offer some ideas, talk about ways you've worked through a similar problem that might apply here. If you've never heard anything like the question asked before, say that to the interviewer, *"I've never seen anything like this before"* or *"We haven't covered this yet at school"*, but don't use that as an excuse to quit. This is **your chance to show that you are eager to engage with new ideas**, so finish with *"But let's see if I can figure it out!"* or *"But I'm keen to try something new!"*. There are many times at Oxbridge when students are in this situation during tutorials/supervisors and you need to show that you can persevere in the face of difficulty (and stay positive and pleasant to work with while doing so).

Types of Interviews

There are, at Cambridge and for some Oxford subjects, several different types of interview that you can be called for. **Every applicant will have at least one subject interview**. Applicants to some courses may also have a **general interview**, especially if they are applying for an arts subject. Either way, you will be asked questions that touch on the course you are applying to study. It may be useful to **look at your interviewers' teaching backgrounds and published work** as this could potentially shed some light on the topics they might choose to discuss in an interview. However, there is absolutely no need to know the intricacies of their research work so don't get bogged down in it. Interviews tend to open with easier and more general questions and become more detailed and complicated as you are pushed to explore topics in greater depth.

Using the Practice Questions

This book contains over 900 practice interview questions. **They are all actual questions that successful Oxbridge applicants were asked in their interview**. However, it is important you take these with a pinch of salt.

They are taken out of context and only included to give you a flavour of the style and difficulty of real Oxbridge interview questions. Don't fall into the trap of thinking that your interview will consist of a series of irrelevant and highly specific knowledge based questions.

Thus, it does little benefit to rote learn answers to all the practice questions in this book as they are unlikely to be repeated. Instead, follow our top tips, take inspiration from the worked answers and put in some hard work – you'll be sure to perform well on the day

---

OXBRIDGE INTERVIEWS ARE **NOT** ABOUT YOUR KNOWLEDGE

THEY ARE ABOUT WHAT YOU CAN DO
WITH THE KNOWLEDGE YOU ALREADY POSSESS

GENERAL INTERVIEWS

A general interview is a get-to-know-you session with senior admissions tutors. This is your chance to demonstrate a passion for Oxbridge; that you have understood the Oxbridge system, have a genuine interest in being a student, and could contribute to Oxbridge if you were admitted. These are more common for arts and humanities applicants, but all applicants should nevertheless be prepared for a general interview.

- This will be less specific than the subject interview. The interviewers will focus more on your personal statement, any essays you may have submitted or have completed on the day of the interview and may discuss your SAQ form if you are applying to Cambridge.

- One of the interviewers may not be a specialist in the subject you've applied for. Don't be put off by this – you aren't expected to have any knowledge of their subject.

- Ensure that you have read your personal statement and any books/journals that you've claimed to have read in your application. You will seem unenthusiastic and dishonest if you can't answer questions regarding topics and activities that you claim to know about. Remember that it is much better to show a good understanding of a few texts than to list lots of texts that you haven't properly read.

- Read and re-read the essays you have submitted. Be prepared to expand on the ideas you have explored in them. Remember, that the interviewers may criticise what you've argued in your submitted essays. If you believe in it, then defend your view but don't be stubborn.

- You will normally be asked if you have any questions at the end of the interview. Avoid saying things like, *"How did I do?"* – Instead use this as an opportunity to show the interviewers the type of person you are e.g. *"How many books can I borrow from the library at one time?"*

What type of questions might be asked?

The three main questions that are likely to come up in an Oxbridge interview are:

- *Why Oxford/Cambridge?*
- *Why this subject?*
- *Why this college?*

You may also get asked more specific questions about the teaching system or about your future career aspirations. This will also be the time for discussing any extenuating circumstances for poor exam results and similar considerations.

To do well in a general interview, your answers should show that you understand the Oxbridge system and that you have strong reasons for applying there. Thus, it is essential that you prepare detailed answers to the common questions above so that you aren't caught off guard. In addition, you should create a list of questions that could potentially be asked based on your personal statement or any submitted work.

Worked Questions

Below are a few examples of how to start breaking down general interview questions- complete with model answers.

Q1: How did you choose which college to apply for?

This question is a good opportunity to tell the interviewer about yourself, your hobbies, motivations, and any interesting projects you have undertaken. You can demonstrate that you have read about the College thoroughly and you know what differentiates your College from the others. The decisive factors can include a great variety of different things from history, alumni, location in the city, community, sports clubs, societies, any positive personal experiences from Open Day and notable scholars.

This is a warm up question – an ice-breaker – so just be natural and give an honest answer. You may not want to say things like, *"I like the statutes in the garden"*. The more comprehensive your answer is, the better.

Good Applicant: I chose which college to apply for based on a number of factors that were important to me. First of all, I needed to consider how many other students at my college would be studying the same subject as me; this was important to me as I want to be able to engage in conversation about my subject with my peers. Secondly, I considered the location of the college as I wanted to ensure I had easy access to the faculty library and lecture theatres. Thirdly, I am a keen tennis player and so looked for a college with a very active tennis society. Finally, I wanted to ensure that the college I chose would feel right for me and so I looked around several Cambridge colleges before coming to my conclusion.

This response is broken down into a set of logical and yet personal reasons. **There is no right answer to this question** and the factors which influence this decision are likely to be unique for each individual. However, each college is unique and therefore the interviewer wants to know what influenced your decision. Therefore, **it's essential that you know what makes your college special** and separates it from the others. Even more importantly, you should know what the significance of that will be for you. For example, if a college has a large number of mathematicians, you may want to say that by attending that college, it would allow you to discuss your subject with a greater number of people than otherwise.

A **poor applicant** may respond with a noncommittal shrug or an answer such as, *"my brother went there"*. The interviewers want to see that you have researched the university and although the reason for choosing a college won't determine whether or not you get into the university, a lack of passion and interest in the college will greatly influence how you are perceived by the interviewers.

Q2: Why have you chosen to apply to study at 'Oxbridge', rather than another Russell Group university?

This is a very broad question and one which is simply designed to draw out the motives and thinking behind your application, as well as giving you an opportunity to speak freely about yourself.

A **good applicant** would seek to address this question in two parts, the first addressing the key features of Oxbridge for their course and the second emphasising their own personality traits and interests which make them most suited to the Oxbridge system.

It is useful to start off by talking about the supervision/tutorial system and why this method of very small group teaching is beneficial for studying your subject, both for the discussion of essay work and, more crucially, for developing a comprehensive understanding of your subject. You might also like to draw upon the key features of the course at Oxford and Cambridge that distinguish it from courses at other universities.

When talking about yourself, a good answer could take almost any route, though it is always productive to talk about which parts of your subject interest you, why this is the case, and how this ties in with the course at Oxford/Cambridge. You might also mention how the Oxbridge ethos suits your personality, e.g. how hard work and high achievement are important to you and you want to study your chosen subject in real depth, rather than a more superficial course elsewhere.

A **poor applicant** would likely demonstrate little or no knowledge of their course at Oxford/Cambridge and volunteer little information about why studying at Oxbridge would be good for them or why they would be suited to it. It's important to focus on your interests and abilities rather than implying that you applied because Oxbridge is the biggest name or because your family or school had expected you to do so.

Q3: What do you think you can bring to the college experience?

This is a common question at general interviews and **you need to show that you would be a good fit for the College** and that you are also really motivated because you have researched the college's facilities, notable fellows and alumni, societies and sports clubs etc. You can mention that you have looked at the website, talked to alumni and current students.

This question also gives the interviewer an excellent opportunity to learn about your personality, hobbies and motivations. Try to avoid listing one thing after the other for 5 minutes. Instead, you should try to give a balanced answer in terms of talking about the College and yourself. You should talk about your skills and give examples when you had to work in a team, deliver on strict deadlines, show strong time-management skills etc. You should also give a few examples from your previous studies, competitions or extracurricular activities (including sports and music).

Q4: Tell me about a recent news article not related to your subject that has interested you.

This can be absolutely anything and your interviewers just want to see that **you are aware of the world in which you live** and have a life outside of your subject. You could pick an interesting topic ahead of time and cultivate an opinion which could spark a lively discussion.

Q5: Which three famous people would you most like to be stuck on a desert island with?

This is a personal question that might be used by your interviewers as an 'ice-breaker' – you can say absolutely anyone but try to have a good justification (and avoid being melodramatic). This is a really **good chance to show your personality and sense of humour**. This is also a good question to ease you into the flow of the interview and make yourself feel more comfortable.

Q6: Do you think you're 'clever'?

Don't let this one faze you! Your interviewers are not being glib but instead want to see how you cope with questions you may not have anticipated. You could discuss different forms of intelligence, e.g. emotional vs. intellectual, perhaps concluding that you are stronger in one over the other.

Q7: What experiences do you have which suggest to you that you'll cope well with the pressures of Oxbridge?

The **interviewers want to hear that you know what you're signing up to** and that you are capable of dealing with stress. If you have any experience of dealing with pressure or meeting strict deadlines, this would be a good opportunity to talk about them. Otherwise, mention your time management skills and your ability to prioritise workloads. You could also mention how you deal with stress, e.g. do you like running? Yoga? Piano? Etc.

Q8: Why are you in this room right now?

There are hundreds of potential responses to this type of question, and the interviewer will see this as a chance to get to know your personality and how you react to unusual situations.

Firstly, **take the question seriously**, even if it strikes you as funny or bizarre. A good response may begin with: "There are many reasons why I am in this room. There are lots of smaller events and causes that have led up to me being here". You might choose to discuss your desire to attend Oxbridge, the fact that you have travelled to the college to take your interview. You might choose to discuss the interviewer or college's taste and budget when it came to selecting the chair you are sitting in, as that determined why and how you have come to be sitting in that particular chair, rather than any other chair. You might then simply mention that you were invited by the interviewer to take a seat.

A weak response to this type of question would be to dismiss it as silly or irrelevant.

Q9: Let's say you're hosting a small private party, and you have a magical invitation which will summon anyone from time and space to your dining table. Who's name do you write on the invitation?

This is a fairly straightforward question to get in a general interview, so use it to show your personality and originality, and to talk about something you are really passionate about.

If you are asked a question like this, give an answer that is relevant to your application. This is not the time to start talking about how you are a huge fan of Beyonce and would just love to have dinner together! You should also avoid generic answers like "God".

If you would love to meet Obama and know more about him, consider what that would be like. Would he be at liberty to answer your questions? Might you not get more information from one of his aides or from a close friend, rather than the man himself? As this is a simple question, try to unpick it and answer it in a sophisticated way, rather than just stating the obvious.

Q10: What was the most recent film you watched?

This question seems simple and appears to require a relatively short answer. However, a good candidate will use a simple question such as this as an opportunity to speak in more depth and **raise new and interesting topics of conversation**: "What I find particularly interesting about this film was…. It reminded me of….. In relation to other works of this period/historical context, I found this particular scene very interesting as it mirrored/contrasted with my previous conceptions of this era as seen in other works, for example… I am now curious to find out more about… This film made me think about…etc."

Whilst it is extremely important to respond accurately to the questions posed by the interviewer, do not be afraid to **take the conversation in the direction led by your personal interests**. This sort of initiative will be encouraged.

Q11: How do you think the university will evaluate whether or not you have done well at the end of your degree, do you think that this manner of assessment is fair?

This question invites you to show your potential and how diverse your interests are. There are three aspects of this question that you should consider in order to give a complete answer: "end of your time here", "measure" and "your achievements". You may want to discuss your hobbies and interests and potential achievements regarding various aspects of university life including academia, sports, student societies, jobs, volunteering etc.

Then you may want to enter into a discussion about whether there is any appropriate measure of success. How could you possibly compare sporting excellence to volunteering? Is it better to be a specialist or a generalist? This ultimately comes down to your personal motivation and interests as you might be very focused on your studies or other activities (e.g. sports, music). Thus, multiple things would contribute to your success at university and your degree is only likely to be one way to measure this. Finally, it might be a great closing line to mention that getting your degree might not be the "end of your time here".

Q12: Tell me why you think people should go to university.

This sounds like a very general question at first but it is, in fact, about your personal motivations to go to university. You don't need to enter into a discussion about what universities are designed for or any educational policy issues as the interviewer is unlikely to drive the discussion towards this in a general interview.

The best strategy is to **discuss your motivations**- this could include a broad range of different things from interest in a certain field, inspiring and diverse environments, academic excellence, opening up of more opportunities in the future and buying time to find out more about yourself etc. As it is very easy to give an unfocused answer, you should limit yourself to a few factors. You can also comment on whether people should go to university and whether this is good for the society.

Q13: I'm going to show you a painting, imagine that you have been tasked with describing this to someone over the phone so that they can recreate it, but you only have a minute. How would you describe the painting in order to make the recreation as close to the original as possible?

This question is very common and surprisingly difficult. **You can take a number of approaches**. Ensure that you have a concrete idea of the structure you will use to describe the painting. For example, you could begin with your personal feelings about it, then the colours and atmosphere the painting creates, then the exact objects, then their respective position and size. It does not matter which approach you take but this question is designed to test your way of organising and presenting your ideas.

You could also comment on the difficulty of the task and argue that human language limits you from adequately describing smell, taste, sound, and vision. Modern language applicants may have read about Wittgenstein, in which case, they can reference his works on the limitations and functions of language here.

Q14: Which person in the past would you most like to interview, and why?

This is a personal question but try to **avoid generic and mainstream answers**. Keep in mind that you can find out much more about a particular period or era by speaking to everyday citizens or advisors for politicians or other important figures. It is much more important to identify what you want to learn about and then set criteria to narrow down the possible list of persons. This question opens the floor for developing an analytical, quasi-scientific approach to your research.

Q15: What's an interesting thing that's been happening in the news recently?

Whilst this question may be asked at a general interview, it's a good idea to come up with something that is related to your course. Instead of going into technical detail with an interviewer who may be from a completely different discipline, it is better to give a brief overview of the article and then put it into a broader context.

For example, an economics applicant may want to discuss the most recent banking scandal. A physics applicant may want to discuss a recent discovery.

A **good** candidate might say something like "That's a great question, there are lot of really interesting things which have happened recently. For me I think the most interesting one is the confirmation of increased magnetic movement in muons at the Fermi National Accelerator in America.

This is mainly interesting for two reasons, I think that it as always interesting when you have examples of the standard model perhaps not working as it should. It's seemed like there have been problems with the way we understand everything working for some time now, but actually being able to perhaps find a new force, and write new laws of physics is incredibly exciting! The other reason this in particular is interesting is because it shows some of the strengths and weaknesses of the scientific process. Even though this magnetic movement has been detected in multiple experiments for over twenty years, it is still not something which we can consider confirmed, because this movement has not been confirmed to the five-sigma level of certainty needed to announce an actual discovery. This rigour helps ensure that we don't have incidents like the Pons and Felischmann Cold Fusion scandal, but does also mean that we will have waited more than two decades to start re-writing the textbooks at the point that this can be confirmed, assuming of course that it ever is. Events like this one really show how thorough and reliable scientific work can be, but also that in areas like theoretical physics things can be very slow to change."

The answer should not be a complete analysis of the issue but an intuitive and logical description of an event, with a good explanation of why it is interesting to you, personally. They really want to see here your enthusiasm for the topic of the article in question (and hopefully the topic of your chosen course) as well as your ability to reflect in a mature way on its most general themes.

Q16: Can people be entirely apolitical? Are you political?

In general, you should avoid expressing any very extreme views at all during interviews. The answer, *"I am not political"* is not the most favourable either. This question invites you to **demonstrate academic thinking in a topic which could be part of everyday conversations**. You are not expected to present a full analysis of party politics and different ideologies. It doesn't matter if you actually have strong political views; the main point is to talk about your perception of what political ideas are present and how one differs from the other.

With such a broad question – you have the power to choose the topic- be it wealth inequality, nuclear weapons, corruption, human rights, or budget deficit etc. Firstly, you should **explain why that particular topic or political theme is important**. For example, the protection of fundamental human rights is crucial in today's society because this introduces a social sensitivity to our democratic system where theoretically 51% of the population could impose its will on the other 49%. On the other hand, it should be noted that Western liberal values may contradict with social, historical and cultural aspects of society in certain developing countries, and a different political discourse is needed in different countries about the same questions. Secondly, you should discuss whether that topic is well-represented in the political discourse of our society and what should be done to trigger a more democratic debate.

Q17: One of the unique features of the Oxbridge education is the supervision system, one-on-one tutorials every week. This means a heavy workload, one essay every week with strict deadlines. Do you think you can handle this?

By this point, you should hopefully have a sound understanding of the supervision/tutorial systems. You should also be aware of the possibility of spending long hours in the library and meeting tight deadlines so this question should not be surprising at all. It gives you an opportunity to **prove that you would fit into this educational system very well**. Firstly, you should make it clear that you understand the system and the requirements. On average, there is one essay or problem sheet every week for each paper that you are reading which requires going through the reading list/lecture notes and engaging with wider readings around certain topics or problems. Secondly, you should give some examples from your past when you had to work long hours or had strict deadlines etc. You should also tell the interviewer how you felt in these situations, what you enjoyed the most and what you learned from them. Finally, you may wish to stress that you would *"not only be able to cope with the system but also enjoy it a great deal"*.

Q18: If you had to live in the world of a book you have read, which book would it be, and whose role would you take?

This question is an ice-breaker- the interviewer is curious to find out what type of novels you read and how thoroughly you are reading them. You want to show that you are capable of thinking on your feet, talk them through why you've chosen their particular world, does it have advantages which outweigh its pitfalls. For example, if you say you like Robin Hood, it is a world in which you could carry out noble deeds in an idyllic setting, but you also have to deal with poverty, homelessness, and a brutal regime. If you would like to live here, then tell them why. As for the character, centre in on who you want, for instance Robin himself, explain his situation briefly as becoming an outlaw, resisting the authorities, and aiding the poor and his fellow men. Would you like to take his role because you would like to do the things he did, or do you feel that you could 'be' him differently, or even better? Would you be able to learn or grow from entering your chosen world, and being a certain character - think of what course you are applying to, and see if there are particular skills which you think this experience could teach you, empathy, if you're applying for medicine, or social responsibility, if you're applying for economics & management, as examples.

The main point is to be able to **give a very brief summary of the character and the world in which they live in**, (especially if you choose a less well-known work), and have a good and interesting justification for choosing them.

Q19: Do you think that we should give applicants access to a computer during their interviews?

This is a classic open question for an insightful debate. The most important thing to realise here is that **Oxbridge education is about teaching you how to think** in clear, structured and coherent ways as opposed to collecting lots of facts from the internet.

Internet access would provide each candidate with the same available information and therefore the art of using information to make sound arguments would be the sole decisive factor. On the other hand, the information overload can be rather confusing. In general, a braindump is not helpful at the interview as it does not demonstrate in-depth understanding and analysis of any problems. At the end of the day, it comes down to the individual candidate, i.e. what would you look up on the Internet during the interview? Would you want to rely on unverified knowledge? How reliable is that information on the internet? How could you verify this information?

Q20: What was your proudest moment?

This is another chance to highlight your suitability for the course, so try to **make it as subject-relevant as possible**. *"I felt proud to be awarded first place in a poetry competition with a sonnet I wrote about…"* (if you're applying for English). *"I recently won the Senior Challenge for the UK Mathematics Trust."*, *"Achieving a 100% mark in my AS-level History and English exams – an achievement I hope to emulate at A2".*

Of course, it's not easy to pick one moment and this is not a question you might have expected. You could also argue that you can't really compare your achievements from different fields e.g. your 100% Physics AS-level and football team captaincy, but be careful. You should always try to settle on one in the end, this will show the interviewer that you are able to answer the questions you are given, even if they are very challenging, which is a vital skill. A useful tip here is to talk them through your thought process, there are several competing moment which could be your proudest, and you need to work out which one was the best. Try separating out the ones which impressed others versus those which were more personal to you, and decide on one which, overall, was the most impactful. This way, you have talked through a number of impressive things with the interviewer, but you have shown critical thinking skills and attention to detail in providing a definitive answer.

Q21: Would you ever use a coin-flip to make a choice, if so, when?

This question can be quite tricky and aims at revealing how you make decisions in your life, your understanding of abstract concepts, rationality and probabilities. You should begin with answering the question from your perspective, you can be honest about it but give a justification even if you never want to make decisions based on luck. Try to **give a few examples when tossing a coin could be a good idea**, or would cause no harm. Then you can take the discussion to a more abstract level and argue that once all yes/no decisions are made by tossing a coin in the long run, the expected value should be fifty-fifty so you might not be worse-off at all and you could avoid the stress of making decisions (although this is very simplistic).

You could also reference the stock markets where high returns may be purely luck-dependent. On the other hand, **rational decision-making is part of human nature** and analysing costs and benefits would result in better decisions in the long-run than tossing a coin. In addition, this would incentivise people to conduct research, collect information, develop and test theories, etc. As you see, the question could be interpreted to focus on the merits of rigorous scientific methodology.

31

Q22: If you had omnipotence for a moment, but had to use it to change only one thing, what would it be?

This question tests your sound reasoning and clear presentation of your answer and the justification for it. There is no right or wrong "one thing" to choose. It is equally valid to choose wealth inequality or the colour of a double-decker bus if you argue it well! It should be noted that if you've applied for social sciences, it is a better strategy to choose a related topic to show your sensitivity to social issues.

Firstly, you should choose something you would like to change while demonstrating clear thinking, relevant arguments. Secondly, you are expected to discuss how, and to what extent, you would and could change it. Again, a better candidate would realise that **this is not necessarily a binomial problem** – either change it or not – but there may be a spectrum between these two extremes. Once you've identified the thing you'd like to change, talk them through why. A good way to make sure you always do this is by thinking aloud, and walking the interviewer through the way you would reach this conclusion yourself.

Q23: Oxford, as you know, has access to some very advanced technology. In the next room we actually have the latest model of time machine, if we gave you the opportunity to use it later, when would you go?

This is a question where you can really use your imagination (or draw on History GCSE or A-level). **You can say absolutely any time period** in the past or the far future but you must have a good reason for it which you communicate to the interviewer. This doesn't necessarily need to be linked to your subject.

For example, *"I would love to see a time when my parents were little children and see where and how they grew up. I'd ideally like to stay for some time to gather as much information as possible. This would be really valuable to me as I'd get to see them when they were people without children, just as they themselves were developing, and could give me opportunities to better understand them. I think understanding ones parents is often a good way to help you understand yourself. The pursuit of self-understanding never stops, but this opportunity would give me a unique chance to improve that."*

Choosing something personal or creative will make you stand out and you are more likely to get interesting questions from the interviewer if you are able to involve them in an intriguing conversation. It is also fine if you choose a standard period like the Roman Empire or a time which has not yet come to pass, say the year 4000, if you have a good reason.

Q24: Should interviews be used for selection?

This question may appear slightly inflammatory on the surface, considering that you are answering it in an interview, to an interviewer who likely believes in the merit of interviewing for selection. However, remember that the interviewer is interested in your opinion, and will not take offence providing you respond in a measured way, providing examples/evidence. Another important thing to remember for any question that addresses interviews and/or selection, is that what you are currently sat in is not the only form of interview, and what you are being selected for is not the only form of selection. As a result, you could wildly disagree with interviews for selection in most situations, but agree with them in the situation you are currently sat in, or vice versa.

"One up-side to using interviews for selection, is that it forces the interviewee to think on their feet (providing the questions aren't known to them in advance), which can demonstrate their real-world knowledge of a subject and is likely to bring out more honest answers about themselves. One down-side is that an interview is quite a short and high-pressure situation, as a result, an interviewee could easily make a number of mistakes or say something inappropriate and tarnish the interviewer's opinion of them. By extension, interviews rely somewhat on the opinion of the interviewer, therefore, are prone to bias."

This would be a good answer, as it addresses one for and one against aspect, justifying each point with an explanation. However, a great answer would be one that takes this further, and considers interviews' appropriateness for different types of selection.

"In some situations, the ability for an interviewee to make a mess of the interview due to the short time they are with the interviewer, and the pressure they are under, is a bad thing. This is in the same way that an entire year's work boiling down to one exam is often criticised as a way of measuring someone's academic ability. However, if the interview is for something that requires working in that situation, such as a politician who will be subjected to questions and interviews throughout their job, then an interview is a great way to measure their suitability."

By considering the appropriateness of an interview in different scenarios, you are not only demonstrating your breadth of consideration, but also your ability to remove yourself from your own head and think outside of your current situation. This question could, however, specify a type of interview and/or a particular thing being selected for. In this case, make sure you stick to that specific concept. You may address an alternative concept for comparison, but always bring the conclusion back to the question's specific elements.

Q25: Would you ever choose to go to a party rather than write an essay for university?

At first glance, this might feel like a trick question. As an interviewer, they are likely a practicing academic at the university and could well be a subject tutor you could end up having! However, it's important to remember two things. Firstly, tutors are human too and like to have fun occasionally. Secondly, all universities have 'parties' that are sanctioned by the university or an individual faculty, therefore, it's perfectly fine to want to go to parties! There are a couple of distinctions to make when constructing an answer for a question like this, and they hinge on the importance of each element.

In isolation, you might consider it impossible to argue that a party is in any way important. However, there are lots of ways in which it could be. This could a big, once in a lifetime faculty ball, it could be a party for a close friend's birthday, it could have valuable networking opportunities, or it could simply be a party you really could do with as you're feeling a bit down at that moment. The other aspect of this question is, of course, the essay. When picking something over something else, you should be considering the importance of each thing in isolation to the current situation, rather than just the concepts in general. For example, if the essay is due tomorrow and the party is a small get-together down the hall which is going to result in you not sleeping properly and not being able to finish the essay in time, then it would be quite difficult (although not impossible in the 'right' circumstances) to argue that you would pick the party over the essay.

Under some circumstances, the party might be a well-deserved break from your work, and not directly impact your ability to submit the essay by the deadline. For example, if an essay is due at the end of the following day and the party is that night, it might initially seem sensible to finish the essay first and relax after. However, you won't be able to go to the party tomorrow afternoon once you've finished the essay, as it won't be going on then. So, in that case, it would make sense to go to the party and then finish the essay the following afternoon before the deadline (providing you have enough time to do so). This sort of decision-making is more likely to go approved by an interviewer if the party has some kind of important element (e.g., a big, one-off organised event or a birthday party), but even if not, it is important to be able to back your decisions. As long as you are completing the work to a high standard and on time, it's also important that you enjoy yourself!

Q26: Who do you think has the most power: Biden, Merkel or Adele?

Answering a question like this first rests on your knowledge of each person. You don't need to know a great deal about them, but it is important you know what their role is. If you don't know that, make sure you ask the interviewer! Once you have established who each person is, you need to address any words in the question that have multiple interpretations. In this case, that word is 'power'. In order to answer the question, you need to decide how to measure power. As with all of these types of questions, you are welcome to pick one definition and go with it, or address the fact that there are multiple definitions and briefly approach each one individually. You can always make a comparison/conclusion at the end of the latter to potentially pick the 'best' definition for that particular situation.

When defining power, there are two key starting points. The first is how many people are aware of what each person says or does. This is probably the easiest to answer.

"If you consider power to be the potential of each person's words or actions to affect others, then the most influential would probably be Adele. Her music and name are known worldwide so, while she is probably not known by as many people in the US as Biden is, her reach is more global and likely through to a younger audience. More people will have heard her, and responded in any number of different ways, even turning off the radio is affecting others. However, as Biden progresses through his presidency and makes more headlines, that could easily change!"

Due to the simplicity of this definition, in this case, it is probably best to address at least one other definition of influence. One alternative definition is how much those who hear what that person says or sees what they do, will change their thoughts or long-term actions based on it.

"If defining power as how much people will change their actions or thoughts based on the actions and words of that person, then the most influential person is probably Biden. As the Amercian president, the majority of the US population will be brought into his words and actions, even if it is to vehemently disagree with them!"

You could go on to explore whether power can be just as valid when someone disagrees with the words or actions of an influential individual, or how many more people would someone need to affect a little bit to make them more powerful than someone who influences a smaller number of people a lot. The important thing is that you explore your thought processes aloud, and see them through to a conclusion each time. The conclusion doesn't need to be right, as with a concept like this it is hard to be 'right', it just needs to be some kind of decision (even if that decision is there is a tie!).

Q27: What would you say was "your colour"?

With a question as basic and seemingly abstract as this, there are two ways you can approach it. The first is to delve into the question in-depth and explore each concept and its origin. The alternative is to answer the question succinctly and give a clear reason for your conclusion. Below is an example of the latter.

"I believe that red is a colour that represents me best as it is my favourite colour. I think it came about as my favourite colour because my parents' car when I was a child was red, as was the front door on the first house I remember living in, so I always associated red with my family and home".

That would be enough detail to give a valid answer. You have given the basis of the reason (that it is your favourite colour), and then discussed the origin of that reasoning. Alternatively, you can choose to explore the question in much more detail. The first concept to approach when doing this, is the idea of representation. Is this self-representation, how others would represent you, or perhaps how you relate to what the colour typically represents in society. Below is an example of a succinct approach to all three of those concepts, something you could state after outlining the three concepts aloud.

"For myself, the colour green represents me best because it is my favourite colour, I own lots of green clothes and decorations in my room and would love to have a green house! If other people had to choose, I'd say they would pick blue because I spent a lot of time in rivers in my parents' canoe, and enjoy spending time in the sea on holiday. If I had to be represented by a societal norm, I would day that red best represents me because I have a fiery temper."

While, in the real interview you would probably approach each of these in a bit more details, this gives a basic outline of how you would separate the three concepts. You don't have to address every concept in your answer but, as usual, it is always good to outline all the concepts in the beginning to demonstrate to the interviewer that you are thinking comprehensively. Remember, when you are addressing multiple concepts in an answer, it is all too easy to drift away from the origin of your thoughts. Bring it back each time by answering the actual question at the end of each of your thought processes, in the context that thought process has been discussed in.

Q28: What shape is man? What shape is time?

On the surface, this question seems impossible to answer because it is simply too abstract. There is no shape that fits the shape of a person, and time isn't a physical concept. However, this is a test of how you address something seemingly impossible to answer. There is no wrong way to answer this question, providing you actually answer it! The important thing to remember is to get started with answering it quickly, the longer you spend pondering the wider concept, the more difficult it will be to get started!

Addressing each question individually is important and something you need to conclude on so, as a result, it is easy for you to separate two concept discussions by addressing one per question. When considering the first question, you can start by providing the obvious answer, and follow-on by delving into the concept more deeply.

"There is no named shape that is the shape of a person, so you would refer to 'man' simply as being 'man-shaped'. We refer to things in this way all the time, so not having a named shape to represent something shouldn't limit you. One important differentiator is that 'man' is not an exact shape, as every person is different. Therefore, if your definition of shape must be precise such as a square having four equal length sides with four ninety-degree corners, then that would not be possible to apply to 'man'. However, a shape like an oval doesn't have explicit parameters, so is closer to the idea of a shape which could define 'man'."

There are clear caveats to this answer, such as an oval having the strict rule of no straight edges and being entirely symmetrical, but the consideration of two different types of existing shape definitions is a great way to start the discussion. When moving that discussion on to consider time, it becomes even more abstract. You could open the discussion with the fact that time is not considered a physical concept, thus it would be inappropriate to allocate it a shape. However, you then open the discussion around space-time, where time can be considered represented physically. An interviewer may not choose to entertain such a discussion, as it is not exactly psychology related, but making sweeping and abrupt statements like that are best avoided anyway. A better way to open the discussion might be to explain that time is often considered a circle (history repeating itself, the circle of life etc.). While it would be inappropriate to state that time is a specific shape, acknowledging these ideas demonstrates your ability to think conceptually and compare it to real societal discussion.

Q29: Do things have to have specific names?

When answering why, the first thing to consider is 'what's in it for the user'. In this case, what is gained by naming things.

"One reason why things have names is to avoid having to describe them every time we refer to them. Once you have learned what the name refers to, conversations can be had much more quickly, and more easily across different languages. Rather than having to learn all the terms that describe a thing, you would only need to learn the name of that thing in order to tell a person about it in a different language."

You can centre the entire discussion around this idea of what we gain from something, but it is important to broaden your horizons a little if you want to make the discussion as interesting and engaging as possible. You may consider a few gains we make by naming things, but the next step is to consider the origin of naming things and the reason for the concept. The first reason is that we gain something from doing it, so it justifies the effort of coming up with and learning the names, However, another example which would explain the origin of naming something is that we want to take ownership of it. By giving something a name, it can be recognised by that name and associated with one person as its 'owner'. This could be considered the origin of naming, whereby everyone would have a different name for the few things they considered to be there. Gradually, through communication, perhaps we established it would be easier to have a unified naming process, such that there were fewer names to remember. This could have led to the origin of possessive pronouns, to go with these unified names.

None of this is necessarily true, and would be almost impossible to prove either way due to how long-ago naming things came about as a concept. Discussions of this type do, however, demonstrate your ability to consider both the value and the origin of a concept or action and link them together. The importance of a question like this, is to evoke a discussion of the abstract that you can tie together into a coherent conclusion. As such, it is vital that regardless of the content of your discussion, you conclude with an actual answer. This is welcome to be a brief touch of each of the discussion points you have made, as it is often impossible to make an explicit decision on which is 'right', but it needs to be clear and concise.

"I believe things have names because it was a way of identifying them as our own, which developed into a way of communicating what they were between people who didn't know of each other's possessions. It stuck as a concept, because it enabled shorter discussions through not having to fully describe a thing each time it was mentioned."

Q30: Do you read any international publications, do you think there is a value to doing so?

This question requires honesty above all else. This doesn't mean you couldn't implicitly overstate quite to the extent that you read a particular publication, but you absolutely should not discuss something you haven't actually read. Many of the interviewers you will speak to will ask this question because they are very well read, thus could easily pull you up on a particular publication. As a result, you need to have actually read an international newspaper or publication to answer this question. It would be best if you have read at least one of each, but if you have only read one, open with that.

What the interviewer will be looking for is your critique of the publication. It would be a bonus if it is psychology-related, but don't think it to be necessary. The important thing is that you recognise and address the context under which the publication is written, and how that might influence what they write about and how they write about it. When critiquing an academic paper in an essay, these are the sorts of things a tutor will be looking to see, and it is what the interviewer wants to assess your ability on at this stage. This isn't to say that you should construct your entire discussion of the publication around this critiquing, but it is definitely something you should include.

"I read [American Newspaper] online quite regularly, and tend to focus on the 'social issues' section of the paper. It is interesting to read about American social issues because some of them are so similar to our own, whereas others are so distinctly different. One article I read in the most recent version [don't be this specific if you're not sure it was] *highlighted the ease with which someone could buy a gun as a non-American citizen, meaning that someone who's history is unknown to American authorities could enter the country and buy a weapon with bad intentions. I wonder whether gun culture contributes to xenophobia and racism, as the risk that someone coming into the country with bad intentions poses, is potentially much higher than if the same thing happened where guns weren't accessible to the public."*

While this is a very simplistic discussion of a point and you would want to delve into some more detail and evidence in the real interview, it demonstrates how you can bring a psychology them to a seemingly unrelate article. The next stage in your discussion would be to critique the paper itself. With gun culture being alien to a UK resident (if indeed you are one), you could consider your views on the topic to be biased. You could also make a suggestion to rectify that, by discussing the article with an American person or someone who is in favour of guns being legally accessible to the public. This last bit is important as it is key to consider how you can broaden your views in a practical way. If the context is right, you can link it to how you might do this during your time at university.

Q31: Can you hear silence?

There are two elements that can be considered in almost any question which touches on biology in a psychology interview. The first is the biological element, and the second is the concept that we experience/express as a result or in anticipation of that biological effect. In this case, there is the biology of hearing something, and the interpretation of that into neural signals. In this case, how you explain the biology is very much dependent on your biology knowledge. Unless it is something you have mentioned in your personal statement or in the interview, the interviewer won't expect you to have comprehensive knowledge of the biology behind hearing. However, they will expect you to have a general understanding that sound travels in waves, and those waves are interpreted into neural signals (which we 'hear') by bones in your ear.

When considering this from a biological perspective, then you can be pretty conclusive in your statement that we cannot hear silence. If there are no sound waves, then we do not 'hear' anything from our environment. However, this doesn't mean that we don't interpret the silence as something other than nothingness, from the neural signals we receive. Without making any sweeping statements about the complicated biology around neural signalling, it would make sense to assume that neurons aren't ever 'silent'. Things in biology are rarely as cut and dry as being 'off' or 'on', so you could use that train of thought in the following discussion.

"I imagine that neurons are never at a point when there is no transmission of chemical between them. It is more likely to imagine they have a 'resting rate' of transmission, which is then greatly increase when 'active'. As a result, even when there is no noise, you might assume there are still some signals being sent between neurons related to hearing. In order to create a silent environment, humans have gone to great lengths to create sound-deadening material. Therefore, one could assume that silence is not something you would come across in a natural setting.

If the human hearing system has not evolved to consider true silence, when faced with it, its reaction will likely be to 'hear' the 'resting rate' of signals that would normally never be reached due to ambient noise. With that in mind, while you cannot actually hear silence because there are no sound waves to hear, the experience of true silence is likely to manifest as some kind of ambient sound."

Making one point per statement in a discussion like this enables you to create an argument that is easy to follow. This is beneficial for three reasons. Firstly, the interviewer can take note of every point you have made. Secondly, the interviewer can see you are proficient at organising your thoughts. Thirdly, the interviewer can be invited to target a new discussion (even if that is to disagree with you) at any one of your points. The more discussion the better!

Q32: You mentioned having good thinking skills in your personal statement, can you tell me how many golf balls can you fit in a Boeing 787 Dreamliner?

This question is testing a few things, all related to your thinking process, despite its seemingly pointless nature. The first thing it is testing is the comprehensiveness and commitment of your subject consideration. What the interviewer will be looking for is you to exhaust all aspects of the question, in order to work towards the answer. Part of this is considering the physical nature of the objects in mind. The two elements in this question are the plane, and the golf balls. To consider the physical size of the plane, it might be best to get some clarification from the interviewer if you don't know the size of the plane. The number will be very different between a double-decker transatlantic plane compared to a private jet! If you know the size, make sure you state it out loud, it doesn't really matter whether you are right or not, just that the interviewer knows what you are working from. When discussing the golf ball, make sure you also give the rough size you are working from.

The next step has two options. The first is to take a mathematical approach, based around volume. The other is to consider all the places you could put a golf ball on a plane (overhead storage, under seats, in cockpit etc.). Depending on your maths confidence, the choice would be yours. Don't worry if the maths you do isn't exactly right, just make sure you talk through each step out loud and ensure that the number you come out with at the end seems believable. If working through the different places a ball could go, try to attribute a number to each one (e.g., 300 golf balls in each overhead storage area, 300 passengers so 100 areas, 30000 total golf balls in overhead storage), and make sure you write it down! It's far too easy to get caught up in the line of sums, without being able to add them together to an answer at the end!

Once you reach a point of concluding, ensure that your answer appears believable and answer the question! Don't let yourself tail off at the end of your last consideration and not actual provide a number. It doesn't matter (within reason) what that number is, as long as the methods you used to get to it made sense.

Q33: How would you work out the number of flights passing over London at this moment?

This question is testing just one thing, that being the degree to which you can work through a large series of thoughts, considering all possible options. While it is vital that you give a numerical answer, the value of that answer (within reason) doesn't really matter, what matters is how you got to the answer. When beginning this question, it might be helpful for you to outline some parameters. If you know how many airports London has (6), then you can start from there. There will definitely be more than 6 planes over London as they will be coming and going from each airport. So, from your starting point you can work out a realistic maximum.

If you know anything about airport scheduling then absolutely discuss it, any colourful insights into your life will be memorable for an interviewer. However, most people won't have that kind of insight so will be starting from scratch. It would be safe to assume that there is a gap of at least two minutes between planes landing, in order that they can taxi off of the runway. At the speed planes travel, they could probably traverse London in 15 minutes or so. Considering of the 6 airports, there are maybe 10 runways, assuming planes are always nose to tail coming in and out, you could sum 7 planes per 'queue' times the 10 runways, making a total of 70 planes.

It doesn't matter if this is entirely wrong, it may be hugely more than this or hugely fewer. The important thing is the steps taken to get to that value. If you want to extend your discussion, you can go on to review the number you have reached. If you look up at the sky at any given time, you can only see a couple of planes at most, and your view extends quite a few miles in every direction. As such, you might choose to assess that 70 seems like too many, and perhaps halve your answer. If you add in the explanation that maybe there is a 4-minute gap between landings, rather than the originally assumed 2, the numbers would add up. Being comprehensive and explanatory in your thought processes is vital and will be most well received by an interviewer.

Q34: How many deliveries are made in the UK every day?

As with any numerical question, the value is your method, not the answer. However, you must give an answer to 'complete' the process. To reach any kind of answer to the scale that this will be will take some considerable calculations. If you have any prior insight (such as knowing how many they delivered last year, or how many your local post office receives), then outline and apply it aloud. Each bit of information you can bring to inform your calculation will not only likely make it more accurate, but also impress the interviewer that you have such niche knowledge and have thought to apply it.

When starting your calculations, it can be helpful to set parameters. You can assume that not every person in the UK receives something every day, so the number is likely going to be less than the total UK population (if you know it accurately, great, if not it can be generally helpful to know it's around 70 million people). Your next point of consideration is that commercial mail exists as well. While much of mail is sent via email now, businesses still account for a lot of the mail sent each day. As such, you may choose to reconsider your original 70-million limit, to account for commercial mail.

None of the assumptions and considerations you make matter in their accuracy to reality, only in their abundance and degree of thought. Within reason, in a question like this, the more times you reconsider a particular point, the greater depth of understanding it demonstrates to the interviewer. When you have made all the considerations you think are reasonable (it can be helpful to write them down to keep track), make sure you conclude with an actual value. Once you have a value, it can often be insightful to reflect upon that relative to a reasonable assumption you might pick out of the air. If this calculated value and the 'random' value are distinctly different, perhaps spend a moment discussing why that might be, relative to the calculations and considerations you have just undertaken.

Q35: Have you been to this college before?

This question is unusual, in that it is not testing anything in particular. It is far more of an exploratory question which seeks to bring out your experience of university and the college, as well as your expectations for it going forward. When answering any question based on your experiences, it is important to be honest. You can embellish the truth in part if you wish, but always ensure that the core of what you're saying is true. The interviewer will probably expect you to have visited Oxford at least once before the interview but it is not a problem if you have not.

If you have not ever visited the college before, the interviewer will want to know what attracted you to it, and that will likely be the next question. As a result, your considerations should immediately be looking towards why you were interested in the college, as soon as this initial question is asked. The best way to approach that, is to describe in what context you have seen the college (e.g., through the university website) and what it was that you liked about what you saw/read.

If you have visited the college before, the first thing to outline is under what context. If it was a family trip to Oxford and you looked around as a tourist, it is fine to focus on the 'tourist things' that you liked about the college e.g., the architecture. If you visited quite recently (during the time you might be expected to have been thinking about university) or as a school trip, where the focus was a little more on the academic side, then make sure you address some of the 'non-tourist- aspects too. It is fine to talk about the grounds and the architecture, but having done some reading around the library, subject foci and alumni/faculty members will go a long way. This is one of the few questions where it wouldn't really be fitting to conclude by answering the question. Answering the question should be the very first thing you do, everything that follows is simply an extension of that. One key thing to make sure is that you don't end up talking too far into the subject. It may be that the interviewer was simply asking this as a yes/no question, precursory to a more in-depth question. With that in mind, try to read the interviewer's body language to see if they were expecting you to take the reins on the discussion!

49

Q36: Do you think that Oxford/Cambridge will suit you?

This question is testing two main things. The first is your understanding of (and, by extension, your reading up on) the university, and your self-awareness. You want to ensure that the overriding message of this answer is 'yes', as that is the whole reason you are applying. However, don't be afraid to touch on some elements that may not be 100% positive. For example, if you feel like you don't have much in common with the stereotypical student of the university, you can say that! However, what is important is to express your realisation that the stereotype isn't the reality.

If you want to go down this route of discussion, the safest is way to is to describe your experiences once you have arrived. By the time you have gone into your first interview, you will have had quite extensive contact with some other prospective students. More than likely, you will have found some people with things in common with yourself, take that on board I your discussion. The more recent the experience and the more truth behind it, the better! If this process of meeting your fellow interviewees has squashed some doubt about whether you would fit in, that's a fantastic result and you should definitely share it!

The next part is to make sure that you have read up on the university, and to make that clear! If the university is very research heavy, match that up to your own academic interests! The same goes for if they have a particular department that is of interest to you. Don't be afraid to add a little more personality to the discussion, perhaps the location is convenient for you in some way, but make sure your answer hinges on the more impactful content.

"After my undergraduate degree, I would really enjoy pursuing a PhD in psychology. I'm not sure exactly what I would want to specialise in yet, but the opportunity to be surrounded by practicing academics to discuss that with is invaluable. In addition, I'll be able to stay on my undergraduate campus for my postgraduate studies, and have access to some incredible research facilities and equipment. In addition, the university is only 45 minutes' drive from my home town, so I'll be able to visit there easily for birthdays and other special occasions!"

Remember, this question is about why the university is the right fit for you. You could easily be asked why you are the right fit for the university, and you would have to phrase your answer slightly differently. To explain why the university is the right fit for you, you should be assessing why the features of the university fit into your life and personality. If you're answering why you're the right fit for the university, then that answer is the other way round!

Q37: What do you think you'll be doing in a decade? How about in two decades?

No interviewer will expect you to have an actual plan for the next 10 or 20 years of your life. Instead, what they're looking for is an understanding of how you gaining your degree might set out a path for you in life. This is far more about understanding your options than it is deciding which one you are going to pursue. It is important to distinguish the sections of your answer between the 10 and 20-year mark. Remember if you wanted to do a PhD, you wouldn't likely finish that until around 8 years from the point that you're in this interview. As such, if that was your plan, you wouldn't be far into post-doctoral research/your first 'proper' job in the first 10 years. It is important to articulate details like this, even if you haven't definitely decided you want to do a PhD. Any understanding of your options in this way demonstrates to the interviewer that you have considered these things.

If you are more concerned with the industry you want to go into than any postgraduate studies, then discuss how you might want to pursue success there. At the 10-year point, if you have spent 6 years of that in an industry, what would you like to have achieved. You have the classic milestones such as being a team leader, running your own project, owning your own home, or any other 'standard' aspirations. However, you should try and add in some things which are unique to you and your preferred industry. If you wanted to go into marketing, something that is quite common for psychology graduates, then it would be great to aspire to have one of your projects on national television, or up in the store of a 'household name' business.

It is, however, important to remember that the interviewer is likely to be an academic, and is likely to (be it potentially implicitly/subconsciously) want you to aspire to do the same thing. As a result, you should consider how you 'tune' your answer to appease those who are listening to it. I would never expect a tutor to reject an applicant on the basis that they didn't want to pursue studies beyond undergraduate, however, it is easier to engage with someone on a topic they are interested in. The more engaged you are with the interviewer, the more likely they will remember and the better a conversation they will have with their peers after you are gone. This isn't a hard and fast rule, but it is human nature to frame memorable things in a positive light (unless of course it was objectively bad!). in sum, you want to approach this question with honesty, but make sure that you consider your audience!

Q38: What is your favourite activity outside of school?

This is a question which 'assesses' your personality outside of academia. It's great if you have genuine hobbies which are subject-related, but most people don't and no interviewer will expect you to. What they are looking for is ways in which you unwind, what environments you choose to put yourself in (rather than those which are thrust upon you!), and how competitive you are. If every hobby of yours involves playing a competitive, spectator sport to a high level, then the interviewer can deduce that you are outgoing, competitive and have an interest in exhibiting your skills. This is very different (although by no means better/worse) than someone who's hobbies are all quiet activities to pass the time that you engage with alone.

As you discuss your interests, remember that the interviewer will likely be comparing their stereotypical view of someone who has these interests, alongside their experience of you in this setting. If you are describing yourself as confident and outgoing through the activities you like to do, but are aware that you have been shy in this setting, it could be a good thing to highlight that! Having a high level of self-awareness is a great sign of emotional intelligence and will only be another point in your favour!

When talking about your interests, it is always beneficial to highlight any achievements you might have made in them. This doesn't mean you should tune the entire conversation into a list of your achievements (as that wasn't the question!), but it can be useful to highlight where you have committed yourself and gained success. In addition, spend some time on the less usual hobbies. This is the perfect opportunity to inject some real personality into the interview and, you never know, the interviewer might even share an unusual hobby of yours which you can engage on!

Lastly, it can be a good idea to describe how you are going to continue pursuing those hobbies through university. The interviewers don't want someone who is going to drop everything and become a sheep when they arrive on campus, they want someone who is going to bring something new to the table! As a result, whether it's simply a hobby you'll keep up in your own time, or a club that you'd want to set up in your college, make sure you outline how you'll go about keeping these things up! Make sure these are realistic and measured against the amount of commitment you will need to bring to your academic studies, but by all means dream big!

Q39: How will your fellow college residents see you?

There are a few ways in which you can contribute to college life as a student. One, which could be easily overlooked when considering college life specifically, is simply being a friendly and approachable person. When talking in the context of college life, it's easy to forget the things that make you a contributor to a pleasant society in general. When it comes to college-specific things, it's good to open with some more general points, with some demonstration that you have read up on college-specific things as well.

What this means is first considering what makes a good contributor in any small community. You could contribute by applying your skills in a particular sport (or otherwise) to the college team, you could apply your academic ability and commitment to success to enhance the college's academic rankings. You could even include something like experience in party-planning or finances to contribute to the college ball (should there be one). The next step is to introduce some college-specific things, to demonstrate that you've done some reading around the college, and to highlight your specific suitability.

An easy (although predictable) one would be if the college has any particularly successfully (or perhaps even unsuccessful, although that would be more difficult to find out!) sports teams. You could highlight this if you have an interest/skill in any one of those, and highlight that you would be keen to join in. Some of the less predictable things would be societies outside of sport, or whether your college has a chapel and you'd like to be involved in that. There is a wealth of different things which a college could be interested in having someone contribute to, it's just a case of matching one up from your research to something you're interested in. The important thing to remember is that it doesn't have to be something you have dine already, it could be trying something totally new!

Lastly, you want to make sure you can contribute to the college after you leave. Something that many people wouldn't consider is going on to be a respectable and successful person in your industry, adding to the college's notable alumni. As with any question that requires you to speak well of the college/university, it is a fine balance between selling yourself as an admirer of the college, and seeming over the top or fake. Strike the balance well by practicing talking around these kinds of subjects, you'll soon develop a way that works for you.

Q40: Why do you think we structure the course in the way that we do?

This question doesn't try to hide what it's assessing at all. One of the big indicators of someone who is committed to the application process (and, by extension, the university) is how much preparation they have done for the interviews. The first thing you should have looked at when deciding which course to choose, is what the actual course content in. There are two sides to a course decision, the first is how it will help you get to the next stage if your education/career (if you have planned that far ahead!), and the other is whether it will interest you while you study. The latter can only be answered by exploring and reading around the course content.

When talking about the course structure, it is best to keep the objective details to a reasonable level. You don't want to sound like you're simply reciting a list of modules, nor do you want to risk getting muddled and saying something that is objectively wrong. You are much better off making a point which you have come to the opinion of through your reading, and then evidencing it in the discussion thereafter.

"I can see from reading up on the course that it focusses a lot on social psychology in the first two years. This was one of the things that attracted me to it, as I think undertaking a social science independent study in third year would be really interesting. The focus on social psychology seems to come from the disproportionately high number of modules which approach topics in the field, when compared to subjects like perception."

Above is a bit of a clunky answer, but one that demonstrates you've read around the course content and are very happy with what you have read (which is arguably the most important bit!). You could construct an answer in a more coherent manner, by opening with the number of modules on one particular subject, highlighting that it appears to be a particular focus of the course, and then finishing with why that is a good thing for you. However, when opening with the number of modules on a course, it sets up the answer to feel too over-prepared. Your preference between them is, of course, your own and either will make a good structure to answer a question like this.

As aforementioned, the most important bit is to highlight why the course content works for you. Make sure to not have that as the conclusion of your answer, because that isn't the question, but always make sure it is included.

Q41: What would you say was your single greatest weakness?

Answering this question well is very difficult. There are two ways in which you could go wrong. Neither of these ways would necessarily be terrible, but they are best avoided if possible. The first way is to give an answer that is simply a positive attributed in disguise. An example of this would be 'admitting' that you can sometimes be too much of a perfectionist or be too detail oriented. These are things which would certainly be bad traits under certain circumstances, but the combination of the fact that in a lot of cases they are good and that they have been presented as 'sometimes' being an issue, makes them far too weak as answers.

The other way in which you could answer this question in a non-ideal way is to overshare on your weaknesses. The interviewer doesn't want to hear that as soon as there's a test around the corner you have a complete meltdown and only just drag yourself through. If your weakness has something to do with an event you'll face at university, you're best-off underselling it slightly (only if it's really bad of course!). if this is the case, it would also be beneficial to explain what you're doing, and will continue to do, to work on that weakness. Self-awareness of a real weakness is a great sign of the potential for personal growth, but the growth only comes if you actually act to solve the problem!

In an ideal scenario, you will have a genuine weakness that you are working on fixing, that doesn't really have anything to do with university. That way, you can have an honest conversation with the interviewer, without it having any chance of jeopardising their view of you as a competent student. However, this isn't normally possible and you will likely have to talk around a weakness that could affect you as a student.

As a result, you want to focus on what you are doing to rectify this weakness, and the timeline over which you are acting. The latter is very important, no interviewer will expect you to start university as a perfectly formed student, but they would be very keen to see some kind of commitment from you to have worked on that weakness prior to starting your course. It might be that you know you're a slow typist, so you're going to take a touch-typing course over summer. Or it could be that your handwriting is bad quality, so you're going to spend your last few months at school comparing your handwriting every week and looking to see an improvement over time.

There's any number of things you could list as a weakness, just remember that it needs to be honest (and an actual weakness!) but something that is fixable (or at least manageable) in a sensible time-frame.

Q42: You have mentioned a number of personal strengths in your statement, which is your greatest?

Answering this question involves just as much care as answering what your biggest weakness is. It is far too easy to list a generic skill like 'essay-writing' and explaining how it will benefit you in your degree because that is something you will spend a lot of your time doing. The key to answering this question well is finding a balance between bragging and being too modest. If you undersell your strengths, it demonstrates a lack of confidence and perhaps an indication that you might not be as good as you appeared on paper. Oversell your strengths, and it suggests a lack of self-awareness and an arrogance towards your own ability.

To balance this answer properly, you want to find a couple of strengths to 'warm-up' with, that are related to your main strength. Alternatively, you can find one main strength that is backed up with 'auxiliary' strengths. Here is an example of the former, followed by the latter.

"Leading up to my GCSE's, I spent a lot of time doing creative writing in my spare time. I was able to apply those skills and experiences to my English work, as well as my longer answer questions in other subjects. Through all that, I've built up a keen interest and strong ability to write engaging texts on a wide range of topics, making me a good essay-writer. I would say this is my biggest strength in academia."

"My biggest strength in academia is essay-writing. I enjoyed writing through school and wrote lots of stories as a child. By the time I got to my GCSE's my experience and developed proficiency enabled me to excel in English, and at the longer-answer questions in other subjects. I have continued this success into my A-Levels, securing a really good grade in English."

Both of those answers highlight the same strength, but present it in a different way. The latter is for those who are more comfortable 'selling' themselves, the former for those who struggle more with that. One important thig to note is that moth answers highlighted this as being a strength in academia. If you are going to pick that, it is totally fine, but I would open with a statement that highlights it. The interviewers know that you are more than what you can do at school, so will often be looking for non-academic strengths to answer a question like this. If you highlight in the beginning that it is specifically an academic strength, then it prompts them to ask if you have considered a non-academic one too. If you have, feel free to explain that you opened with the one you did because it is your biggest strength, and then explain your other one.

If you want to go ahead and discuss a non-academic strength, of course feel free to do so! It is often easier to add personality in this way, but is sometimes harder to evidence how you have been strong. However, if you use a similar structure, you should be able to present it as a convincing strength.

Q43: How will your experiences from the Duke of Edinburgh scheme benefit you during your time at university?

This is a question that many interviewers will be keen to ask, if you have something like a Duke of Edinburgh mention on your CV/in your personal statement. It may sound a little like they are trying to belittle the achievement by asking it in a sarcastic way, or to try and trip you up. Rest assured that is not the case, they are simply interested to see how you view the skills you have acquired through the program, and how you would apply them to the entirely different environment of studying for a degree.

The key to answering this question well, while it seems obvious, is picking out genuinely applicable skills and experiences. This means valuing relevance over and above the extent of your experience/skill. If you try to shoehorn a skill to fit your university studies, just because it was a large focus of your scheme, your answer will come across ill-fitting. It is important to be prepared for a question like this because it is quite likely to come up, if it is something you have discussed in your personal statement or have on your CV, and it is something quite difficult to come up with off the cuff.

To establish will skill to select, it is best to consider what you have actually done compared to what you will be doing in your degree. If you spent time orienteering and doing crafts, that's not something that fits the bill, however big a part of the scheme it was or how much you enjoyed it. However, if you spent one of the nights up on your own, devising a plan of action and getting everything ready for the following morning, that is something that can be very easily applied to your degree.

"On the last night before our long walk, our team remained very disorganised and we still hadn't got a route fully together, or decided exactly what we needed to pack. I decided, rather than have a frantic rush in the morning, to work into the evening and night to prepare the map route and set up a packing list for each of our team. I had to do this on my own as the rest of my team were getting early nights, so had to rely on my own intuition and conviction behind my decisions. Even though I was tired the next day, I was happy that we were able to set off with a clear route and could have all of our things packed without having to think about whether anything important was missing. I think having to work late, on my own and being able to make those independent decisions has prepared me for the independent projects I will have to take on in my degree."

You could easily have continued the explanation further, regarding the applicability of skills and experience to situations in degree studies, but this demonstrates how you can apply the experience of one isolated event, better than you could trying to apply an irrelevant experience. Remember that the relevance is so much more important than the abundance. It is much easier to oversell how big a deal the event was, than oversell how applicable it is to your degree!

Q44: Why choose Oxford or Cambridge, if you know that other universities are less competitive, and may mark your work much more generously?

There are two ways to approach this question. You can answer successfully discussing one or both. The first point you could make is that you may not actually do better elsewhere. You will likely have spoken in that interview, previous interviews or your personal statement, about how the environment of your chosen university will give you the drive to push forward and excel. At a university where perhaps that drive is not present to the same degree, you may not be pushed in the same way. This is a tricky answer to phrase, as you don't want to come across like you are unable to self-motivate, but if you feel like it applies to you then convincingly portraying that self-awareness will be received well. However, if you don't feel confident discussing that, or it doesn't apply to you, then there is the bulk of the answer to approach.

When answering the main part of this question, you need to consider the value of the university beyond the grade on your degree. If you are confident in yourself that you can achieve a first class result regardless, then that's great. It wouldn't necessarily be the best structure to lead with that, as it would be easy for that to appear arrogant. However, it is a good way to round off your answer, if you are confident talking about that. Approaching the value of the university is all about understanding what it will bring you along the way. If you want to be an academic at that university, then the grade relative to any other university is not really relevant. If you want to learn about your field in the most all-encompassing way possible, then the grade you get is not really relevant to that part of the experience.

However, it is important to acknowledge that as something you have considered. Expressing that awareness will be well-received by an interviewer. The key is to balance it against the personal points you are making. You may wish to make those points after acknowledging your concern around the topic, or you may wish to save it until the end, rounding it off as something that has been weighed up and dismissed based on your conclusion. Most importantly, you should demonstrate that you have the self-confidence to know you can do well in any environment, and not feel the need to establish a different one.

Q45: Cambridge is very intense; do you think your current approach to time management will be sufficient?

There are lots of ways in which you can say you will manage your time. However, the interviewer is going to have heard them all before. The way to make your answer convincing and stand out, is to give evidence of where you have learned these techniques and where you have successfully applied them. It would be a good idea to pick a few techniques for organisation, stress management and timekeeping (although there will. Be some overlap with organisation), and prepare some examples for when these techniques have worked for you in the past. While it would likely make your answer too convoluted if you tried to do this for every technique, it can inject some personality into the answer if you talk about where you learned one of the techniques, particularly if the story is interesting!

"One challenge I am sure that I will face is having to prioritise work. In this sort of situation, it's important to manage explicit deadlines, as well as the importance of each piece of work. During sixth form, I have been a private tutor. Having to manage marking my students' work and completing my own has been very challenging at times. I have mostly chosen to prioritise my students' work, as I have already had discussions with my teachers and they are happy to be lenient with my deadlines, providing they are not exams or coursework!"

By giving a real and honest example of a difficult situation, you'll connect with the tutors a lot better than if you try to make something up on the spot. Once you have explained the situation and experience, as above, it is then important to explicitly apply this to your degree experience.

"From this experience, I am confident talking to tutors and asking them for help with my schedule. In order to stop myself getting too stuck, I would make sure I reach out to a tutor when in need, and ask them to extend my deadline. I would make sure that I am prioritising the work that leads on to future work, so that I don't fall behind on a series of pieces."

By demonstrating your understanding of how you might prioritise something, this gives the interviewer further evidence to suggest what you are saying is something you actually have had to do. In addition, you are showing the confidence to stand up for your decisions, even if that means asking for help.

Q46: What have you read in the last 24 hours?

As with any question that asks you directly about an event, honesty is the best policy. However, it is completely realistic to assume that you may not have read anything on the morning of your interview, or the night before apart from your interview preparation notes. With that in mind, consider this question to be asking more 'what have you read very recently', rather than specifically this morning. That is, unless you have the confidence to be fully honest when, by all means, be exactly that! If you are going to be entirely honest, just ensure that you're not wandering down the road of oversharing. Remember, while the interviewers are friendly and they want to have a pleasant conversation, they are still assessing you! Saying something like "I've actually not read anything in the last 24 hours, I've been a little busy, but just the other day I read some of *The Count of Monte Cristo* in my spare time" is a good way to remain honest while still giving the interviewer something to play off, and giving you something you can explore in depth.

You should make sure you discuss a text you have read recently, and ensure that your discussion is realistic. The interviewer is not going to believe that you have spent your entire morning reading the full works of a particular psychologist, or a novel from cover to cover! The best approach to picking a text is to have read something very recently in preparation for your interviews, and discuss that! If the text is relevant to your interviews, then there's no real reason to spend a lot of time highlighting its relevance. However, if the text is a little more unusual, then by all means explain its relevance to the interviews.

If you choose to discuss a text that has nothing to do with interviews, that's fine too! The interviewer will appreciate the fact that you're reading for pleasure, not just for work! However, the text you discuss should either have an element of psychology, or an element of personality to it, for maximum impact in the interview discussion. The more you can recall about what you read, the better. That's not to say you should go about reciting it verbatim, but it enables you to discuss its content with confidence. If you open with a single point about the text after a brief description of its context, the interviewer may ask you to expand or continue, in which case that gives you the starting point from which to begin your full discussion. If they don't respond in any way to your initial point, try to make you second point psychology related. It may be that they are simply interested to know what you have read recently; in which case they may not pry beyond your initial description. Don't worry either way, all interviewers are different in the way they will want to explore what you have read and how you interpret it.

Q47: What would you say was your greatest personal challenge in life? How did you handle it?

This question is supremely personal, and you should make your answer as such. In an ideal world, you will have had a challenge which comes to mind immediately and you will have no need to prepare any thought on it at all. However, in most people's lives, there are a large number of small challenges, rather than one outstanding one. In this case, the thought you should put into this question is regarding how you overcame one of those challenges. The interviewer is looking to understand a bit more about your background, and build knowledge on how you deal with difficult situations. If you have a challenge that was not quite as big as your biggest ever challenge, but you handled getting over it in a much better way, then that might be your better bet to pick!

As with any of these personal questions, depending on your confidence, you may choose to be 100% honest. It may be that the biggest challenge you have faced was one that you did not overcome well, one that may have beaten you. That is completely fine, as long as you talk about what you learned from that experience. It is no good discussing a difficult situation that wasn't handled well, and then simply going on with your life as if nothing happened! The interviewer will be looking for honesty, self-awareness, self-reflection and the ability to better yourself after a setback. It will be very common for you to come across aa seemingly impassable challenge in your degree, so the interviewer wants to know what experience you have dealing with that kind of situation.

If there is an element of independence to your overcoming of the challenge, highlight that it might be that due to not having the support you might have had in other situations, you didn't handle the challenge as effectively as you might have otherwise. That's fine, but highlight what you learned from the experience and how you would go about approaching it differently next time! It is vital that there is at least an element of self-reflection in your answer. It might be that the challenge happened very recently, and you haven't had enough tie to process it and become better at tackling situations like it. It might be that your biggest challenge was preparing for this interview! If this is the case, then make sure you reflect on that. Don't be afraid to put yourself on the spot to evoke some more honesty out of your answer.

There are three stages to a good answer in this question; situation, specific challenge (and why it was challenging) and what you did/would do next time to overcome it.

Q48: Do you think that the impact of a good teacher can stretch beyond the walls of a school? Who do you think was your best teacher?

Of course, it doesn't matter who your best teacher was, it certainly doesn't need to be the one who is teaching you the subject you're applying for! What matters is how you have assessed them to be your best teacher, and the extent to which you understand how they have influenced you. A poor answer is one that doesn't address any of these elements in any detail, as follows.

"My favourite teacher was my year9 maths teacher. She inspired me to do better in maths and got me from really struggling at the beginning of the year, to being almost top of the class by the end, and really enjoying it!"

A better answer, is one that considers each element of the question in some detail, with a degree of reflection into why you have the thoughts that you do. Below is an answer that does this.

"My favourite teacher was my yr9 maths teacher. She inspired me to do better at maths by simply letting me get on with it, my teachers in years before had always tried so hard to engage me in the lesson when working on the board, and as a shy student I just shrank away and disengaged from the lesson. As soon as I was left to my own devices, I realised I could do it when I wasn't put on the spot! Since then, my confidence grew a lot and by the end of the year I was asking to go through things on the board! I'm not sure how she knew to treat me differently than my previous teachers, but she definitely had more patience. Maybe she saw that my homework was always right but my classwork wasn't and put the pieces together to work it out!"

This answer demonstrates a real insight into why a teacher treated you how they did, and what the result of it was. It also implies that you are a good independent learner (which is always a bonus to slip into an answer!). When you are discussing why a teacher has treated you a certain way, it is important not to consider any of your own assumptions to be fact. Remember, the interviewer is likely also an educator, and they may see that your assumptions which you have made out to be fact, are likely wrong. It is, however, important that you outline what your views on how they treated you are, as even just the fact you are considering the reasons behind teachers' actions is a great way to better understand yourself and how you work best.

Q49: What are your long-term plans in life?

This question is incredibly open, and doesn't need to be answered like a 'where do you see yourself in x years' question. You can answer this question entirely unrelatedly to academia and work if you like. If your goal in life is to own your own home and have a family, say that! The important thing is to ground it around how this degree will help you get there. It could be something as simple as the degree with unlock doors in the job market that you wouldn't normally have been able to enter, or it could be that the degree will teach you how to work hard and independently, which will help you achieve things in later life. Whatever angle you approach it from, it is a great idea to include a piece about your degree studies.

However, you want to be honest with these plans as a question as open as this is a perfect opportunity for you to discuss something memorable to the interviewer. Maybe you have always wanted to be a clown, so working a job which pays well will enable you to go to clown school at the weekends and learn! It doesn't really matter what it is, as long as it's honest. If you start talking about something because you think it will be memorable, rather than because it is the truth, the interviewer will likely see right through you, so don't!

It is totally fine to have 'boring' aspirations, everyone's life is their own! If your aspirations in life are somewhat mundane, make that part of the explanation!

"I know it seems pretty mundane, but what I'd really like is to have a house, family and a stable job by the time I am thirty. This degree will teach me the skills I need to do well in the working world, unlock access to a job that I will enjoy, and enable me to earn the money I need to own my own home."

It isn't the most personality-injected answer, but if the above answer is honest then it is totally fine to go down that route! Obviously, if you have an honest ambition that is a little more whacky then discuss it, but don't feel like you have to make something up to be memorable! Honesty is the best policy, but try to make a link between whatever you're discussing and your degree studies. It doesn't have to be forced if it really doesn't work, but ideally you want your long-term plans to be tied into your degree, to some extent!

Q50: If you had to name your three greatest strengths, what would you pick?

This is a very open question. Because of this, it would be best to make at least one of these skills something to do with your degree and another something very personal to you. Beyond that, the floor is yours! When answering, for each skill you should explain what that skills is, where it originated, and how is has/will be useful to you. When talking about how it will be useful, that's where the degree studies bit comes in! Below is an example of how to outline one of these three skills.

"One of my top skills is my ability to type very fast and very accurately. I started typing pretty young because my mum worked from home and I used to use her keyboard to type fake emails while she was on her lunchbreak. I had to touch-type to a degree because I wasn't tall enough to see over her desk! When I started school, I used to get into accidents a lot so spent a few terms in various casts. Whenever that happened, I had to do all of my schoolwork on a laptop. Since starting sixth form, I've done all of my work on my laptop and have really honed my typing skills. These will definitely come in handy when writing essays, as I can much more easily and accurately write down citations!"

This answer brings some personality as it describes the origin of the skills, from an amusing childhood story to current working conditions in sixth form. If you are lucky to have a skill with such an extensive back story, then absolutely discuss it, even if perhaps you wouldn't consider it one of your top three skills! The clearest way to explore these three skills is to tell them as three individual stories, if you outline the skills first and go into the stories after, it will be too easy to get muddled and lose track of where you are. It would be great if you had skills which spread across a variety of disciplines. For example, in addition to the skill explained above, you could have one which relates to your social skills (e.g., recognising when someone is upset, even if they're trying to hide it) and one which relates to your physical ability (e.g., your proficiency at a certain sport). Of course, it would be all too convenient if that were the case, so don't try to bend the truth too much to get it to fit this model. It is better to be honest in a question like this, providing your answers have some degree of interest and relation to your subject!

Q51: How much should you charge to wash all the windows in London?

This question is not looking for an exact answer; instead the interviewer is inviting you to take them through your thought process as you make an estimate. Ultimately the tutorial experience is all about reasoning through often ambiguous or tricky problems, and this is an opportunity to demonstrate that you can do this.

A standard applicant might estimate the total surface area of windows in London, the average surface of windows washed per hour, and the hourly labour costs of window washing and use these to provide an answer. What will set a **good candidate** apart from a standard one is the quality of reasoning behind the numbers they come to. In this specific question, you would want to recognise that residential and commercial buildings, flats, and houses all have different numbers and sizes of windows. You may also want to consider other factors, such as London being a distinctly urban area, and windows potentially needing to be washed on both sides.

Remember, these are just some possible considerations; there are all sorts of factors you could bring into the discussion.

For example, let us assume that there are 8 million people in London, and the average household is 2.5 people. This would mean that there are about 3.2 million households in London. You might then assume that the average number of windows across all residential and commercial buildings works out at 7.5 windows per household, and that the average surface area is 80cm by 50cm. To account for washing windows on both sides, you would multiply by 2 to give you the total surface area. Multiplying various decimals live might seem a bit daunting; feel free to round numbers where appropriate (and explain to the examiners why you are doing this). So in this example, you would calculate 3 million x 8 x 0.8 x 0.5 x 2 which would be about 19.2 million square meters of window.

From there you could discuss per hour labour costs, and the estimated surface area of windows you could wash per hour. Again, nuance is the key to making your answer stand out. Factors you might want to consider include (but are not limited to): skill required in window washing, cost of materials, cost of living in London, competition within the London window washing market, or whether the labour market is seasonal. Introducing these considerations offers you the opportunity to show not only that you are logical and rigorous, but also creative. To conclude this example, let us say you assume a wage of 10 pounds per hour, and 50 square meters of window per hour. This would give you a total cost of 3.84 million pounds.

A **weak answer** may have a very similar structure to a strong answer but lack the justification for numbers chosen. Other pitfalls to avoid include making simple calculation errors, and failing to use common sense when estimating numbers. For example by assuming that a population of 8 million people in London means that there are 8 million households. Avoid the temptation to be funny (e.g. answering "I have better things to do than wash windows"); this will not go down well.

Q52: How many piano tuners are there in Europe?

Although questions like this might seem initially daunting, the goal here is not to accurately estimate the number of piano tuners in Europe but rather to demonstrate clear, well explained reasoning.

In other words, a **good applicant** will offer sensible numbers backed up by a brief explanation as to how they chose these figures. For example, you could estimate that there are 750 million people in Europe, about 2.5 people per household, and therefore a total of 300 million households. Then by assuming that something like 1 in 50 households have a piano, you would estimate the number of pianos in Europe as around 6 million. Factors to consider when selecting these numbers could include how popular an instrument the piano is, or the cost of a piano. From there you could ascertain the number of piano tuners by dividing the average number of times people need their pianos tuned in a year by the number of pianos a piano tuner is able to tune in a year. When creating these numbers you could consider factors such as how long it takes to tune a piano, or how many days a year a piano tuner works (these are just a few examples, feel free to introduce your own ideas). For example, you could estimate that it takes a piano tuner 2 hours to tune a piano and they work about 8 hours a day, five days a week, for 50 weeks a year. This would amount to 1000 pianos per tuner per year. So, to carry out 5 million piano tunings you would need about 5000 piano tuners in Europe. Great answers could also introduce interesting considerations such as the potential impact of the increasing popularity of electric keyboards, and whether technological changes have led to an oversupply of trained piano tuners. Answers that contain deeper exploration like this help a candidate by showing nuanced, creative and forward-looking thinking.

A **poor applicant** will be thrown by the ambiguity of this kind of question and may just guess a number, or fail to use common sense or basic general knowledge; e.g. not offering even a rough idea of the population of Europe, or merely asserting the number of pianos tuned per year rather than estimating it logically. More generally, students should avoid the temptation to waffle when uncertain. What differentiates a weak from a strong answer, at least in part, is that the strong candidate will adopt a systematic and deductive approach to answering the question.

Q53: India introduces a new population control policy to address the gender imbalance. If a couple has a girl, they may have another child. If they have a boy, they can't have any more children. What would be the new ratio of boys to girls?

Obviously, the nature of this answer may vary substantially between applicants – a political scientist and a mathematician are likely to give very different answers. However, the essential thing is to be able to clarify and justify the assumptions that you are making when you answer this question.

For example, a **good quantitative candidate** might decide to discount any parental preference for one gender or the other, and assume that there is perfect compliance with the policy. From there, the candidate would note that every birth has a 50% independent probability of resulting in a girl and a 50% independent probability of resulting in a boy. This would mean that half of all families stop at one child, and the rest go on to have another child which also has a 50% chance of being a girl. Putting aside practical considerations, this process could repeat infinitely - although the probability of an unbroken chain of girls converges towards zero. The big thing to note here is that with each pregnancy the probability resets to 50/50. However, even when offering a quantitative answer the candidate should still acknowledge practical limitations (e.g. having infinite children is not possible).

By contrast, a **good humanities candidate** may choose to focus on questions of citizen preferences, and the state's ability to enforce policies. You could draw on your real-world knowledge to consider instances where similar policies have been implemented. For example, sex selective abortion is illegal in China and the number of children per household is restricted, yet there is still a gender imbalance. A weaker answer might use this evidence to simply conclude that the policy in India would be ineffective; a stronger answer would acknowledge that the policy would have some impact, but could use the example of China to argue that this may not be enough to make the gender balance 50/50.

More broadly, a **weaker answer** is likely to contain some of these elements but fail to identify key assumptions, or make implausible assumptions (e.g. parents having infinite numbers of children). Candidates who choose to use examples should also be wary of relying on anecdote rather than reasoning. For example, a weaker answer may use the example of China to discuss the effects of birth control policies on sex ratios, but simply argue that because sex ratios remain imbalanced in China they will do the same in India; it would be more useful to explore the similarities and differences between the two countries and their policy environment, rather than making a blanket correlation.

Q54: Why are manhole covers round?

As with many of the more unusual questions you may be asked, the key here is not to find the answer, but rather to demonstrate the ability to engage with ambiguous questions and reason logically. The key advice for questions such as this is to always try to tackle the question head on, engage with the hypothetical, and ask yourself why this specific question is being asked. This should hopefully help you to avoid the sort of woolly and non-committal answers that questions such as this often provoke.

A **strong candidate** would focus on the core of this question: what is distinctive about the circular shape (as opposed to, say, a square)? A good candidate will also avoid the trap of getting hung-up on the empirical question of whether all manhole covers are round – there is no need to go beyond an acknowledgement of this doubt. Focusing instead on the unique features of circles would allow the candidate time to offer a range of explanations as to why manhole might be round. Possible explanations could be that you do not need to worry about the orientation of a circle when replacing it back on to the hole, circles can be rolled which is useful since a manhole cover is usually heavy and made out of metal, or that round manhole covers are less likely to fall down the manhole. A great candidate will be able to specifically link this answer back to the purpose of a manhole. For example, the cover being easy to roll is likely to be important if you only have one person working on the manhole, or when a manhole is deep and so preventing things (people, or the cover) falling down the hole is very important.

A **weak answer** could take several forms. Candidates who attempt to debate whether manholes are all round, are unlikely to meet with much success. Although under certain circumstances disagreeing with the premise of a question can be a fruitful tactic, this rarely tends to be the case when the premise is a factual claim. Other weak approaches include offering a vague answer such as `tradition` or `culture`. Answers such as this one fail to engage with the core of the question; a good warning sign is that your answer could apply to a broad range of other questions. If this is the case, your answer is probably lacking in specificity.

Q55: How many times per day does a clock's hand overlap?

There many ways of getting the answer other than the one provided below; however, more important than the specific method is walking through the steps in your reasoning clearly and logically. This does not just demonstrate your thinking process to the interviewer, but will also help you to avoid making silly mistakes by jumping to an answer too quickly. If you find it hard to structure your thoughts in your head, consider taking a minute to write down your thought process on a piece of paper.

A **good answer**: On a 12-hour clock face the hour hand completes two full circles in a day, and the minute hand does a full rotation every hour; i.e. 24 rotations in a day. Having established these facts, one approach is to visualise the first time the two hands cross. If you start from midnight with the hands in the same position you would need to wait for at least one full rotation before they intersect. Since the hour hand is moving from midnight to 1am the intersection would be at roughly 1:05 (it would actually be a bit later since the hour hand would actually be at the 1 when the minute was at the 12). Now we know that the two hands cross at approximately 1.05 we can visualize the next overlap which would be when the hour hand is at about 2 and the minute hand is at about 10 minutes past (again the numbers are not quite exact). What you might notice here is that the overlaps happen at about 65 minute intervals. There are 14400 minutes in a day (60 x 24), so if you divide 14400 by 65 you get a little over 22. Therefore the total number of overlaps would be 22.

As noted above, a **weak answer** may occur due to simple calculation error or trying to jump to the answer too quickly. For example: "The minute hand goes around the clock 24 times in a day, so it presumably crosses the minute hand once each time. So that would be 24." Many candidates may slip up on this question by choosing a seemingly obvious answer. The larger lesson to draw from this is that if a solution seems obvious, ask yourself whether it is likely that the interviewer would get any value from seeing you solve this problem. Not only the content, but also the brevity may be a warning sign that your answer is on the wrong track.

Q56: You are given 7 identical balls and another ball that looks the same as the others but is heavier than them. You can use a balance only two times. How would you identify which is the heavy ball?

Although questions like this may seem somewhat intimidating the best way to approach them is to start by slowly working step by step. You do not necessarily have to start with the correct method, but try to work towards it and rule out less useful approaches as you go.

A good candidate might start by noting that they do not know how much heavier the heavy ball is. From this information they can deduce that placing 3 balls on one side of the scale and 4 balls on the other may not give us precise enough information. Instead, for a more accurate approach we must start by placing an equal number of items on each side. If one places three balls on each side, then whichever side is heavier must include the heavy ball. However, if the balance is equal then the heavy ball must be the ball that was not placed on the scale. From here a candidate could deduce that either they had solved the problem, or they would need to repeat the experiment with the three balls on the heavy side of the balance. In this instance, the candidate would compare two of the balls from the heavier side and set the third ball aside. If either of the two balls on the balance was heavier we would have our answer, or if they were equal, the remaining ball that the candidate had set aside would be the heavier ball.

By contrast, **a weaker candidate** may use a process of trial and error instead of taking a step back, drawing conclusions from their thinking and using these new conclusions to inform their next move. Note that not all strong candidates will immediately come to the solution; the difference between the strong and the weak candidate is that a strong candidate will be able to course-correct as they go and spot the nature of their error, whereas a weak candidate may not be able to identify where they made a mistake.

Q57: What is your favourite number?

This question is a great opportunity for you to demonstrate enthusiasm for your chosen subject. For example, as a mathematician you may find a specific number theoretically interesting, as a historian you could pick a specific date, or as a biologist you might pick a number that represents an interesting phenomenon in the natural world (e.g. rate of bacterial reproduction). When answering the question, take care to pick something that you genuinely find interesting and can talk about at length, rather than something you think will sound impressive. Make sure the interviewer remembers you for the whole content of and justification for your answer, not just the opening line.

Although personal stories are unlikely to harm you, choosing your grandmother's birthday, a football player's jersey number or the numbers you always pick for the lottery is unlikely to strengthen your application. The important thing to remember when confronted with an unexpected question is to take a step back and think about how you can direct the conversation to something that will bolster your case for admission.

Finally, although it is important to draw in interesting content about your subject, a good candidate will also answer the question. A **weaker answer** might use the answer as a springboard to offer a prepared answer on an unrelated topic. For example, cite a historical date and then simply talk about their interest in that historical period. By contrast a **strong answer** might talk about the role numbers play in memory, or the importance of quantification in history. These answers are stronger because they focus on the core of the question and justify why the number is a relevant feature of the answer, rather than the number being an afterthought. Directly engaging with the question is important as it shows that you are responding authentically and in the moment, rather than seeming like a poor listener or an overprepared candidate.

Q58: Who am I?

This is a good opportunity for a candidate to demonstrate they have thought about their college choice and know who the tutors in their subject area are; this is a chance to show that you are thoughtful and engaged with your chosen degree subject.

Good answer: 'You are Professor X, you work in the field of [biomedical science, economics, etc]. I think more specifically you work in the subfield of [human anatomy/microeconomics] and some of your research looks at [cerebral cortical development/auction theory]. I was really excited about applying to this college because, as I mentioned in my personal statement, I am particularly interested in [the role of cortical development in conditions such as dyslexia/the application of auction theory to public goods tenders].'

This is a good answer because it shows that the candidate has serious academic reasons for applying to a college, and has begun to develop interests within their subject area. Of course, this is contingent on these interests being real. Do not bring up research if you do not understand it; this is likely to lead to embarrassment! There are other ways to answer this question. For example, a tutor might state on their college webpage that they love working with undergraduates, or you may have seen them give an inspiring talk at an Open Day. These are also valid things to bring up about a tutor, as they have chosen to put this information in the public domain.

A **weak answer** could go in a lot of different directions. For example, the student might attempt to move in an excessively abstract direction (e.g. what is the nature of identity?) - this might be OK if you are in a philosophy interview, but less so for subjects like maths. Alternatively, the student may simply not know who the interviewer is. You will typically be interviewed by fellows at the college, so you should have the opportunity to have a look at their research. Additionally, you are normally told who your interviewers will be prior to the interview, which should give you an opportunity to look them up.

Q59: Is there any question that you wished we had asked you?

This question is a great chance to highlight an aspect of your application that you would like to talk about. For example, you may have written about a specific book on your personal statement that you think you can speak about further in an interesting manner, or you might have written an extended essay which demonstrates your interest in and understanding of a specific subject. Thanking the interviewers and expressing enthusiasm about the content can also be a nice touch. However, it is inadvisable to simply state your desire to go to Oxbridge, or launch into abstract declarations of your love for the subject. These should be demonstrated through actions not words; over the top displays of emotion are more likely to make an interviewer uncomfortable than convince them to admit you.

More commonly, however, what will differentiate a strong from a weak answer is not the topic but rather the manner in which you talk about it. For example, a **strong answer** should highlight an aspect of your application in a concise manner that directly underscores your commitment to the subject and shows intellectual maturity. However, you do need to make the case as to why you want to discuss this; it should not come across as simply a desire to introduce impressive things you have done. Ways to avoid this include explaining why a given activity demonstrates your curiosity about your subject, or perhaps an interest in the process of academic research.

A **weaker answer** could come in many different forms. Any answer that strays into boasting or flattery is unlikely to make a favourable impression. If you genuinely do not have any topics you would like to discuss it is fine to admit to this; interviewers know that the interview experience can be stressful and not all candidates (even strong ones) will relish the prospect of further interview questions!

Q60: What are you looking forward to the least at this college?

This is a question where you can be honest to a certain extent, but must remain balanced. **Poor answers** are likely to fall into one of two extremes; the 'fake problem' or the 'too blunt'. Interviewers are unlikely to believe the candidate who claims that they are least looking forward to a choice of modules because they wish they could choose everything (is that really the worst possible thing you could think of?). As a result, this attempt to avoid admitting to any negative or undesirable opinion risks coming off as insincere. However, veering too far in the opposite direction is also inadvisable. Saying you are worried about the workload before you have even arrived is likely to raise red flags and make interviewers wonder whether you will be able to cope with the pace of Oxbridge.

By contrast a **good answer** will strike a balance between sincerity and oversharing by stating a genuine concern - but ideally one that does not relate to academic concerns. For example, you could quite reasonably express concerns about financial stability, being able to find a common cultural community, or other similar considerations. If these are genuine concerns, they are things a college will be interested in knowing so that they can try to help solve them. If you are struggling to find an appropriate concern, while not ideal it is OK to say that you will miss your cat, home cooking, or that you are mostly very excited about going to university and so do not yet have anything you are very worried about.

Ultimately, this sort of question serves two functions for interviewers: it helps them to decide whether students are applying for the right reasons (academic work not college balls), but also to make sure that they are aware of applicants concerns. Colleges really do want to make themselves accessible and friendly places, so this is a time when it can be appropriate to raise a concern or question that may have been bothering you.

Q61: Who has had the largest influence on your life?

Questions such as these should be answered in a way that is first and foremost plausible, and secondly makes the case for you as a candidate. Ways you can make that case include demonstrating that your interest in your chose subject is deep and long-standing (i.e. you didn't apply on a whim and you have specific subject interests).

Weak answers may come from candidates too eager to impress interviewers with their passion for their subject. Very few people are likely to believe that Marie Curie has had more influence on your life than a family member, or caregiver. It is important to remember that seeming genuine is just as important as seeming intelligent (if not more so). Other ways candidates can provide weak answers include being too laconic, or unreflective. Failing to relate the answer to your current subject interests, while not something that is likely to be penalised, might be a bit of a missed opportunity.

Explanation is the key to a **good answer**. For example, you might quite plausibly be able to say that your mum has been the biggest influence on your life, briefly discuss non-academic ways in which she has influenced you and then discuss how she has had a role in your intellectual development. Maybe she encountered problems when finding work that made you want to become an economist to better understand the labour market. Perhaps at a certain point she stopped being able to answer your questions about the world, and as a result you wanted to become a biologist. Ultimately, the connection you make will depend on both your subject and your chosen person. Of course, sometimes a connection to your degree will not be obvious, and that is fine. It is better to have a natural seeming answer than forcing a subject matter connection where none exists, and running the risk of seeming disingenuous.

Q62: If you were me, would you let yourself in?

Although some people might feel a temptation to answer 'no' to stand out, this is not the time for being wacky. Instead, treat this as an opportunity to advocate for yourself while also addressing any perceived weaknesses you might have. Each candidate will vary in the traits that make them distinctive, so answers will differ substantially between candidates. However, a **strong candidate** should start by considering qualities that Oxbridge might look for in a candidate, and then assess themselves against this framework. Not only does this directly answer the question, but also demonstrates to the interviewer that the candidate is a structured and rigorous thinker.

For example, you might start by defining a 'good' candidate as having both a deep interest in their subject, and academic aptitude. You might then illustrate your interest in your subject by referring to your personal statement and extra-curriculars. This could include addressing any weakness (e.g. mixed GCSE results) with reference to a mitigating or balancing factor (e.g. a strong focus on science subjects, and strong predicted A-levels). Any suggestion that a weakness is either acceptable or irrelevant should be backed up by a plausible explanation; if you believe that an explanation will simply sound like an excuse, it may be better to not raise it at all.

A **poor candidate** may have woolly reasoning or be unable to explain what makes them distinctive - many candidates will have excellent marks and a good personal statement. It is also inadvisable to speak negatively about other candidates (even in broad brush terms). For example, I am X unlike all of Y who are the same. You can make points about your own distinctiveness without coming across as mean-spirited or negative. Remember that these interviewers will have to teach you; they do not just want to know you are clever, they also want to know that working together will be an enjoyable experience.

Q63: What do you think my favourite colour is? Why do you say that?

Although many questions offer the opportunity to demonstrate your interest in your subject, in certain circumstances you may have trouble doing so naturally. Again, answering the question and demonstrating good listening skills is key. In situations such as these, rather than offering a tangential and canned answer, think of critical thinking strengths you can highlight through your answer. In this instance, good deductive reasoning and clear communication can help you demonstrate to your interviewer that you are a clear and logical student who will fare well in tutorials.

A **good answer** may discuss how a favourite colour might influence someone's clothing or room decoration choices. This would not be simple reasoning, such as "people will wear their favourite colour", but would introduce nuance by considering limitations to the evidence that they are using. For example, if you really like bright pink or bright green you might not wear that colour in a professional setting, or just limit it to somewhere inconspicuous such as a tie, or a pair of socks. Importantly, although a good answer will consider limitations to reasoning it *should* come to a conclusion. A candidate who twists themselves in knots of uncertainty will come across as a messy thinker who is not able to weigh competing pieces of evidence. By all means acknowledge weaknesses in your logic or contradictory evidence, but you should offer a guess.

A **weak answer** might suffer from a lack of nuance; or conversely a candidate may be so aware of the limitations of their reasoning that they offer a long-winded reply that ultimately comes to no conclusion. Other pitfalls include coming across as combative or annoyed by a seemingly irrelevant question. Although the interview experience can be stressful, being polite and upbeat is key; these are people you will have to work with.

Q64: What is a lie? How do I know what you just said isn't a lie?

In questions that ask you to offer definitions of complex concepts, a great way to start is by using examples to explore your initial intuition. Interviewers are unlikely to expect you to have a ready-made definition; many of these concepts are the subject of intense academic debate! What *is* important, however, is showing that you are a creative thinker who can course-correct and explore their own thinking in a structured manner.

For example, a **strong candidate** might start with a definition such as "a lie is a statement that is knowingly false", and then use specific examples to test whether this definition fits across a range of contexts. For example, what does it mean to lie to oneself? What is the role of intent in the definition of lying? Are 'white lies' still lies? These are just a few examples of questions a candidate might raise, and there are no definitive right or wrong answers. Instead, the important feature of a good answer is that a candidate can navigate from the intellectually abstract definition to a concrete situation with fluency, demonstrating both strong conceptual thinking and an ability to drive their own intellectual process. The use of examples is a great way to do this because it allows you to ground your answer in everyday experience and may help you to tease out weaknesses or contradictions in your thinking. Again, coming to a conclusion (or at least a specific definition) is critical to a good answer. You can certainly acknowledge weaknesses or uncertainties, but a good candidate should be able to weigh evidence and come down on a side.

By contrast, a **weaker candidate** is likely to be less reflective about the quality of their own answer, and perhaps rush to a conclusion (or be unwilling to come to one at all). One mistake that candidates often make is thinking that an interview is a debate; that they are obliged to stick to and defend their original statements. In fact, it is often a great idea to let your position evolve if you change your mind. Tutors are looking for people who are open-minded and intellectually flexible.

Q65: If you could keep objects from the present for the future, what would they be?

Rather than taking this as a whimsical or warm up question, use this as an opportunity to highlight your passion for your subject. This will naturally vary from candidate to candidate, but the broad lesson is that even seemingly off the wall questions can be used to strengthen your case for admission.

A **good answer** from an historian might, for example, highlight their thoughts about the importance of sources to future generations of historians. A biologist may be interested in species preservation and want to keep a patch of the Amazon. In instances where material objects might be less relevant to your subject (e.g. as an economist, or a theoretical physicist), you could show creativity by suggesting an item emblematic of a phenomenon you find interesting (e.g. promotional material from the sharing economy, or the computer used to carry out complex calculations).

A **weaker answer** could take many different forms, but failing to relate your answer to your subject or poorly justifying your choice are common errors. Many weak answers use the same examples as stronger ones, but simply fail to fully explain why they selected the item. For example, a biologist simply saying "I would preserve a tree in the Amazon because I think that the biodiversity in underexplored areas of the rainforest is enormous, and I think deforestation might eradicate our chances to access this knowledge" does not fully demonstrate that the candidate understands what they are talking about. Their answer remains very general and does not specify what sort of information they are concerned about preserving. A candidate in this position could easily strengthen their answer by drawing on examples of findings they have read about, thus demonstrating that their example is not a vague concern about the environment but rooted in specific knowledge indicative of a deep curiosity about their subject.

Q66: What is more important – art or science?

As with many abstract questions, a **good answer** will offer clear reasoning, an acknowledgement of alternative positions, and an explicit conclusion. For example, you may believe that *generally speaking* science is more important than art because science is central to material improvements in people's well-being. You might then acknowledge some weaknesses in this position, e.g. that this is not true of all science (certain forms of pure mathematics have no known practical application), or that art can be critical to social or moral progress. Finally, do offer a rebuttal (e.g. physical life is the basis of all other values and so although art is important, medical advances are necessary to enjoy art). These are just a few examples of arguments that could be raised, and a compelling case could be made on either side.

A **weaker answer** may offer the same general reasoning as the strong answer, but simply fail to offer much justification. Another common trap is listing the advantages and disadvantages of both disciplines but failing to explain how you weigh these different considerations. This is a question that may arouse strong feelings in many candidates who want to demonstrate their interest in their chosen subject; however, you should be careful about coming across as brow beating, or arrogant. Even if you – as a scientist – believe that art can only exist because of scientific progress, there are ways to explain this view without seeming dismissive of something that many others value enormously. The same applies to humanities students who believe that life only has meaning due to art – beware of sounding pretentious! Once again, always remember that your interviewer may tutor you in the future, so coming across as friendly and open-minded is just as important as seeming clever. Launching into a tirade is more likely to make you seem unreflective than passionate.

Q67: If you could have one superpower, which one would it be? Why?

Seemingly random questions can often be used as an opportunity to talk about your interest in your subject. One way of answering this question would be to think of a problem that you face in your field, and select a superpower that would help you resolve it. Obviously, omniscience might do this, but probably also makes for a less interesting answer.

As with other questions of this variety, what will differentiate a good answer from a weak answer is not the topic chosen, but rather the explanation given. For example, a historian could talk about their desire to time travel; but what would distinguish a good answer from a weak or commonplace one would be the justification. For example, a **weaker candidate** might simply say "I am interested in Napoleonic history so I would love to be able to observe the Battle of Waterloo". While the candidate may talk specifically what they would like to see and demonstrate strong understanding of Napoleonic history, enthusiasm for historical facts is not the same as showing a scholarly approach.

By contrast, a **strong candidate** might discuss their desire to go to a specific period and then relate this to an interest in collecting oral history sources. In an answer such this, the student not only explains their reasoning and relates it to a specific personal interest, but they also display good knowledge of the problems scholars of their subject might face. All of this suggests a mature thinker who would do well at university.

Although a time travelling historian might seem like an obvious example, similar answers can come from a variety of disciplines. A physicist might want to be able to observe unobservable events, a biologist might want eyes with the power of microscopes. Ultimately this sort of question is very open to interpretation and the strength of the answer will lie in the justification.

Q68: Would you ever go on a one-way trip to Mars? Why/why not?

As ever, you should treat every question as an opportunity to highlight why you would be a good candidate for admission. Even questions such as this, which may appear to be utterly random, can often be related back to your chosen subject. However, it is also fine to inject human concerns into your answers; it is always important for your reply to seem natural.

For example, a **good answer** from a biologist might talk about their desire to know more about microbial life on Mars, and their interest in the findings of the Mars Curiosity Rover, but ultimately conclude that they would rather rely on earth-based study than abandon their family. The student expresses enthusiasm for their subject, but also sets out quite reasonable limits on what they are willing to sacrifice for science. This honesty may come across as more credible than the candidate who claims that they would be willing to abandon their family and friends. A word to the wise: if you do raise specific examples (e.g. microbial life) then be certain that you can talk about them in more depth if probed. For non-STEM candidates, a clear relationship to your subject may be harder to draw; but creative thinking should allow you to find one. For example, historians might draw parallels with prior explorers of the globe, and philosophers could establish an ethical framework for evaluating such a choice. However, even if you cannot think of a link to your subject, remember to offer clear reasoning and a conclusion.

A **weak answer** could fall into any of the pitfalls mentioned above. Although it is fine to answer that one would indeed take a one-way trip, making sweeping claims such as "I love physics so much I would abandon my family and live alone on Mars" may ring somewhat hollow. Other weak answers may simply fail to grasp the opportunity to relate their thinking back to their subject. While this is unlikely to actively harm the your chances, it would be a missed opportunity.

Q69: Does human nature change?

Questions which ask candidates to discuss abstract concepts are a great opportunity to demonstrate to your interviewer that you are a structured thinker, who can engage with high level concepts and not get muddled. To answer this question well, the candidate needs to explore what people mean by the term 'human nature'. The candidate may also want to explore what is meant by the term 'change', and under what circumstances their answer might vary.

A **good candidate** might, for example, discuss whether the use of the term 'nature' implies some unchanging essence. There are a variety of strategies a candidate could adopt to do this effectively, including looking at examples of when people use the term 'human nature' and what they tend to be explaining when they do this. Alternatively, the candidate may want to provide a direct definition of human nature (e.g. the basic motivations of all homo sapiens). Strong candidates will also seek to define the parameters of their answer. Rather than simply providing a yes or no conclusion to their answer the candidate may offer a qualified response, e.g. "Yes, human nature can change over time, but a single individual cannot change their nature". While this is just an example, answers such as these show to the interviewer that the candidate has thought deeply about their answer and is able to generate a rigorous conceptual framework on the fly.

Weaker answers are likely to fall into one of a few different traps. Some candidates mistake conversations such as these for a debate and try to defend their instinctive initial answer; however, this can often come across as intellectual inflexibility, or arrogance. Showing willingness to engage with new ideas and revise your own when confronted with (reasonable) criticism can be a strength. Other candidates struggle with the lack of structure provided by this question and will throw out a range of possible considerations but be unable to draw them together into any coherent answer. Taking a minute before answering the question to jot down some thoughts can be a good way to give your answer more structure.

Q70: Define 'success' in one sentence.

This question, like many of the more abstract questions asked, is an opportunity for the candidate to showcase the quality of their thinking when confronted with an unfamiliar topic. Beyond simply showing clear and logical reasoning, candidates can also excel by using this question as an opportunity to emphasise their passion for their subject through their choice of examples.

For example, **a good candidate** might start with an initial definition that is further refined as they reason out loud. One way to do this would be work through a few examples to test whether the definition of success they came up with holds true in each case. An answer would be enhanced if the examples the candidate chooses not only draw on their subject matter expertise, but are also a little unusual. For example, an art historian could, of course, discuss whether Van Gogh (who died in penury) can be considered a success; but this is an example even a non-subject specialist might come up with. By contrast, selecting an artist from a period the candidate mentioned in their personal statement would allow them to demonstrate that their interest has real depth to it.

As with many with many of these abstract questions, a **weak answer** to this question is likely to be caused by a lack of structure, or under-explanation. A good answer and a weak answer may start off with the same definition; but where the quality of the answers will diverge is in the explanation of how a candidate came to that answer. A weaker candidate may offer examples of success as evidence, whereas the good candidate will use examples to pick out specific features of what could and could not be called success. Returning to the Van Gogh example, the strong candidate might point to the tension between the lack of recognition during his lifetime and his subsequent acclaim, and then examine whether or not we would call him a success if he had been famous during his lifetime and then forgotten. By contrast, the weaker candidate's exploration may be limited to noting that 'success can happen outside of your lifetime'.

Q71: Is there such a thing as truth?

Applicants can adopt one of two strategies to answer this question well. As ever, students can draw examples from their own subject to illustrate their answer; for example, mathematicians might want to talk about proofs, and historians might want to talk about source reliability. Alternatively, students can take this as an opportunity to simply show clear reasoning, and good verbal expression. The best applicants may be able to combine these two approaches.

A **good candidate** might start with a simple answer that they explicitly state they plan to refine. An example of such an answer would be "I think there is such a thing as truth, and I will define truth as a statement that describes a situation that exists or has existed in the world". From there, the candidate might use situations which appear to be truthful but do not cohere with this definition to examine whether it is possible to come to a meaningful definition of truth. For example, they might examine whether statements which are mildly inaccurate can be called truth and whether it is possible to make truly accurate statements (e.g. can we say that 'the cat jumped on the table five minutes ago' is a lie, if the cat jumped on the table 6 minutes ago?). Good candidates will also note that certain domains might have 'truth' and others might not. For example, do moral or aesthetic statements have truth value?

A **weaker applicant** is likely to offer a less thoughtful answer. The weakest answers are likely to be characterised by brevity: "Yes, because I can say that this chair is here, and it is. That's a true statement". Although you may believe this to be true, it is always worth fleshing an answer out by exploring where you could be wrong. Less obviously weak answers are likely to suffer from a lack of structure. It is very possible for a candidate to raise a few interesting thoughts but fail to explore them comprehensively or organise them well. While intellectual promise is helpful, without clear explanation a candidate's answer may simply be interpreted as scattershot.

Q72: You are shrunk down so you're the size of a matchstick and then put into a blender with metal blades. It is about to be turned on – what do you do?

This question can be used to demonstrate all sorts of different skills, from creativity to analytical thinking, and could even show how you are able to apply subject knowledge to an unusual problem. The physicists, biologists, and engineers out there may want to ask clarifying questions about the scenario to gain more information, such as the density of the shrunken human body. If you can explain why these questions are relevant and how they influence your answer, then ask away – it is often an excellent way to engage.

For those for whom there may be no obvious subject connection, a **good candidate** could simply work through the problem by breaking it down into component pieces. As with any non-traditional question there is no single correct way of doing this. For example, certain candidates might identify that there are two solutions: break the machine or avoid the blades. They could then discuss which of these two solutions would be more likely to succeed and then select that solution. Other equally successful candidates might consider whether someone is trying to blend them intentionally - and if not, how someone so small might be able to attract the attention of the person about to turn on the blender. Candidates are, of course, also expected to show basic common sense; just because a situation is fantastical does not mean that they can posit absurd solutions. Candidates should try to consider realistic features such as the centrifugal force of the blades, or strength of the machine relative to someone the size of a matchstick.

Weaker candidates are less likely to be let down by the content of their answers, than by the lack of enthusiasm, intellectual curiosity, or flexibility that they demonstrate. Note that even the good candidate may not find a satisfying solution to this (rather strange) problem; but what they will do is explore a variety of ideas, and demonstrate the ability to evaluate their own thought process while remaining engaged with the interview.

ECONOMICS

This interview will require you to demonstrate passion and a genuine desire to study your chosen subject. You can be asked to discuss a source extract, a diagram or a mathematical problem.

In E&M interviews, business-related questions will also feature, where applicants have to tackle basic problems related to the operation and management of a firm.

An economist may be asked economics-related questions or questions from a related subject, such as mathematics, business or even politics and history. An applicant for Economics and Management will be asked questions on both economics and business/management. (The **interviewers understand applicants may not have studied economics** before – be prepared to explain why you think you want to study economics and show through extra-curricular reading or activities how you've fostered your interest). Before the interview, it should be clear which subject will be the focus of any interview.

Candidates are not expected to have studied the subject they are applying for previously at A-level. Instead, candidates should have good general knowledge and to demonstrate interest in and enthusiasm for studying economics (and business in the case of E&M applicants), to demonstrate logic and critical thinking, and to communicate clearly and effectively.

Many of the questions asked in the interview will be a larger question, with many smaller sub-questions to guide the answer from the start to a conclusion. The main question may seem difficult, impossible or random at first, but take a breath and start discussing with your interviewer different ideas you have for breaking down the question into manageable pieces. Don't panic. **The questions are designed to be difficult** to give you the chance to show your full intellectual potential. They will help guide you to the right idea if you provide ideas for them to guide.

This is your chance to show your creativity, analytical skills, intellectual flexibility, problem-solving skills, and your go-getter attitude. Don't waste it on nervousness or a fear of messing up or looking stupid.

For economics, the questions will usually take one of a few possible forms based on highlighting skills necessary to 'think like an economist'. The six main question types are:

- Critical reasoning questions ("Tell me what your view on ... is").
- Normative questions ("Should the government do the following?").
- Practical questions ("How would you determine that...").
- Statistical questions ("Given this data...").
- Questions about proximate causes (mechanism; "How does...") and MultiMate causes (function; "Why does..."), usually both at once.
- Quantitative questions for example from game theory or economic principles.

The questions also have recurring themes because they are also prevalent topics for economic and management theory and research: markets, money, development economics, profit maximisation of a firm, game theory, unemployment and inflation, growth theory and international trade.

WORKED QUESTIONS

Below are a few examples of how to start breaking down an interview question along with model answers.

Q1: I'm going to give you £50. You have to offer some of it to another person, but you won't get to keep a penny unless they accept the offer, with that in mind, how much of your £50 would you offer to them?

This is a mathematical question that will, therefore, require a numeric answer. The most important feature of a strong candidate is the ability to answer the question directly and from an analytical point of view the interviewer set through the phrasing of the question.

Applicant: So, I'm looking for a nominal value between 0 and £50 to be offered to the other person. This seems to be a question related to the field of game theory; the area that focuses on understanding optimal strategic decisions and their modelling. Unfortunately, I'm not familiar with the tools of this discipline but I will try to tackle the question using my basic economic intuition and mathematics. I understand that economics primarily deals with incentives, and here the two participants have very different incentives. Let me consider both of them and then outline who will get their way or what kind of a compromise they will reach. Both me and the other person want to get as much money as possible, but we both can't get the £50, **there is a trade-off**.

We also have different ways of achieving our aims: I set the amount, the other person decides whether to accept or not. The other person can stop me from having any money whatsoever; this seems to be a strong tool against me. So I will have to make the other person happy otherwise we will both walk away without anything. Given this, how can I get the best outcome for myself while navigating through my dual objective: getting money, but satisfying the other one? I have to give the person something, even though I don't want to.

Anything I give should make the other happy since the alternative is 0. Therefore, mathematically, I should probably offer the least amount: £1. But would that be acceptable? At this point, I could consider other, alternative methods to understanding cooperation that can better deal with phenomena like envy, fairness, altruism, etc.

Assessment: The student immediately sets the context and frame of the question, which suggests a very strong candidate who is not trying different things but knows the direction of the answer. Identifying the relevant area in Economics for the question is a nice touch that doesn't require extensive prior knowledge of that particular field, but still shows that the student has a general understanding of what belongs to the subject.

The interviewers don't expect you to be an expert in a niche field. Instead, they want you to apply your existing knowledge and experience to a new problem.

A good candidate will always **draw from multiple disciplines** and apply the seemingly most relevant knowledge they have. Structuring the answer is always key, most importantly, to make it easier for the interviewer to help with the solution. If they know what the plan of attack is, they can guide the applicant in the direction that leads to the correct answer most easily. An outstanding candidate goes beyond conventional wisdom and demonstrates real outside-the-box thinking by having the ability to challenge seemingly fundamental assumptions. In this particular example, the candidate could point out that there are many people to whom getting the highest amount of monetary gain might not be a primary goal, hence making the simple mathematical analysis problematic.

Q2: You've mentioned globalisation in your personal statement, how would you define it, and what would you say the benefits of it might be to ordinary people?

The main challenge in this question is clearly the broadness of the topic. This is a subject hundreds of academics and other pundits have written hefty books on. How does one answer this question in 2-3 minutes so the response has sufficient content but is still structured?

The important thing to keep in mind here is that sometimes the applicant's first response serves only as a discussion starter. There is no need to include everything you would want to talk about in excruciating details, the interviewers only want to hear a few points they can start from. Then they will drive the discussion in a direction they want to.

Applicant: Let me start by clarifying the concept of globalisation. It's a household concept by now, but I'm not sure we have a universal agreement on what is meant by it. To me, globalisation is the process through which national and regional borders become increasingly irrelevant, as a result of culture, business and general economic activity all become more homogeneous and are formed by actors unrelated to any single country. This definition allows me to capture the different aspects of globalisation each of which requires a different analytical perspective: sociology, economics, politics, international relations, etc.

From an economics point of view, **the average citizen gains in two main ways from globalisation**. First, the citizen benefits from the diversification of products and services available for consumption at lower prices. Second, the broadening of opportunities allows citizens to have a better match between their skills and their occupation.

I will first consider the benefits of free trade. The emergence of transnational corporations and wider political movements supporting globalisation have put increasing pressure on governments to allow for greater freedom in international trade. This has resulted in an unprecedented expansion of consumption goods and services available for all customers. Just think about all the exotic fruits, spices, and craft goods one can buy even in their local Tesco. International competition, another benefit of globalisation, has furthermore allowed all goods to be priced competitively on a global scale, leading to significant price drops. This process clearly benefits the average citizen.

My second point relates to the tendency that globalisation comes with the **expansion of cross-border mobility** too. This happens for a range of reasons: better and more easily available information about opportunities abroad, the internationalisation of communication (English as lingua franca) and the transnational HR procedures and multinational corporations. The average citizen benefits from being able to find a position more ideally suited for them than before globalisation had emerged.

Having said that, I believe it's important to note the likely negative consequences of globalisation too: the threat of dumping in developed countries, the threat of exploitation in developing countries or diminishing cultural diversity are just a few on the list.

Assessment: The interviewers most likely have already interrupted the interviewee by this time somewhere. They might be interested in a discussion on free trade, the applicant's thoughts on multinational corporations, etc. But by presenting a clearly outlined structure in the beginning, the applicant ensured that the interviewers know that a strong and well-argued presentation would follow had they not interrupted. It is also advisable with such a complex question to take some time before starting the answer, this allows any applicant to articulate any thoughts in a more organised manner. A focus on the economic arguments is also important as this is an economics and not a sociology interview, and the points, therefore, need to be chosen accordingly.

Q3: I'm going to show you a teapot. Feel free to examine it in as much detail as you'd like - once you've done that, tell me about whether you could value it.

An odd question that clearly is not interested in specific knowledge, but rather pushing the applicant way out of their comfort zone. A question like this can easily appear on both an Economics and a Management interview as it requires out-of-the-box thinking and independence to solve challenging, unfamiliar problems, crucial in both fields. Each student would answer this question differently; the only important point is to show confidence and originality in an answer.

Straight Economics Applicant:

I can certainly look for a suitable price for this teapot from my perspective. However, the valuation different individuals assign to the same product often vary significantly and also with changing circumstances too. Therefore, my monetary valuation is not going to be a universal one.

I would start by stating that the monetary value of the teapot will fundamentally be linked to the concept of a market. I am not looking for the intrinsic value (i.e. the 'usefulness' of the teapot) but the ideal monetary amount it should be exchanged for. Thus I turn to the basic knowledge I have about the market and try to understand how those will determine the optimal exchange price of the teapot. There are two key factors on a market: supply and demand. I will consider both of them in relation to our example.

I know that if goods are supplied widely, its prices or monetary value will be lower than of goods in limited supply. Consider the example of water vs. diamonds. It's not that diamonds are more 'useful' than water, but that they are only available in a very limited amount; hence their supply is constrained. Whereas, water is essential for life but is abundant in supply. Consequently, diamonds have a much larger monetary value than water. In our case, a teapot can probably be bought in any large department store, however, its cracks and tea marks on its side make it unique. Therefore, one could argue that the supply of this teapot is extremely limited, indicating a high monetary price.

Equally, demand for the teapot is also probably fairly limited. While these qualities are visually pleasing, it is probably fair to assume that there aren't many who could appreciate its artistic beauty. Modest demand suggests a low monetary value, as people would not be willing to pay much for the item. This **concept of willingness-to-pay** is a central one for our analysis, and we would have to conduct a more thorough investigation into the existing demand for an artistically cracked teapot.

The two sides (supply and demand) put together suggest that **this teapot should be valued similarly to other niche products** with both small demand and supply. Such products include pieces of art, rarities or unique luxury products (e.g. custom made sports cars or watches).

Assessment: This is an economist's take on the question who tries to analyse the problem with the tools provided by the discipline. The question provides a great opportunity to enter a discussion on markets and prices, complemented by a basic summary of the forces present on a market. With such a question, a specific, numeric answer is not necessarily required as the process of understanding the determinants of prices is much more important. A clear outline, clarification of definitions and real life examples all add to the answer and the image communicated to the interviewers. But once again, many alternative answers could be presented here. The important point is that the applicant shouldn't feel intimidated by a seemingly unrealistic and unsolvable question.

Finally, if the starting point of the question is already ridiculous, then the applicant is free to make unrealistic assumptions too, as long as those can be defended somehow (e.g. the artistic cracks on the teapot add extra monetary value to it).

Economics and Management Applicant:
From a firm's perspective, it is crucial to understand the underlying processes that determine the monetary value of a product. In our situation, the monetary value is equivalent to finding the price of the teapot. I am going to consider three methods to establish that value:

- Pricing based on competition
- Pricing based on cost
- Psychological pricing

The first method seems to be the most obvious to me as it simply builds on the competitive tendencies in a market. This would require us to look at any other seller of similar teapots and record their prices. Afterwards, we simply have to decide if we want to undercut them or simply price it according to their set monetary valuations. Online retailers and, in this particular case, used goods' resellers can both provide a starting point.

Secondly, I could simply figure out how much it costs me to produce it if I'm a decision-maker in the company involved in the creation of the product. Then I would add some profit margin on my costs and that would give me the monetary valuation of the teapot. The **production costs,** in this case, could include raw materials (porcelain, paint, etc.), labour costs, electricity, rent for the workplace and so on. A profit margin is required to make it worthwhile running the business and provide a payout to the company's owners.

Finally, I have read about behavioural economics before, for example in the book *Freakonomics* or in *Predictably Irrational.* These books showed me, how psychological factors play a crucial role in our perceptions of prices. The idea about the **relativity of prices explains the lack of a fundamental link between products and their monetary value**.

Therefore, the **prices of this teapot could be anything in a wide range**, depending on the psychological connections I create, through procedures such as *anchoring*.

Assessment: The student always has to tailor the answer to the subject of the interview. One of the most important requirements on an interview is to show that the applicant is capable of analysing problems from the perspective of the given discipline. Thus, in this case, the student had to demonstrate the ability to consider the firm's view, collecting thoughts around basic concepts that an applicant might be familiar with: costs, competition, etc. The brightest candidates shine through their ability to complement the basic materials with extra reading and real life examples.

Q4: Considering recent events, do you think that the creation of the Eurozone was a good idea?

A good response: "For me, the main objectives of the Eurozone were to improve trade between European nations and to provide more economic stability for those nations involved. I think the European Union has been successful in the first of these goals, however, when addressing the latter, it is clear that the last two decades have been rather turbulent for all Eurozone countries, especially considering the issues with the COVID-19 vaccine rollout. Proponents of the Euro may argue that weak nations such as Greece would never have survived the economic crisis of 2008 without the presence of the Eurozone, but others may argue that a lack of control over individual countries' monetary policy contributed to the severity of the recession. One interesting aspect of the Eurozone process is that it has highlighted the high geographical mobility of labour in many European nations..."

Assessment: This is an extremely open-ended question, which provides the candidate with the opportunity to talk about a multitude of topics and issues. It is easy to get side-tracked with such an unstructured question, but the applicant should make sure they answer the question. However, there is potential for them to talk about areas that interest them, and display their enthusiasm for the subject in doing so.

Candidates should, however, be wary about trying to suggest they have a substantial knowledge of areas that they don't, in reality, know much about.

This question may be followed up with further questioning by the interviewer on more specific aspects of the questions, and the least helpful thing a candidate can do when trying to impress a tutor is falsify knowledge of certain topics and then get 'caught out' doing so.

It is worth bearing in mind that not only is the tutor looking for intelligence; **they are looking for someone that they are happy to teach for the next few years**. Personality can be a factor in determining their decision: arrogance or attempting to deceive a tutor may not be looked upon fondly.

Q5: What would you say if someone used the fact that people who went through higher education get higher wages to argue that going to uni makes you rich?

This question invites the applicant to address a situation closest to what an economist is qualified for. Take a dataset and form a hypothesis. Then test the hypothesis using the dataset to form a conclusion and thus, provide policy recommendations. In an interview, a student might be asked to perform any part of the above process or to give an account of an understanding behind the approach in its entirety. In this case, an externally formed hypothesis and policy recommendation needs to be evaluated. The key, once again, is not to go into a detailed discussion about econometrics, but to demonstrate some basic aptitude for numerical analysis.

Assessment: In my answer, I am going to focus on the plausible conclusions that can be drawn from a statistical result – in this case, that individuals who go to university have a higher average salary than those who don't – while I am going to take the statistical result itself as given. We could, and ideally should discuss the methods used to arrive at that result and. of course. their validity, but this would be too time-consuming in the current circumstances.

We can illustrate the result on a graph that would look something like this. [Draws a simple x-y diagram with a 45-degree line from the origin and with scattered points around it. The axes would be labelled: earnings and education]. More education is *correlated* with higher earnings.

This is an important result; making us wonder about the likely benefits of education towards people's wages and their living standards, which is one of the government's primary objectives.

However, as we know it well, **correlation is not causation**. While the former simply means that two variables change their values similarly, the latter means the changes in one variable lead to changes in the other variable. Basic statistical methods, such as a simple graphical illustration as seen before, are only able to show us *correlation*; we don't know why education and wages are high at the same points. More advanced statistical analysis would allow us to go into further details and hopefully enable us to form statements about *causation,* too. With the information given in the question, it could well be that there is **reverse causality**; a situation where causation actually runs reversely. Those who are richer might decide to go to university as they can afford not to earn wages while studying.

Equally, it could be that there is a third, unknown variable that affects both variables. For instance, the geographic area individuals live in: urban citizens can have both higher wages and better access to higher education when compared to rural inhabitants.

In both of these cases, we would see a correlation between education and wages, but that would not mean that education causes higher wages. Therefore, I would say we need to **further investigate the data** to understand whether in this case, there is indeed a causal effect running from university education to higher earnings.

Assessment: This question allowed the applicant to demonstrate a number of vital skills. First of all, priorities needed to be set. The applicant had to understand that there is no time to address all aspects of the question, from data analysis to recommendations.

Second, the applicant could make use of graphs, the confident use of which is a fundamental skill any aspiring economist or management student should have. Third, the basic notion: *correlation is not causation* was required for the answer. This is a concept all applicants should feel comfortable about as it's the basic principle of statistics.

The interviewee could also shine by bringing in originality in trying to come up with reasons other than education → wages. In an interview situation, the interviewer would likely specifically ask about this rather than expecting the applicant to feel the need to list examples, but the importance of original thoughts is evident nonetheless. Finally, the applicant needed not to forget that the question was: "What would you say?", therefore, the answer needed to be specific. Had the applicant stopped before the last paragraph, some points would have been taken away for not directly answering the question.

Q6: Do you think the government should privatise the NHS?

This question provides an opportunity for the applicant to present their understanding of the issue, but they must be wary not to be drawn into giving a political argument. The focus should be placed on the economic impacts of privatisation, rather than personal opinions. The applicant has to formulate an argument about a topic that is both important and probably relatively unfamiliar for most A-level students. As always, it is not the factual knowledge of healthcare economics which is required, but **good structure and critical thinking**.

Applicant:

Privatisation is the act of transferring assets from public ownership (effectively state ownership) to private owners through the sale of the assets. Political parties from the left and the right have had a long-standing debate over the desirable extent of public ownership of certain strategic companies and sectors, e.g. schools, hospitals, utilities or public transportation operators. Out of these, the transfer of the healthcare provider, the NHS, has been one of the most controversial topics in UK politics, effectively since the creation of a universal health care provider shortly after WWII.

There are strong reasons for both supporting and opposing the transformation of the healthcare system into a market-driven system. However, I still believe that the arguments against it are stronger, thus I would not support the privatisation of the NHS. I have **three main reasons** to believe so: adverse effects on doctor-patient relationships, social injustice, and insecurity of continuous provision.

Firstly, I have always thought that **doctors choose their profession very differently** from what economists assume about rational agents, who only care about monetary reward. They are dedicated to helping the sick and doing everything they can to do their jobs best. If the NHS was privatised, there is a good chance business owners of hospitals would introduce measures to motivate doctors to think more business-mindedly. This would, however, endanger the personal trust patients need to feel when they see their doctor about their health.

Secondly, allowing private owners to supply healthcare services would threaten with them **seeking profits above patient care**. They could increase prices of services as demand for basic health services is inelastic (we are all willing to pay nearly anything for the health of our loved ones). While the well-off could probably still pay for their healthcare, with higher prices many would not be able to purchase even basic services.

Finally, a private owner might decide to continue the supply of profitable services and cut back on others or even shut down loss-making hospitals in less developed areas. This could mean that **healthcare is not universally available across the UK**, undermining citizens' inevitable right for equal treatment.

Of course, privatisation doesn't have to take such an extreme form and it can also be heavily regulated to improve some of the above-mentioned areas. Yet, the potential problems are so serious that **even if the NHS is not an economically viable business and costs the State a lot, it should remain in the public domain.**

Assessment: The applicant started with placing the question in a historical and political context, which is always a good idea with questions of this sort. It shows the interviewer that the applicant didn't just memorise arguments for topics but actually understands how things come together. A clear structure and a strong stance are also qualities of a strong applicant. Of course, such a question is bound to lead to a discussion where the interviewer challenges the applicant and comes up with strong counter-arguments. The applicant is expected to respond to those challenges, but not to give up their stance unless factually proven wrong.

Another good response: "There are economic benefits and costs of privatisation, which would be particularly emphasised in the case of a large institution like the NHS. The benefits of privatisation may include the potential for improved competition in the healthcare provision industry. Improved competition has benefits for an economy as it means that firms have an incentive to improve efficiency and innovate. This could mean lower costs for consumers and an improved service. However, it could be argued that this is a welfare issue and that health care would be underprovided to poorer citizens in a free market. It may also be reasoned that the high barriers to entry make healthcare provision a natural monopoly and that privatisation would lead to one firm dominating the market and exploiting its powers to overcharge. I would not support privatisation of the NHS as I do not think healthcare is a good that should be made excludable based on price."

Q7: Let's say I'm the CEO of a major company, what do you think my biggest concern will be?

The applicant has to show the ability to 'think like a manager' and to analyse questions from their perspective. With such an open-ended question, the challenge is not to find something to talk about but to be able to make a proper case out of it with valid reasons. There is no wrong answer, only insufficient reasoning.

Good Applicant: Chief Executive Officers are the people in charge of the overall business and with the final say on most daily issues, where the Board of Governors doesn't intervene. The pressure and responsibility on them are tremendous and finding a way to prioritise their tasks and problems is crucial. CEOs serve as the **ultimate link** between the company's employees, owners and customers. Therefore, rather than any individual task of their own, I think it's the management of opposing incentives and goals which are the biggest problem facing CEOs.

The workers in the company strain themselves to achieve better working conditions, higher wages and are often trying to minimise the work effort they exert. Shareholders seek a return on their investment. Thus, they expect the CEO to deliver growth and, most importantly, profit which is already in conflict with higher wages and less work. Customers care the most about price and quality.

The former needs to be low to attract customers, but high to have profits and pay wages. The later is costly to produce and requires stringent work effort. Finding the perfect middle ground is challenging and requires constant monitoring and re-evaluation from the CEO.

This is a big problem for CEOs because other challenges are one-dimensional, e.g. developing future growth plans, creating more equality between workers, fighting competition, etc. Whilst these are all difficult areas, the desired outcomes are obvious. In the case of managing different interest groups, it's often **unclear what outcomes CEOs need to achieve**.

Assessment: After demonstrating familiarity with the main stakeholders in a firm (CEO, Board, workers), the applicant took a clear stance and named a topic thought to be the most difficult. This was then analysed from the point of view of the CEO or any other business professional. The applicant didn't lose track of the question. And by mentioning other potentially important topics, a wider familiarity with the subject could be highlighted. After this intro, the interviewer would likely invite the applicant to further discuss those other areas and compare their relative importance.

Q8: Would you be able to tell me about the relationship between restrictive monetary policies and the bond market?

A good response: "I may be wrong but I believe that restrictive monetary policy involves raising short-term interest rates. I don't know if there is any formal relationship between interest rates and bond prices, but if I was investing in bonds at a time with high interest rates, I would expect higher returns in order to stop me investing the money in a bank instead. Therefore, I would imagine that the **price of bonds would probably fall** in order to make them more attractive to investors who might otherwise save their money in a bank."

Assessment: The main point of this question is to identify an interviewee's ability to determine relationships between two ideas and their understanding of how economic mechanisms allow policies to work. The candidate shows the interviewer that they are not completely certain on the topic, but this is perfectly acceptable – the tutor is attempting to test thinking skills and not knowledge. The logical, step-by-step approach shows that the candidate remains calm and methodical even when presented with unfamiliar information. Given the testing nature of the Oxbridge courses offered, it is important for tutors to establish the ability of potential students to work under pressure.

Q9: You've mentioned an interest in counter-factual history, what is the point of it?

- Counter-factual history is the history of *what if?* It challenges the historian to consider what would have happened had something else occurred. Common counter-factual examples include: *What if Germany had won the First World War?*

- Consider the merits and limitations of this type of history.

- The advantages are that you can consider crucial turning points – such as battles, political events or wars. An event is significant if the *What if* leads to a drastically different turn of events.

- They are an interesting and engaging way to deal with the past.

- However, some would argue that creating stories or ideas is not good history. We should be evaluating the evidence of what did happen, not following a distracting path of what might have happened.

- History is about the events, people, and changes which occurred in the past. Arguably, counter-factual history is a subversion of that.

Q10: What do you know about economic theory? Tell us about Classical economic theory, how do you think it compares to the theories of economists like Keynes?

Keynesian economists believe that the immense resources of the state should be deployed during periods of economic slowdown (recession). Classical economists, on the other hand, believe that the interference of the state distorts the working of the market to an extent that any well-intended policy will actually further hinder economic recovery and that, where possible, government spending should be limited and taxes cut.

It would be good to use a relevant example from current affairs. In 2008, Gordon Brown used a **fiscal stimulus** (Keynesian) to attempt to kick-start the economy – he brought forward capital spending and cut VAT to boost consumption. While in 2010, the Chancellor, George Osborne, began austerity to restore confidence in UK public finances and reduce the budget deficit while supporting monetary expansion through the reduction of interest rates to facilitate business lending.

Who are classical economists? Friedrich Hayek *A road to serfdom*, Milton Freeman (negative income tax), Adam Smith *The Wealth of Nations*.

Who are Keynesian economists? Paul Krugman or Nicholas Kaldor (and obviously John Maynard Keynes).

Q11: Have you ever heard of the term 'rational agent' used to describe a consumer - can you think of examples of consumers being 'irrational'?

A good response: "To answer the question, we must first understand what rationality is. In my view, a rational decision is one that makes sense based on the facts or evidence presented to the decision maker. In the case of addiction, the facts available to the addict are the feeling which their addiction gives them — which may be seen as benefits, and the associated costs of the addiction.

If the benefits to the addict outweigh these costs, then it may be argued that addiction is rational. However, it could be suggested that an addict has a distorted view of these costs and benefits, and, therefore, their ability to think rationally is compromised."

Assessment: This response is well-structured and focuses on attempting to answer the question at hand. By initially outlining a definition of rationality, the candidate displays that they fully understand the question and are engaging with it critically. The response shows a consideration of both sides to the argument without being side-tracked into an irrelevant discussion. One area for potential improvement is the conclusion where no definitive answer is given. Tutors will be looking for students who can articulate their own opinions, and the lack of a conclusive response may suggest that an interviewee does not possess these skills.

Q12: Inflation is often talked about as a bad thing, but governments don't try to prevent inflation from taking place, why do you think this is?

A good response: "0% inflation may seem like a good idea as lower prices provide consumers with the opportunity to get more for their money. Price increases are often poorly received by consumers as they have to reduce what they buy. However, there is often a **trade-off between inflation and economic growth**, and aiming for zero inflation may lead to stagnation in an economy. Inflation only forces a reduction in consumption when prices are rising faster than wages, so a government may compromise on inflation – such as the Bank of England have done with their 2% target – in order to ensure that economic is being achieved."

Assessment: The candidate effectively pre-empts, and dispels, arguments in favour of 0% inflation goals. Given that this is probably a topic that the interviewee has never had to tackle before, it is advisable to ensure they can present a structured logical argument before attempting to answer. This may involve asking for a moment to think, and a good candidate should not be discouraged from doing this as it gives themselves a moment to collect their thoughts.

This response is clearly well organised and thought through, which is clearly preferable to a rushed and illogical answer, even if it comes at the expense of a momentary pause. The candidate has the opportunity to show the extent of their understanding by referring to current policies or additional knowledge from further reading.

Q13: Economics is often thought to sit between the humanities and the sciences, do you think economics should be classed as a social science?

A good response: "I would define a social science as any academic discipline that studies human interactions using scientific methods. Economics seems to fit this definition. Firstly, it is clearly the study of a human phenomenon; the core issue at the heart of the subject is how humans allocate resources. The methodology used is what provides the science part of the description in my view. Economics is based on quantitative analysis and modelling, and much of the theory is built upon scientific methods. Some people might disagree with the description of economics as a social science. They may argue that it has no real scientific grounding given that there is often very little irrefutable evidence to prove an economic theory. However, I believe that this is inevitable in any study of humanity as **human behaviour is so unpredictable** – and that if economics is not a social science, then neither is any other field of study."

Assessment: A clear definition, even if it is one the candidate has concocted rather than one taken from a textbook, shows a real understanding of what the question is asking. This is a very difficult question to answer given the vague nature of a 'social science' and the difficulty in pigeonholing an entire subject such as economics. However, by considering how well certain criteria are met and assessing contradictory points of view, the interviewee is able to display their ability to grapple with testing problems and use logical reasoning to answer the question at hand. The answer may have been improved by suggesting alternatives to the description provided (e.g. "perhaps a better description of economics is as a series of 'fads and fashions'…")s and then assessing the credibility of those alternatives.

Q14: How much do you think CEOs should be paid?

A good response: "I do not know a lot about current CEO pay levels, but it would seem to me that any **employee should be paid based on their contribution** to the firm. If the CEO has a serious positive impact on the business, for example, if they are responsible for securing high levels of profits, then they deserve a large salary. However, if they have no greater impact than any other employee, then they should not be compensated any more generously. If the cost of paying a CEO outweighs the benefits they bring, they are being overpaid."

Assessment: The candidate is honest in their response, acknowledging the fact that this is a topic they know little about. However, by applying more general economic intuition, they are able to provide a concise argument, and more importantly, demonstrate their ability to engage with unfamiliar concepts. This is a very attractive skill to an Oxbridge tutor and is preferable to an interviewee who attempts to deceive an interviewer into believing they know a lot about the subject.

Q15: Moving away from the UK, let's take a look at OPEC - do you think that a cartel is a wise choice for running a global market?

A good response: "Am I right in the understanding that OPEC is the organisation that maintains oil prices?" [Interviewer: *"Yes, that's right."*] "In that case, I believe that OPEC has run the oil market relatively well. However, I do not believe that the market has even been close to efficiency as many OPEC members have made large profits on the back of the cartel, and in a perfectly efficient market, these profits would not occur. Large price fluctuations, particularly the fall in oil prices, in the last 18 months suggest to me that OPEC does not have as much control over the industry as it would like…"

Assessment: Asking for clarification on a question is not something a candidate should be afraid to do. It displays a willingness to fully understand the concepts that they are dealing with, and so would not be frowned upon in most scenarios.

If the topic in question was of a very basic level, there may be some questions raised, but tutors will not expect a candidate to know about every economic issue and will be expecting some gaps in their knowledge. In this case, the student was right to establish exactly what the question was before attempting to answer. Bringing in **knowledge of current affairs** regarding oil prices also displays interest in the subject, and this enthusiasm for the subject will be taken well by interviewers.

Q16: The economy of scale is a widely acknowledged concept, where average unit costs decrease as a company's output level increases - do you think the opposite, a 'diseconomy of scale' if you will, could ever exist?

A good response: "If average costs are rising as output increases, this suggests that it would be beneficial for firms to stay small. I think we can see plenty of examples of cases where it is beneficial for a firm to stay small. If a company would have to increase its spending on marketing greatly in order to sell any additional goods produced, then the average costs of those products may rise and the company would be suffering from diseconomies of scale.

Assessment: Some applicants, particularly those who have previously studied economics, will have a good understanding of this topic whilst others will have almost none. However, the interviewer is not using this question as a test of existing knowledge, but rather will be looking at the way in which it is approached. The ability to apply theory to real life is important and this question may be designed to test that ability. The candidate excels by showing good real world knowledge.

Q17: What do you think is the difference between a floating currency and a pegged currency, what difference would switching to a pegged currency have?

A good response: "A pegged currency is when a country chooses to set its own currency as a direct proportion of that of another economy, usually when a less developed economy aligns with the exchange rate of a more established country.

This means that an economy has more stability in their exchange rate, which can lead to less volatility in the balance of payments. However, it means a government cannot use economic policies to affect its exchange rate, so they are more susceptible to shocks from external factors – particularly from the nation they are pegged to. It also means that government policy elsewhere has an impact, so the pegged country needs to ensure congruence between the two nations' objectives."

Assessment: The candidate clearly shows a great understanding of the topic, which may not have been covered in any real depth during A-Levels or equivalent. They are able to present a balanced argument even in a short answer and draw on a variety of ideas. To improve, the applicant could refer to real life examples, which shows that they have read around their subject and can be an indication of enthusiasm for the subject. However, in a situation where they don't know any examples, then considering the types of nation that might use pegged currencies – "a less developed economy" – is a good alternative which still displays good understanding.

Q18: You're the new Chancellor of the Exchequer - you've been appointed on the promise of growing the economy, would you pursue this from the demand side or supply side?

A good response: "Classical economists believe in a vertical long-run average supply curve, and thus would argue that demand side policies are useless in stimulating growth. However, I feel like the Keynesian model is more realistic and demand side policies can be effective when an economy is not at full employment. Despite this, I believe that supply side policies usually stimulate more long-term sustainable growth rather than one that boosts to economic performance. If a government is seeking growth, I think supply side policies would be preferable."

Assessment: This answer is good and comes to a solid conclusion, but seems to lack the depth to impress an Oxbridge tutor. To improve, the candidate could spend more time analysing why a government may disagree with their viewpoint, and then providing evidence to support their own argument.

Another extension to the answer may be to consider the circumstances under which one approach is more suited than another. Questioning the context surrounding the question shows an inquisitive nature and shows that the candidate is analytical of information presented to them. In this case, a conclusion along the lines of "if a government is facing *situation x*, it should pursue *policy y*..." may add some substance to the arguments presented.

Q19: Would 0% inflation be a good thing or a bad thing?

This question is looking to assess both your basic knowledge of a simple economic concept (inflation) and then your ability to use this knowledge to answer a difficult hypothetical. You should first make it clear that you can clearly and coherently explain what inflation is and why it exists. Then you have some scope to come up with some issues that might arise if there was no inflation. You can be imaginative here but to a degree, as your answers must be rooted in economic knowledge.

Good Applicant: Inflation is the sustained rise of the price level, or the average price of goods and services, in the economy over a period of time. It can also be understood as a fall in the value of money as, after a period of inflation, a fixed amount of money now has less purchasing power. Inflation therefore means that, over time, our money becomes less valuable and so it encourages consumers to spend and keep their money flowing through the economy rather than save it for long periods of time. This is known as inflation 'greasing the wheels' of the economy. If there was no inflation and purchasing power didn't change, then there is less incentive for consumers to spend and it is more likely that they will delay spending and keep their money in banks where they will make a standard interest rate return on it. This could cause the economy to become stagnant with less spending. Inflation is also a signal of a healthy, growing economy and if there was no inflation then this could signal to markets that there is no economic growth which could cause uncertainty and falling consumer confidence.

A **poor applicant** might respond with a simple view that no inflation might be considered a good thing because prices will stay the same and they prefer it when things are cheaper. They might be able to identify that most central banks aim for a small but stable level of inflation, but not go into any detail on why this is the case and what the benefits of inflation are. They may also confuse no inflation with deflation, and this is something to avoid.

Q20: A lot of economics revolves around the use of economic models, do you think these are used too much?

This question is trying to get you to explore concepts relating to the method of economics rather than pure economic concepts themselves. It is important to not let the wording of questions like this sway your answer too much. The question is clearly leading you in a negative direction (to criticise the use of models in economics) but you need to make sure that your answer carefully considers both sides of this debate. Also, you will be interviewing with an economist so you shouldn't try to dismantle the whole nature of models in economics but instead you should be trying to understand why economists use models and what the benefits are.

Good Applicant: Economists use models to simplify the complicated world so that they can understand and analyse specific impacts and effects in economic systems. Economists are attempting to explain how changes in policies or incentives will affect behaviour and the wider economy, but they are unable to use controlled experiments due to the huge amounts of other influencing factors. This is why they use models – to simplify reality and run experiments of what will happen and what the causality effects may be. The issue with these models is that their conclusions rely on lots of assumptions that are made to simplify the model, but that are extremely unlikely to hold in reality. This is why it can be argued that economists rely too heavily on models as they are unlikely to accurately predict reality. This is an issue, but it is one that economists are aware of and constantly trying to address. One way in which they do this is by testing models against empirical data to identify which models are best and most accurate. If a model is found to not represent reality well, there is still something to be learned about the economy and by explaining what is different in reality compared to the model.

A **poor applicant** would be someone who may identify the issues with models and their strict assumptions but does not explore in any detail why economists still use these models and what their benefits can be despite the assumptions. Furthermore, a poor answer would not take into account the idea that economists are aware of the limitations of models and actively seeking to improve and test them. Finally, a poor answer would be one that criticises the use of models but does not provide any alternative or guidance for solving this problem.

Q21: If economics is a social science, does it follow that sociology is a valuable tool for studying economics?

This question is looking for you to identify what sociology is and how it relates to economics. Economics is considered to be a social-science, and this question is looking for you to explore the 'social' side of this understanding and how this might benefit the study of economics. You are able to ask the interviewer to clarify what exactly they mean by 'sociology' if you are not clear of the definition.

Good Applicant: Sociology is the study of social life, change and the social causes and impacts of human behaviour. From this definition, it is clear that sociology will be useful for developing a study and understanding of economics. Economics is ultimately concerned with how scarce resources are allocated in a society with unlimited desires, and so an understanding of social structures and behaviour will help to answer this question of allocation. Much of economics, specifically microeconomics, is focused on individual behaviour and decision-making. Basic economic models use assumptions of perfect rationality, but this is clearly unrealistic, and an understanding of sociology can help us to unlock this assumption and better understand human decision-making. Economic agents and markets exist in the context of society, and thus sociology will help to understand some of the external effects that are difficult to include into traditional economic models.

You could go either way with this question, but the important thing is to make sure that your answers are well supported. You could argue that the most useful areas of economics are the purely mathematical, model-based studies and that sociology has very little to offer here as these complex models use a set of assumptions to remove the societal impacts. However, if you did argue in this way, you would still have to show some awareness for the interaction of economics and sociology but explain why this is not that important (e.g. because assumptions of models remove the sociology-based impacts).

A **poor applicant** might simply state that sociology is not useful for economics without any real explanation or detail. They might also argue that sociology is useful because economics is flawed. Better answers are those which explore the links between sociology and economics and how they interact and overlap with each other.

Q22: How do we measure GDP - do you think this is reflective of reality?

This question is looking for you to show some level of understanding of what GDP is, how we measure it, what the limitations to our measurement techniques may be, and why economists care about GDP at all. If you did not know exactly how we actually measure GDP, feel free to ask the interviewer for some specific methods as this question is more focused on evaluating the potential flaws in these methods rather than knowing them off by heart.

Good Applicant: GDP is supposed to be a measure of the total value of goods and services, known as output, in a country or economy. This method of measurement is likely to be easier in a traditional, manufacturing-based economy where we can measure the value of the physical output of all goods that are produced. This, however, is likely to be much harder in a more developed, service-based economy like the UK. This is because there is likely to be some value created, especially in innovative tech firms, that is difficult to quantify and include in the measure. GDP will also fail to include the underground economy and so the measure of production will always be an underestimate. The final point to note, is that while there are some limitations to measuring GDP, it is still an important metric as it allows for consistent, cross-country comparisons to be made which is important for economists to assess relative economic performance.

The question is phrased in such a way that it is assumed you know how we 'actually' measure GDP, and the interviewer is looking for you to assess whether this 'measurement' really makes sense/can come close to representing total output in an economy. You should still look to show how GDP is actually measured, but the bulk of this answer should be debating whether measuring GDP is actually possible/should be done.

A **poor applicant** might not fully grasp what GDP is and why economists care about trying to measure it. They might say that we just add up all of the purchases in the country and so it is actually an easy measure, showing no consideration for what 'value' might be missed from those transactions.

Q23: If you were evaluating the UK's productive potential, what would be the main influences on it which you could identify?

This question should be familiar for those who are taking the Economics A-Level course. This question is looking for you to show an understanding of a fairly basic economic concept and give the standard explanation of what might influence productive potential. From here, however, you should look to extend your answer beyond the A-level course and discuss some other factors as well as potentially questioning the definition of productive potential altogether.

Good answer: The productive potential or capacity of a country is the total potential output if all resources and factors of production are utilised to their fullest efficiency. There are a number of factors which can influence productive potential. The size and productivity of the workforce are both key factors, as a larger and more productive workforce can produce more total output and more output per worker. The size of the workforce depends on the number of economically active people which is influenced by the age structure within the country as well as levels of net migration. Labour productivity, or output per worker, depends on the education, training, and motivation of the workers. Furthermore, labour productivity depends on the interaction of labour and capital, and a change in the quantity and quality of capital stock will also impact productive potential. There are also factors outside of the quantity and quality of factors of production that influences productive potential, including the level of political stability and security within a country.

You could develop this further by questioning the method in which we would measure productive potential in an economy. With technology advancing at an increasingly rapid pace, it seems that traditional measures of productive capacity might be outdated as the potential output of a country in the long-term is likely to be constantly changing.

A **poor answer** will just recite the textbook definition of productive potential which is that productive potential depends on the quantity and quality of the factors of production.

Q24: What, if any, is the value of government debt?

For this question, you should be looking to show a clear understanding of why governments have debts and what it means for a government to be in debt. From there, you need to show a clear understanding and consideration of both sides of this argument before giving your opinion on whether countries should or should not have debts. It does not matter which side you ultimately argue for, only that you have backed up your answer and that your conclusion follows on from your explanation.

Good answer: We first need to distinguish between an annual budget deficit and national debt. The budget deficit is when, over a year, the government spends more money than it generates through taxation. This deficit is often funded by the issuance of government bonds. The national debt is the net accumulation of these annual budget deficits. The key benefit of government debt is that it allows governments to increase their spending without increasing taxation. This might even be necessary during a recession when tax revenue falls and higher government spending is required. If the question is asking whether governments should have any debt at all, then the benefits of spending without increasing taxation is a strong argument for some level of government debt/borrowing. However, there are concerns about higher levels of government debt. As it increases, the risk of defaulting gets worse and worse to a point where the government is unable to borrow more. This could lead to a fiscal crisis where the government cannot adequately raise funds through either taxation or borrowing.

Additionally, this question could involve a more moral/ethical-based answer. When a government accumulates debt, it might solve fiscal problems in the short term but in the long-term it will have to be paid back by taxpayers who may not benefit from the debt in the first place.

A **poor answer** would be one that fails to acknowledge both sides of this debate and appreciate why debt is a beneficial and sometimes necessary part of the global economy. A poor answer would also fail to acknowledge the binary wording of this question.

Q25: Should you or I be bothered by inequality?

This style of question is asking you to consider the traditional stereotype of what an 'economist' cares about. You should look to answer the question directly but also question what exactly an economist would care about and why this may or may not be different to what someone else might care about (e.g. a politician). Also, you need to be clear on what it means for something to 'matter' to anyone.

Good answer: Inequality can be referring to income or wealth inequality, and this can be within individual countries or between different countries. Economists are focused on allocating resources in the most efficient way, and this usually involves trying to maximise some sort of welfare function across the economy. In this way, inequality should matter to an economist as it should be an important part of a holistic welfare function. Inequality makes people's lives worse, and therefore economists should look to reduce inequality to some extent in order to maximise societal welfare. Furthermore, inequality has important implications for economic behaviour. Some degree of inequality should, in theory, have beneficial impacts for the economy as it encourages hard work and innovation/risk-taking. This is a key theory that underpins capitalism, but we must be careful to mediate the level of inequality. These benefits will not be felt if there is not equality of opportunities so that those with less are able to work their way up. Economists should therefore care about inequality of outcomes and opportunities.

You can argue for either side of this question, but make sure to show a consideration for both sides in your answer. You should also make it clear that you understand why an 'economist' might think differently to someone else (e.g. economists are trying to maximise welfare whereas a politician might care about inequality in order to be more popular with the electorate).

A **poor answer** is one that does not consider both sides of this question. It feels obvious that an economist should care about inequality, but a better answer needs to adequately explain why this is but also why it may not be the most important consideration.

Q26: If there's a national deficit in the balance of trade, should this trouble the government?

The balance of trade should be a familiar concept form the Economics A-level course, as should some standard arguments for why it does and does not matter. For this question, you need to prove your knowledge of this before being more creative and questioning the role of a trade deficit in modern macroeconomics.

Good answer: A trade deficit is simply when a country imports more than it exports (in monetary terms, meaning the total value of imports/exports rather than the quantity). A trade deficit is not immediately a good or bad thing and it depends on the specific macroeconomic objectives of the country. A trade deficit may be a good indicator of economic growth in the country. Generally, during a boom, the trade deficit will increase as spending in the economy grows and more is spent on imports. The reverse is also often observed as the trade deficit improves due to a fall in consumer spending. However, a trade deficit can also be caused by more damaging structural factors. It can reflect falling relative productivity and capital investment in a country. Furthermore, a larger trade deficit means that the country is more exposed to what is occurring in foreign economies and likely to be less resistant to shocks. A strong economy is one that is resilient to external shocks and a level of self-sufficiency is important – something that is not present with a persistent large trade deficit. Overall, the cause of the trade deficit matters more than the trade deficit itself.

The word 'trouble' in this question is purposefully vague, and it is up to your own interpretation somewhat. You can define 'trouble' in this context in a number of ways, but the important thing is to make it clear what you think makes something 'trouble' an economist. For example, you could argue that something is only 'troubling' if it will affect total overall welfare across the economy, which the balance of trade deficit may not directly impact.

A **poor answer** will not address the reasons behind a trade deficit and will simply debate whether the mere presence of a trade deficit matters. It also may not consider both sides of this argument before concluding.

Q27: Is the Keynesian approach to market intervention correct?

This is an example of a common question/debate in economics that has a wide range of potential answers and discussion points. You should not look to answer this question from every possible angle and cover every relevant point. Instead, you should focus on giving a concise, well-measured answer that looks at one area of this debate. Since this is an economics interview, you should focus on answering this question by using economic terminology and understanding. You can still mention this debate in the context of other disciplines (e.g. politics), but you should make sure the focus of your answer is the economics behind this.

Good answer: This is a complicated question that is difficult to distil down to a simple yes or no answer. The key point for discussion will be why the government is intervening/feels as though they need to intervene in the market, and this will shape whether this should occur or not. Economists have a general focus on promoting efficiency in markets and so governments should intervene if something is preventing a market from reaching its equilibrium. A common example that we see in reality is intervention into markets for goods/services with externalities. The government should intervene to ensure that marginal social benefit = marginal social cost as this is the desired equilibrium. This is an example of government intervention to correct market failure, which should occur. The main argument against government intervention is that they are unlikely to have the correct information about the specific market and their intervention could make the problem worse. The market is the most efficient mechanism for allocation because it does not require any external 'information' – prices automatically reflect scarcity. Government intervention may be beneficial if done correctly, but the lack of information may lead to the government making a wrong decision when they are trying to help.

A **poor answer** would fail to answer this question using the appropriate economic terminology. You need to make use of efficiency and show an understanding of why economists think that 'markets' are the most efficient allocation method.

Q28: *Do you think that it would be reasonable to say that a failure of regulation caused 2008's financial crisis?*

As a potential economics student, you should have at least some level of knowledge about the 2008 financial crisis and the underlying causes. If you did not know in the interview, or you didn't know how it related to regulation failure then it is better to ask for some guidance rather than stumble into an answer that you do not know. The interviewer will give you some impetus, and then you should try to use the information to come to some sort of answer. If you are unsure, then try to keep it brief rather than waffling to fill time.

Good answer: The financial crisis of 2008 has a number of contributing factors and it cannot be said that it was only caused by a failure of regulation. That being said, regulation failure and deregulation were large contributors to the scale of the financial crash. The decade prior to the crash saw steady deregulation of the financial industry as banks sought to not be regulated in a harsher fashion than emerging, non-bank institutions. By 2008, there were severely low levels of supervision and regulation in the financial system and this regulatory failure contributed to the crash. Banks were able to create riskier and riskier financial instruments, culminating in the mortgage-backed securities that collapsed when the housing bubble burst. The banks were also lending to riskier and riskier borrowers with less and less liquidity to cover themselves. All of these factors should have been better regulated and this has started to occur since the crash, but there is still some way to go. Overall, the financial crisis of 2008 was not just a failure of regulation as there are numerous other root causes of the crash, but regulation failure is a key factor.

A **poor answer** would be one that is either too vague about the causes of the financial crisis, but also one that gets too carried away with proving a wide knowledge on the area and does not focus on the specific question relating to the crash and regulation failure.

Q29: Let's suppose that due to a mainframe error, the value of the American Dollar and the Japanese Yen are exchanged instantaneously - what do you think the main outcomes would be?

This question is looking for you to use your standard economic understanding to answer a difficult 'what if' question. There is no correct answer here, so you should focus on being clear with your logic and line of reasoning for how you get to an answer. You have some freedom to be creative here, so do not be afraid to speculate a bit for questions like this. If you don't know the exact (or even rough) relative values of the dollar and the yen, then feel free to ask the interviewer.

Good answer: One US Dollar is worth around 100 Japanese Yen. If these two values swapped overnight, there would obviously be a significant level of panic and a period of adjustment in global markets. While it is difficult to say exactly what happen, we can speculate some possibilities. The US Dollar has now become 1/100th of the value that it previously was, whereas the Japanese Yen is now 100x more valuable. If this suddenly occurred, financial institutions might expect that the exchange rate market would correct these values. Therefore, you might expect that anyone in possession of the Japanese Yen would want to sell it, and investors would want to buy the US Dollar before it increased in value again. This process would speed up the correction process as the difference in value is arbitraged away.

Even if this currency swap was corrected fairly quickly, there would likely be long-term damaging impacts for global markets. The key impact might be a severe loss of faith in the US Dollar. If it instantly dropped to 1/100th of its value once, there is nothing to say that this might not happen again and so the value might drop forever as it is seen as a far riskier currency to hold. Furthermore, this extreme event might undermine confidence in global FX markets generally and we could see investors move their money into other areas.

A **poor answer** would be one that gets too bogged down by the technical details of this question and fails to show any creativity of speculation in the answer. A poor answer would also be one that does not think about the difference in short and potential long-term impacts.

Q30: Sadly we aren't allowed to just sit down with you and play a game of Monopoly, but if we did, how would you try to win? Would your strategy also work in the real world?

This sounds like a slightly less serious question, but it is still clearly grounded in economic theory and, as such, so should your answer. If you are not familiar with monopoly or are not clear on what the best way to win is, then you should ask for clarification on this. The interviewer will be interested in how you apply the method to reality and the subsequent discussion of whether this is possible.

Good answer: In general, the best way to win monopoly is to play it as aggressive as possible. This means buying up every single property that you land on or that becomes available to buy in some way. Your ultimate aim is to acquire sets and owning as much as possible gives you a much larger degree of bargaining power over other players. You should not save any money as it is easy to instantly mortgage and unmortgage properties to pay anything that you owe. To apply this to real life, we need to consider what the overall goal of monopoly is. In order to win, you need to bankrupt every other player and by doing this you accumulate all of the available money and assets. For the sake of discussion, we will assume that the goal of real life is to achieve economic success through accumulation of wealth. The monopoly strategy does have some real-life application. It makes sense to accumulate as many safe assets as possible (property in this case) and then accumulate a steady flow of income in the form of rent. Bargaining power is also important in reality, and a strong set of assets is a useful bargaining tool. The crucial difference in monopoly, however, is that resources (properties) are so scarce and you are one of a small number of people trying to acquire them. In reality, both the pool of assets and potential buyers is much greater. This means that accumulating one extra property has a far smaller impact on your bargaining power. Furthermore, it is useful in real life to have some savings and liquidity to fall back on. You cannot instantly mortgage and unmortgage assets in the same way as you can in the game, and as such having no savings as coverage will increase your chances of going bankrupt.

A **poor answer** will be one that does not take this question seriously and treats it as more of a joke. While the question is not serious in tone, you need to make sure that you are still treating it with care and using it as an opportunity to show your economic knowledge and relate concepts to the specific question.

Q31: There are a wide range of materials which we go to considerable effort to extract from the Earth, one of the most expensive is diamond, while one of the cheapest is steel - why do they have their respective values?

This question asks about two raw materials. While you need to show some level of understanding about each good individually, the question is clearly framed in this way to encourage you to discuss these goods in comparison to each other. They have been chosen as they are both raw materials with a similarly expensive extraction method, and so a comparison of these two goods and the differences in their markets will allow you to form a much better answer.

Good answer: The prices of these goods depend on the relative supply and demand in their respective markets. There are both supply and demand explanations for why diamonds are so expensive. In terms of demand, diamonds are the most commonly sought-after precious gemstone. They are associated with wealth and prosperity, and there have been several successful marketing campaigns that have increased demand for diamonds by making them seem essential for expensive jewellery and engagement rings. The biggest factor, however, is the supply of diamonds. While diamonds themselves are not that naturally scarce, they have an extremely limited supply which has forced up their price. This occurred as the De Beers corporation has maintained tight control (essentially a monopoly) over diamond supply since the 19th century. This limitation in supply means that diamonds are a highly demanded but highly scarce good which makes them expensive.

In contrast, steel is a much more abundant good. It is mainly made with iron, which is a fairly plentiful ore that can be found and extracted. The demand for steel may be equally high, but the supply is so plentiful that demand is outmatched, and the price naturally falls much lower than that of diamonds.

A **poor answer** will not explain the relative prices of these goods, and it will not explain the prices of these goods in terms of the supply and demand forces within the individual markets. It is not enough to just say 'diamonds are rare, steel is more abundant'.

Q32: You are the CEO of new airline, which only flies directly between London and Tokyo - this is a route which no one else in the world currently provides, so how would you work out how much to charge in order to maximise your profits?

This question is not expecting you to give an answer with a specific, detailed knowledge of how airlines exactly set their prices. Instead, it is looking for you to identify some general factors that influence price-setting and how general firms assess costs and seek to maximise profits. You should then give your best effort to apply these general factors to the specific case of airlines. It is fine if your examples are not precisely accurate, you just have to ensure that you have sound, reasoned logic behind your answer.

Good answer: There are several influencing factors for setting the price of this ticket. The first is the general market demand for this type of ticket. The airline needs to consider how many people will be demanding this ticket from London to Tokyo, and what their individual willingness-to-pay will be. Since it is a unique route, the number of people who want to buy this ticket is likely to be low but the few people who want to buy it will likely have a high willingness-to-pay. Another influencing factor would be the price of similar airline tickets for similar routes. We could look at what other airlines are offering for flights to other locations in Japan or the surrounding area in Asia, and either look to match these prices or potentially undercut them (although this could result in a price war). Our costs will also influence this decision, as we have to ensure that the price of the ticket is high enough to cover the cost of fuel/staff involved in the flight. Finally, to ensure maximal profit we need to try and identify the level where marginal revenue of a ticket will be equal to marginal cost. This is a difficult equation to calculate in reality, but it is useful as a baseline to aim towards and be as profit maximising as we can even if we cannot be at the exact point.

A **poor answer** would be one that does not mention multiple factors influencing this pricing decision. Pricing is not a simple calculation (despite that A-Level course often making it appear to be) and so better answers will be ones that recognise the real-life challenges of pricing decisions.

Q33: Tell me about the golden ratio - why do people at banks and investment companies care about it?

This is a very specific question, and it relies on a fair amount of background knowledge. If you have not heard of the golden ratio then you should feel free to ask the interviewer to give you a definition. This is better than trying to waffle your way around it. Secondly, once you have been told what the golden ratio is, you should try to give a potential way that banks/firms may be interested in it. Even if you do not get this correct, you will still be credited for giving a plausible sounding answer that you can back up with some logic.

Good answer: The golden ratio is a unique ratio (about 1.618). It is derived from the Fibonacci sequence and the natural balance of this ratio is abundant in much of nature (e.g. the number of female bees divided by male bees in any hive). This is useful to bankers/investors as we have been able to derive some technical analysis tools from the idea that there is a unique balance to this ratio. The best example for financial markets is the use of the ratio to assess whether a chart is showing significant recovery or resistance. For example, if a stock falls from 20 to 10, we can check whether the stock reaches 38.2% recovery (up to 13.82), then 50% recovery and then 61.8%. If it passes these boundaries, then the recovery is usually very strong.

This answer is very specific, and it relies on a lot of background information about investment strategies. If you didn't have this knowledge, however, you can still give a well-reasoned answer to this question. If you asked what the golden ratio was and the interviewer told you that it was the ratio 1.618 that provides balance and solidity in nature, you could still relate this to banking and investment. One response could be that this ratio may be how banks/investors split their investments between their top two best-performing funds. It could also be how they split investments between less risky and more risky investments. The idea is to come up with some way in which a specific ratio could apply and be used in financial markets.

A **poor answer** would be one that fails to correctly describe the golden ratio and does not ask for any clarification. A poor answer would also try to argue that the golden ratio is not used in banking (to their knowledge). Even if this was the case, the question has asked you to come up with some way that the ratio can be used and so you must do this rather than question its use in general.

Q34: How would you try to predict economic changes, if you could, do you think this would help you avoid depressions?

This question is looking for you to illustrate a clear economic understanding of what a recession/depression is, why economists care about them and what the potential warning signs for one may be. It is important to clarify that recessions are fairly inevitable in the boom/bust cycle, and the question specifically wants to focus on avoiding depressions as this is the more severe version of a recession (lasting for at least a year rather than months).

Good answer: Predicting recessions is extremely difficult, with economic forecasts often being compared to weather forecasts in that there is an element of unpredictability that we cannot control for. Even with all the economic information and signals in the world, some recessions are not able to be predicted – such as the recession caused by the global pandemic. This does not mean that we should give up on predicting economic recessions entirely, and there are some warning signs. A key signal that we can use is the financial yield curve. An inverted yield curve (when the long-term yield is lower) has been an accurate predictor of every US recession since 1970. However, there is a small sample size of this and the reasons behind this prediction are still only theories. I would argue that the prevention of periods of depression is more reliant on accurately identifying when a recession is beginning rather than trying to predict it long into the future. If we can identify the beginning of a recession, then governments and central banks can start implementing policy earlier to counter the negative output effects.

The best answers to this question will be those that not only identify practical ways/metrics that can be used as early warning signs for recessions and depressions, but also go further to identify what could be done to prevent/mitigate the depression once it has been identified.

A **poor answer** would fail to appreciate the unpredictability of recessions/depressions. Furthermore, there is a certain inevitably to economic recessions and they are not necessarily an absolutely bad thing for the economy – this is something that a poor answer would not appreciate and instead give a simplistic view on why recessions are bad and how we can prevent them.

Q35: Do you think that a country which can fund its own space programme should receive international aid from countries like the UK?

This question combines some economic discussion with some ethical discussion, and it is important that you can answer from both of these angles. You should try to give a nuanced answer that appreciates both sides of this discussion while also understanding the perspective of a country that relies on aid.

Good answer: There are two fundamental reasons why countries give foreign aid (either humanitarian or developmental) to other countries. The first is for a moral reason – the protection of life and support for the most vulnerable global populations. The second is for economic reasons as developmental aid given to countries will generally be in the form of an investment which will bring benefits to the donor country in the future. The question is implying that countries with international space programs should not be recipients of aid as they should have enough funding of their own (since they can set up a space program). This view is extremely binary and simplistic. From a moral perspective, we should still look to support the most vulnerable even if their own government has prioritised something else (e.g. space travel). Secondly, countries with space programmes may still have large amounts of inequality between sectors/regions and require developmental aid to bridge these gaps. If the country already has the space program, these are significant sunk costs, and they would not be able to reverse this decision and spend the money on developmental support instead. The funding of the space program could be considered as government failure, and government failure is not a significant reason to stop providing aid in any form.

This answer phrases the decision as purely binary with only two options (to give aid or not). You should show that, in reality, this will not be the case and there might be other approaches that we would want to take. For example, you could argue that the foreign aid that we give should be correlated with the GDP per capita of the recipient countries. This would mean that countries who were previously reliant on aid, but then rapidly developed and developed space programmes should have their aid reduced to a more appropriate amount, and more aid could be allocated to countries who need it more.

A **poor answer** would fail to explain why exactly any country gives aid. Furthermore, a poor answer would not be explicit about the nuances involved or show an appreciation for who would suffer most if the aid was stopped.

Q36: How would you assess the scale of the divide between communist and capitalist ideologies?

If you are applying for an economics degree, then you are expected to have some familiarity with these two forms of an economy. You should explain these differences clearly and precisely. You can then be more creative for the second half of the question and come up with some ways in which they are similar (or their outcomes in the real world are similar).

Good answer: Capitalism and communism are both economic and political systems. Capitalism is when trade and industry is controlled by private owners who operate for profit, whereas communism is when all property and factors of production is public (owned by the community) and each person contributes and is compensated equally. The key difference between the two, aside from the private vs public ownership of the factors of production, is the market mechanism (or lack thereof). In a capitalistic society, the level of production and resource allocation is determined by the free market forces of supply and demand. These factors determine the price and quantity of each good. In a communist society, these decisions are made by the government who sets each of these. In theory, the capitalist society requires no government intervention in the markets as they should operate 'perfectly' and lead to the most efficient and overall beneficial outcome.

However, in reality, we often observe market failure that needs to be corrected (e.g. in the case of climate change which is a large-scale externality market failure). In these cases, the government needs to intervene to influence prices and output in the market (in the same fashion to communism). If the government had perfect information, then they would be able to intervene to bring us to the true free market equilibrium. However, since governments do not have full information, their decision becomes similar to the communist government as they both (somewhat arbitrarily) have to choose what prices/output will be.

A **poor answer** would be one that correctly identifies the similarities between these two ideologies but fails to develop the answer and come up with some ways in which the ideologies are similar (either in terms of the underlying economic/political theory or the observed outcomes).

Q37: What do you think are the main factors driving the increasing privatisation of once-public large services like the Royal Mail or NHS?

This question is essentially asking for the pros of privatising large, previously nationalised industries. You should be careful to focus on the specific question at hand and not be distracted by turning this into a full-scale debate about privatisation. Even if you do not agree with privatising these services, you need to be able to understand and appreciate the other side of the debate.

Good answer: The main reason for privatising these large services is to improve efficiency and remove political interference. Large companies are extremely difficult to manage, and this task becomes even harder when the company is not driven by a profit motive as there is less incentive at every stage to be the most efficient and productive. Private industries are motivated by their profit margins and shareholders, and so they have a more direct incentive to be efficient and run smoothy at a low average cost. Privatisation may also occur alongside significant deregulation to promote competition in these markets. Large monopoly power reduces the incentive to innovate and improve and so privatisation alongside deregulation (to encourage new entrants) may solve this. Finally, there is the benefit of raising government revenue through the sales of these services, and this may be spent elsewhere to improve the overall economy/welfare.

You should focus on the specific case of 'large services' and the effects of privatisation in these industries. The two examples given are both large-scale, traditional UK services and so you should also ensure that you answer has something that is specific to this context. For example, you could argue that the NHS is an old service and so there may be more opportunity for dynamic improvements from privatisation.

A **poor answer** is one that simply reels off the basic pros and cons of the privatisation debate, without focusing on the reasons why this may be happening as well as not focusing on the specific nature of 'large' services (e.g. likely to previously be monopolies and so deregulation may be beneficial).

Q38: On Oxford high street there are three coffee shops belonging to the same brand on a single street - why do you think this happens in populous cities?

This question is looking for you to understand a specific market and the actions of one type of firm. Even if you do not know this answer beforehand, you should be able to come up with some economic reasons as to why this would make sense for the firm and their ability to maximise profits.

Good answer: This answer comes down to understanding which areas are most popular for coffee shops, and then understanding how firms will exploit this. Crowded cities are clearly the best location for selling coffee for a number of obvious reasons (high population density, high population of working people who drink coffee regularly, high footfall etc.). In a city, there are certain areas that shoppers will naturally congregate towards when they want coffee. These areas will be in squares, near retail outlets and near other restaurants as opposed to in residential areas. This means that the coffee shop owners want to take full advantage of this demand and, since there are multiple coffee shops, the demand is greater than just one shop. Since the demand exceeds one shop, there is a decision on where to build the second and it makes much more sense to put this shop in the same area with high demand/density of coffee drinkers rather than in another location. This is why we end up with lots of coffee shops next to each other in certain areas of crowded cities, as these are the optimal locations to take advantage of the excess demand for coffee.

The key with this question is understanding why it might make economic sense to have two identical coffee shops so close to each other. We have already mentioned that there is likely to be excess demand, so you then need to explain why multiple shops makes more sense than one big coffee shop (since this seems to go against our standard theory of economies of scale). One major factor in this could be that queueing is a major drawback of getting a coffee and having two coffee shops in a similar but not identical location may split queues enough to increase the amount of customers that they could serve compared to if there was one larger coffee shop.

A **poor answer** would not take into account the supply and demand factors, as well as the myriad other factors as to why certain areas in crowded cities are the most optimal for coffee shop locations.

Q39: You have been tasked with getting rid of the UK's national debt - how would you do it?

The aim of this question is to think step by step about the processes – what debt is, how to eliminate it and whether this is a good thing to do. It does not matter whether you are answering correctly – the interviewer will just want to see that you can think logically.

A bad answer: Would focus solely on listing ways of eliminating the debt – without thinking about their plausibility and potential negative effects. Furthermore, a bad answer would perhaps not think about what national debt actually is, and not attempt to define what it is and who the debt is owed to.

A good answer: First would think about what national debt is – perhaps an answer would include that it is money that the government owes, and think about who it owes this money to: other governments, big corporations etc.

In the simplest terms, the way to eliminate such debt, would be to pay back those the government owes. The candidate would then need to think about what would have to be done to achieve this. The country would either have to reallocate current spending in order to pay the debt off or think about ways to increase the GDP of the country (through industry for example) to then have the funds to pay off the debt. Other good suggestions from candidates could include raising taxes – then discussing the pros and cons of this such as reducing household assets and consumption, which could have negative economic effects.

Lastly, an excellent answer would perhaps question whether the debt needs to be eliminated at all. Thinking about the coronavirus crisis, countries have all increased their national debt hugely.

- Candidates could either argue that yes, the debt needs paying off so that the state can be seen as credible for further investment.
- Or could argue that if the country is in a financially good position, the proportion of debt would be getting proportionally smaller, and so would be less of a pressing issue and perhaps there would be a weaker need to eliminate it. The negatives of raising taxes and potentially increasing inequality may not be worth eliminating the debt

Q40: Why do we use public money to provide healthcare to the elderly?

This kind of question is designed to get the candidate to think quite creatively and see whether it is possible to weigh up quite conflicting arguments.

A bad answer: Would go down strongly on one side of the argument without considering the alternative side at all. The lack of consideration for alternative points of view would demonstrate inflexible thinking.

A good answer: Would discuss what 'NHS money' is – the NHS is funded by the taxpayer. In this way therefore, the taxpayers are paying to keep other taxpayers, the old people alive. Old people themselves are taxpayers, so they are also funding a service that they are using.

The answer would then discuss the pros and cons of doing this.

Pros:

Society is more than the economic value of its members - almost everyone who is funding care for the elderly via tax 'NHS money' will have elderly friends and relatives that they care about. Therefore, it is likely to be a societal preference of this use of NHS money. If this is the outcome that society prefers, surely this provides a argument for using this money to keep elderly people alive.

Could perhaps discuss the fact that children are not contributors to the economy – but huge resources are used to fund their education. Although children will contribute in the future, the elderly have contributed in the past and therefore should not be excluded on this basis.

The elderly pay tax and have been paying tax throughout their lifetime so are just as much entitled to public services.

The NHS keeps many people alive – not just those that are elderly. The elderly are no more at risk of falling victim to a car crash for example – and in some cases their lower level of activity could actually reduce their likelihood of being victim to a random accident.

Cons:

Would argue that the elderly are non-productive members of society, and therefore the money would be better spent on public resources that would benefit those who contribute to the economy.

With the proportion of the population of the elderly growing, this is going to be an increasing drain in resources, if this trend continues.

A good answer would then weigh up these suggested pros and cons (and any creative ones the candidate can think of) and decide on what should be valued more. It is important to note that this kind of question does not have a right answer - being able to think of arguments and weigh up their strengths is the aim.

Q41: What do you think are the main push and pull factors behind human migration?

This question wants the candidate to think both big and small – or in economic terms, the microeconomic factors and the macroeconomic factors. A good answer will think about both the decisions of individuals to immigrate or emigrate – and the larger structural factors that drive such decisions.

A good answer: Individual decision-making towards emigration or immigration will usually be some form of cost-benefit analysis. If the decision is taken to emigrate or immigrate, the benefits from this huge move are seen to be greater than the potential costs. Such individual drivers of immigration and emigration can include financial issues such as a redundancy – the move could be to a new area with job sectors suited to the individual. Emigration or immigration may also be driven by emotional or family ties, such as marriage or moving to elderly relatives. Another reason why individuals choose to immigrate or emigration could be due to a threat of discrimination in the country of origin, for example by a religious or political authority.

The macro factors that drive immigration and emigration can be demonstrated when they cause large-scale immigration and emigration – as therefore these factors are drivers of not just an individual's decision. Whether or not the move will be immigration or emigration, such drivers suggest that the final destination will be preferential to the place of origin. Such drivers can include civil war and unfavourable economic conditions, that could make immigration or emigration an attractive option for large groups. Furthermore, policies of nations to make immigration or emigration cheaper or easier can also provide a macroeconomically favourable environment for immigration or emigration.

An excellent answer would question the scale of the immigration and emigration – as it could be a regional, national or international move. All of these different scales will have varying motivations and varying costs. For example, an international move will be significantly more costly to fund than a national one.

Q42: Here in the UK - we have a fairy well-established system of taxation which is used to fund a range of programmes. How do you think that places like Dubai, which don't use taxation at all, are able to grow at all, let alone so quickly?

This question wants you to think about other ways of development and expansion, apart from tax-generated income. The correct reason for the expansion of Dubai is not necessary, and instead the focus should be on possible routes for funding expansion without taxes.

A bad answer: would just state that Dubai is popular and therefore there is an incentive to invest and therefore expand the city.

A good answer: would think about the reasons Dubai may be a favourable place for investment. Ideas can be creative!

For example, the weather and climate of Dubai makes it an ideal holiday destination, which means that expansion of hotels and the commercial sector is very lucrative. The climate also means that the travel sector can thrive all year round, as opposed to ski resorts that often have quite a limited season. Furthermore, the increase of globalisation and reduction of air travel costs, means that Dubai is more accessible than ever and for global markets.

Geopolitics also provides an answer to this question. Dubai and the UAE are hugely rich in oil, and therefore expansion can be funded through oil revenues as opposed to tax-generated income. This reliance on oil revenues has let Dubai thrive during the age of increased industrialisation and innovation. However, this poses a question about whether the future of Dubai is secure. Global efforts to fight climate change and reduce emissions could reduce the profitability of the oil sector, and perhaps require taxation in order to fund further expansion.

An excellent answer would think about what tax generated income often provides, such as public services and schools. Such services can be privatised, and as such there can be expansion without tax-generated income. The candidate could then go on to think about whether this could apply to other states, and whether tax-generated income is a necessary feature of statecraft.

Q43: You are the infamous pirate captain "Dread {YOUR SURNAME}" and you have a standing rule where if more than half of the crew publicly disapprove of your tactics, they can execute you. You've just seized a large haul of gold, and have to divide it up. How would you distribute the wealth in such a way that you maintain the favour of your crew and get the largest possible share of the booty?

Here, they want the candidate to think of a logical answer, and then question whether the rest of the actors will act in the way that you would expect.

To divide the share to get the maximum and survive – divide the entire share equally between one more than half of the pirates – they will therefore agree and even if others get none, your share will be maximised.

However, you cannot guarantee that even the pirates who get some of the share will be happy with this - for example, one of the other pirates may want the entire share, and therefore will not agree unless they get this. Furthermore, we do not know that you will not die even if more than half of the pirates agree with you – the question does not specify this.

Lastly, a good answer would think of other ways of dividing the treasure – and what would happen on these occasions.

Examples:

Dividing it equally

This would not maximise the individuals share, but would have the highest likelihood of agreement, as there would be no inequality that could be questioned. However, pirates may not be satisfied with this amount, especially if there are many to share the treasure between

Keeping it all

You could potentially therefore use this to bargain with the pirates that are more capable of killing, so avoiding death and maximising the share of the treasure. However, this would be very reliant on perceiving which pirates have the willingness or capability to kill.

Q44: Why do people decide to change careers? If they are moving from a career which relies on extensive higher education to one which requires extensive vocational training, where do you think responsibility for funding their re-education lies?

This question is designed to make candidates think of reasons for changes in employment, and what drives such decisions. The second part of the question, in regard to who should pay for their training is designed for candidates to think about who benefits from such training, and thus who should have the responsibility of investing in it.

Reasons for teachers to become plumbers could be personal – such as the idea that they no longer enjoy teaching and would just like to try something different. Or, it could be a financial choice – such as a reduction in the wages of teachers requiring a change of employment in order to maintain a particular lifestyle.

A move in residence for the teacher could also lead to them becoming plumbers. For example, they could move to an area in which there are no vacancies as teachers, but a great shortage of plumbers. This would mean that they would be unable to continue their previous occupation.

Financially, the idea is that those who benefit the most from their training should be the ones that pay for it. As the benefits of the training will outweigh its costs. Therefore, if the teacher is likely to financially gain significantly from retraining as a plumber, they should be the one to bear the cost. However, if there is a shortage of plumbers, and they are in dire need around the country, perhaps the government should incentivise training. This would provide an incentive for teachers to retrain. Also, in this situation the country would be the one to benefit from the plumbers, and so the teachers should not bear the cost of their training.

An excellent answer would go on to think about whether the person that should pay for the training is the one that actually does pay. This very much depends on the political system – in some countries education and training is subsidised considerably more than in others.

Q45: Do you think that you could ever build an economy which was based entirely on service industries?

Firstly, an answer needs to think about what the service sector actually is. An answer to this would include the aspects of the economy that are not productive, and so do not produce an end product. Examples of this can include the hairdressing industry.

If the economy was to be based purely on the services sector, all other sectors – such as raw materials and industry – would have to be purely imported. Furthermore, as services are very difficult to export – as you cannot really send a haircut across the world, the economy would have a very small export business. This would mean that there would be a huge imbalance between exports and imports.

The next question, now we have determined what it means for an economy to be entirely based on the service sector, is whether this is feasible. This would only be feasible, if the country could afford all the imports necessary for a thriving society, such as food and fuel. These goods would be significantly more expensive than they would be if they were domestically produced, as the cost of importation would have also to be considered.

Furthermore, the inputs of the service industry, such as the food made in restaurants, would have to be imported. This would make the service industry significantly less profitable than in a situation in which the economy was not entirely based on the service sector. As businesses would have to pay higher prices for the inputs that they need, their margins would either be severely cut, or they would have to raise prices. If prices were raised, consumption would decrease as services would become less affordable.

This suggests that an economy entirely based on the service sector may be physically possible, but such an economy will be existing on a significant loss, as factor inputs of the service industry will be at inflated prices.

Q46: Is global overpopulation a problem?

This questioned is designed to get the candidate thinking about an argument and come up with a conclusion based on their own ideas. Like many Oxbridge interview questions, there is not a set answer – the though process is the most important part, so think aloud!

A bad answer: would not fully think about both sides of the argument or would take a very strong stance on one side and not provide the evidence to back up their argument.

A good answer: Would think about both sides if the argument. For example, arguments against there being too many people in the world could focus on the fact that some nations have larger populations due to higher levels of development. Therefore, there are not too many people in the world as not all states have had the opportunity to develop, urbanise and expand to the same extent. Another reason for there not being too many people in the world could perhaps focus on needing more people to fight problems, such as produce more food or innovate more.

The other side of the argument, that there are too many people in the world focuses on the strain on resources that more people bring. This could be in relation to the climate crisis or food production, and how more people may make current availabilities of resources need to be spread more thinly. There may be an upper limit to a population that the planet can support well – and this limit may have already been hit, which can be demonstrated by rises in extreme weather and the deforestation of the Amazon for resources.

The answer would then weigh up these sides of the argument and reach a conclusion by choosing which the candidate deems to be a stronger argument.

An excellent answer would go even further and could think of policies that could either reduce the population – such as policies designed to limit fertility. Or policies that could mitigate the effects of an increasing population on the environment, such as emissions caps on urbanised areas.

Q47. Do you think that the buying and selling of sports players by teams and managers around the world is similar to the buying and selling of people as slaves? Explain why.

This question is asking the candidate to bring more than the object in to question when thinking about sales – the context and meaning of the sale also differentiates it. If the candidate is not clear about the process of buying either option – it is a good idea to ask the interviewer before starting to answer the question. The candidate will not be penalised and it will make their answer better.

The buying and selling of a footballer, while on the surface perhaps sounding similar to the buying and selling of slaves, is hugely different. Firstly, the football player is able to not sign a contract for a sale, if they do not agree with it. For example if they do not want to move because of family commitments or they do not agree with the salary that they will be provided. In contrast to this, slaves are often taken from their homes forcibly, and sold with no freedom of choice in the matter.

Furthermore, the footballer has chosen that career. Whereas a slave would never have chosen to be an unpaid worker. Again, demonstrating that hugely different levels of choice are involved. A sale of a footballer is also often for a set amount of time, whereas the sale of a slave is indefinite – and the bad conditions they can be forced to live in often mean a sale is for the lifetime.

The surface level similarities are that they are both sales involving a human, and both provide the buyer with an employee. However, in the case of a footballer this employee is paid (often extortionately) whereas slaves provide unpaid labour.

An excellent answer may go on to think about perhaps what maintains these differences. For example, if footballers had fewer rights when signing contracts, their choice could be reduced and as such the processes could be more similar.

Q48: Why is a film actor wealthier than a theatre actor?

We can talk about the differences between the actors, the medium, and whether these assumptions will still hold true in the days of streaming.

Good Applicant: It is worthwhile noting that this is a quite dramatic generalisation. The average film actor is wealthier than the average theatre actor, but not dramatically so. However the gap between the wealthiest film actor and the wealthiest film actor is much larger, which is where the assumption comes from.

First of all, the question comes from supply. The live nature of theatre is such that a certain cast can only be at one performance, in one place, at a time. This is not so for pre-recorded film – it can be shown across the world in many cinemas and streaming at home simultaneously. It has the elements of supply over time and space that theatre lacks. This means that the average profit for a film will be much higher, despite requiring only one time commitment. Even if theatre actors acted multiple times a day for years, the issue of space will still be a practical concern.

Secondly, there is the matter of imperfect nature. Considering the nature of a theatre performance as something audiences view once but actors play for weeks, it is clear that no long-running role will be able to keep the same actors indefinitely. Theatre runs also do not always have finite limits since it is dependent on the performance popularity. Thus, except in exceptional cases, we would not expect for audiences to be attending to see specific actors. Instead, performances advertise by location, theme and story. This is exemplified by the fact that the Playbill for a musical would not have its actors names but a movie poster would.

It is important to note that many experts expect these discrepancies to begin closing. Theatre, and all the practicalities involved in it, has long since been criticised for its exclusive nature. Its high entry costs and seating arrangements make it inaccessible to the less fortunate in terms of wealth and disability. In accordance, musicals, an important form of theatre, are expected to be filmed professionally due to the success of the Hamilton recording by Disney. It is difficult to argue that what is posted is not a film, however, considering it is a still capture of – at most – a few performances out of hundreds. It can be concluded, therefore, that the inherently immersive live experience has a different value to society, and will therefore continue to exist, constrained by its nature.

A **poor applicant** may try to attribute this to non-economic reasons, such as difference in quality of acting. Not only is this untrue, it is unlikely to be the basis of the reasoning in an Economics interview.

Q49: Why is deflation a scare to the UK?

This question has three parts – what deflation is, why it is a problem in general, and why it is a problem specific to the UK.

Good Applicant: Deflation is an increase in the purchasing power of an economy's currency that comes from a fall in its overall prices. It can be viewed in contrast to inflation which is widely known as a problem to any who hold cash as inflation erodes its value. Historically, especially in wartime, inflation has been the key problem and deflation, its parallel, has not been seen as such. This has been changing recently.

Firstly, it's important to see why deflation is now considered a problem in general. An increase in purchasing power can be good in moderation when it affects certain staple products, since it increases spending and consumption. It can also reinforce the value of money and encourage saving. However, if it occurs rapidly, economic activity may contract. It may prompt a reduction in consumption since consumers hold out for lower prices, and it has increased the real value of debt. This is especially the case in debt deflation, when continued reduction in consumption hampers circulation of currency and economic growth. This can cause financial crises and recession. Interest rates can tighten, and real-wage unemployment can increase. As with inflation – it often becomes a spiral which is impossible to escape without intervention.

Now we can see why deflation in the UK is a scare. Here is important to note that deflation is thought of as a long-term occurrence. Negative inflation, if it is quickly remedied and does not spiral, is not typically thought of as a scare. However, with deflation the UK faces real issues. Discretionary goods, inessential goods with elastic demand, will not be purchased. In the UK, which has relatively low rates of poverty, purchase of discretionary goods comprises about 70% of all economic activity. If such a significant portion of the economy slowed, it could very well lead to a recession. Essentially, if the initial fall in prices comes from weak demand and not external factors, it poses an issue.

153

A **poor applicant** may state that since inflation is the real problem, and deflation is the opposite, it isn't one with certain constraints.

Q50: You run a sweet shop next-door to a rival sweet shop - you've both been able to drum up considerable loyalty in your customers who will flat-out refuse to shop anywhere else, provided you keep your prices below a tenner per sweet. You each have 10 such loyal customers - but there are 100 potential customers on the street who don't care as much and will buy from whoever is cheapest. With this in mind, at what price point would you have to reach for it to be more valuable to sell everything for ten pounds?

A logical way to go about this is to calculate from the bottom up. This would mean getting a piece of paper and calculating while explaining your process to your interviewer.

Good Applicant: At £10, I would be assured £100 from the loyal customers. Otherwise, I would have 90 customers who I can keep by keeping a price lower than £10. The price at which I would stop undercutting comes from dividing the baseline £100 by the 90 customers. This will give me the amount at which I would be indifferent – just over £1.10. Therefore, at any price lower than this, it would be more economically logical, and more profitable, to sell at £10.

That logic assumes that it will not be a constant bid for lower prices. Realistically, the question allows for the possibility of imperfect information - you cannot always know what your competititor will be selling for, even in the short-term, as they may see your prices and lower theirs once more. This means what we are calculating is an estimation assuming that the price was sufficiently low, and the customers know this, so as to assume that if the price was slightly lower all customers would come there.

All of this imprecision reflects one of the core tenets of microeconomic modelling. Models are not expected or required to be exact to have statistical relevance. They made broad generalisations about rational consumers and perfect information in order to accurately define trends, rather than to elucidate on specific examples. That is to say – the price calculated may not be the case in reality but on average, it will occur. In reality, we may find that the price we choose to switch over at is higher since there is imperfect information, and customers may find that the inconvenience of finding out small changes in price and moving in accordance with them is not worth the time consumed.

A **poor applicant** would make an assumption without attempting a calculation, which would suggest a lack of precision.

Q51: Why are the Chancellor of the Exchequer and the Governor of the Bank of England different jobs? What are the differences between them?

These are two distinct positions in the financial system of England, both of which are relevant to an understanding of it.

Good Applicant: The Chancellor of the Exchequer is a Minister, part of the UK government. They are also the head of Her Majesty's Treasury. It is one of the Great Offices of State and a senior member of the British cabinet. It is nominally what we could consider the finance minister. This position is currently held by Rishi Sunak. Moreover, one of their roles is appointing the Governor of the Bank of England, its most senior position. They are also the Chairman of the Monetary Policy Committee. This is currently held by Andrew Bailey. Both are positions with major economic consequence, but in different ways.

The positioning of these roles within their respective hierarchy is their most crucial difference. The chancellor works within the government. On the other hand, the Governor works within the Bank of England. These are two distinct economic institutions, as outlined in their Memorandum of Understanding. The Bank of England is the UK's central bank. It has been nationalised for over 50 years. Since 1998, the Bank has been an independent public organisation, owned by the Treasury Solicitor on the government's behalf. One key factor where the Bank's autonomy from the government is evident in the monetary policy. They decide the interest rate of the UK officially, as well as other aspects of the monetary policy framework. It works to meet certain targets given by the government, such as the Consumer Price Index measure of inflation, though how it gets there is primarily at its discretion.

This is a summarised depiction of how the Bank of England and the financial sector of the government work independently but towards many of the same goals. Thus, while the roles of their heads are different. For example, the chancellor may have a large role in setting a target inflation rate, whereas the Governor would decide and implement measures to pursue said target. The scope of roles is different, and their positioning reflect that.

Furthermore, the salary and commitments are different. The Chancellor's is around £71,000, though this does not include their salary gained as a member of parliament. By contrast the Governor's is £495,000. This larger salary makes sense with the context of being a less direct servant to the public.

A **poor applicant** would say they have the same job and position and that one may be irrelevant.

Q52: What would be the economic consequences of Scotland gaining independence from the UK? What about Wales?

This question has dramatic relevance now, given that Brexit occurred after Scotland voted to remain in the UK. It has been argued by many that this vote occurred the way it did since the UK was a member of the EU at the time.

Good Applicant: This question is increasingly relevant since the failure of Scotland's last independence referendum was heavily based around the idea that the UK would be remaining in the EU. George Galloway had some interesting points suggesting that Scotland leaving the UK would likely have much more severe ramifications for Scotland than it would for the UK, considering its size of economy.

According to Nicola Sturgeon, Scotland's first minister, Scotland would join the European Union as an independent member. Since they complied with EU law as part of the UK, this process would likely be fast-tracked if they were willing to cede to the EU's demands. Galloway outlined how Scotland in such a large union would lose much of their say. This would also imply a loss of free movement between Scotland and a post-Brexit England, and either electronic or manual checkpoints on the border between them. It is likely this would be a hard border. If Scotland became part of the Schengen Agreement, or generally decreased their immigration control with the EU, passports would be needed to cross this border. Scotland would also be losing some access to the British market. The only alternative to this would be coming to a bespoke agreement with the EU rather than joining it. Considering the priority the SNP – Scotland's primary pro-independence party – has placed on cooperation with the EU, this is unlikely. Economically it provides access to a market eight times the UK's. This is helpful for jobs and living standards. Investments may be affected in the general flux of such an unprecedented change.

With regards to the currency, some advocate for different approaches. Scotland may choose to take on the Euro, which some argue operates only in the interest of the central currencies. It would also need to fulfil certain criteria. The questions arise of separating financial systems and dividing debts and assets. Some economic agents still believe there would be a currency union in place, with strong checks and balances. However, political parties in the UK, as well as the Treasury and Bank of England are fairly unanimous in their worry of an independent Scotland using the pound: the risk two political systems with the same currency is demonstrated by the eurozone. Plausibly, Scotland could develop a new floating currency. It would risk loss of stability of the economy, but allows more flexibility.

Politically, Scotland renounced its sovereignty in the 1707 Act of Union. Since then they have had a separate devolved parliament with a large degree of autonomy except on issues where they have been mandated to defer to the UK parliament. As an independent nation, this parliament will be forced to rethink their reliance on their oil and gas reserves, the prices of which are in constant flux. This would also involve changes and greater control over their military – possibly in appealing to NATO – and health services. To some degree, they have been gradually increasing their autonomy here already and we could expect a smoother transition for it.

Wales, by contrast, would struggle more significantly than Scotland as an independent state. Both would suffer from similar issues, but the issue of poverty in Wales means that the economy does not have the strength for this. It depends heavily on public sector expenditure and infusion of funds, and would need to create new alliances immediately to replace this. It is similar to the event of leaving the EU and its funding, but on a more dramatic scale. Potentially, however, Wales could focus on their positive trade balance on manufactured goods and become more trade-oriented to sustain itself.

A **poor applicant** may try to focus too heavily on Wales, considering that is based on speculation. Avoid this by explaining Scotland's situation and then extrapolating where relevant and explaining key differences.

Q53: How do you predict oil prices will change in the next decade? How about the next century?

It is possible to use the established speculation for oil prices in the next 10 years, as well as global trends, to extrapolate its future more broadly.

Good Applicant: According to experts, the key factors determining oil prices – such as geopolitical turmoil, economic growth, shale production, and OPEC policies – will remain the same. This means that it is possible to predict with reasonable accuracy what oil price trends will occur.

Oil demands have begun to change and will do so in the next decade, but will still peak in the 2030s. This means that oil prices will gradually increase due to its use in shipping, petrochemicals and aviation. Some elements of use will begin to decrease, such as passenger cars. This means demand will continually increase, though likely at a decreasing rate. Moreover, due to limited price variations, growth in US shale production is slowing but will continue to occur for at least the first half the decade. In general, fossil fuels are non-renewable resources that are beginning to face depletion. This means that supply will continue to fall. Both these factors mean that prices will likely increase, though not substantially.

In the long term century view, we will see prices begin to fall. Supply will continue to decrease though at a much slower rate, as less will be mined. Moreover, due to global alarm over climate change, and carbon laws being implemented all over the world, renewable energy will begin to impact the energy scene. It may gradually replace oil use in transport and power, and provided governments align their policy to it, oil demand will decrease. Hydrogen use in particular will limit the demand on oil substantially. As demand falls, we will see oil prices dropping substantially and a corresponding increase in prices of renewable sources of energy.

A **poor applicant** would state that constant market forces of demand and supply would ensure that prices would remain the same.

Q54: What makes the US economy so strong?

There are a few key distinctive features of the American economy that should be explored to describe why America's economy, as opposed to other similarly structured ones, excels in the world market.

Good Applicant: The American economy is known for certain crucial features, notably: competition, consumption, resilience, flexibility, and innovation.

Competition, as in any capitalist country, can provide the fuel of economic growth. It motivates efficiency: businesses produce only those goods that are in demand and have direct incentive to reduce waste and have low prices. Citizens also seek the best jobs and work hard in order to consume the items they most want.

American consumption – while critiqued by many due to its scale – is unparalleled. In every field, including food, clothing and more, the US is expected to spend and consume to excess. This means there is heavy circulation of income and this boosts the economy from the ground up.

Resilience is the feature that ensures that in times of crisis, the other features are maintained. The US has faced some of the largest crises in the world in the last century – natural disasters, wars and the Great Recession. The economy has the durability to withstand such financial setbacks.

Flexibility is inherent in the capitalistic nature of the US system. Bureacratic red tape is minimised, maximising the amount of production and innovation. The government has sufficient regulation to ensure safety and legality, but allows business autonomy for the most part. Only key areas come under government regulation.

Innovation has been inbuilt in the idea of the American dream. Much of the culture of ambition rewards entrepreneurial spirit, meaning the US leads the world in producing new and better products.

A **poor applicant** may focus on one specific time or feature while missing the bigger picture.

Q55: Could you explain to a layman the perceived value of the G8? How would you distinguish it from the G20?

This is a question of contrast. First, give a brief description of what the G8 is. Then explain why the G8 was founded and what they meet to do. Finally, contrast the G20 by explaining what qualifies a country for the G20 but not for the G8, and why the G8 has continued relevance – if it does.

Good Applicant: The G8 is, quite literally, a group of eight countries whose representatives meet frequently to discuss issues of concern. These can be mutual, global and dependent. Most relevantly, socioeconomic development is one of the topics for ministerial meetings. The idea of the specific choice of the G8 is that its major industrialised countries, and between the eight they make up about half of the world's GDP. However, critics suggested that its use is in decline considering the situations of economies has dramatically shifted since the last change to the country line-up. For example, China's economy is currently stronger than that of seven of the eight countries, and yet it is not a member.

The G20 is a similar style of forum, but it has 19 countries and the European Union. They have replaced the G8 as the main economic council of wealthy nations. This means most economic issues and financial crises are discussed there, though political issues may still be solved within the G8. It is said that they are more useful as a means to financial stability given that the world has undergone rapid globalisation since the creation of the G8. Both use arbitrary cut-off lines of wealth, but the G20 increases the representation of countries.

David Cameron said in 2012 that the continued relevance of the G8 in this circumstance is their collective belief in free enterprise to promote economic growth. This explains the G8's roster: all Western countries, excluding Japan, which has been modelled around the US economy since World War II. One could argue that these are countries represent a traditionally Western idea of the model economy.

A **poor applicant** could oversimplify this question. It would be logical to assume that the G20 is simply a larger group of similar-minded countries. It is worth discussing, therefore, the ideological differences between the groups. The interviewer asking about both of the forums in direct succession is a sign that the important parts of the answer will come from their contrast.

Q56: What are the main similarities and differences between the Chinese and Indian economies?

As the two Eastern countries with large and booming economies, comparison and contrast of these economies is incredibly relevant.

Good Applicant: There are a number of historical and socio-political factors that play into the similarities – and differences – we see between these economies today. China is a far larger economy, with a GDP per capita of over $10,000 in 2019. By contrast, India's was around $2000 at the same point. This difference is likely to continue increasing for the time being, with China's GDP growth rate at 6.1% and India's at 4.2%. These numbers not only reflect modernising economies, they represent the wealth of human resource available in the two most populous countries. They also reflect similar unemployment rates.

China has been a closed, centrally planned economy for a long time, and it is only since the 1970s that significant reforms to this have been conducted. This has increased their efficiency dramatically. Price liberalisation, financial decentralisation, autonomy for state enterprises and more have been at the heart of this rapid transformation. One of the key statistics of note here is that shortly before China became the world's economy, it became the largest exporter and trading nation. However, China faces problems such as localised efficiency, an ageing population and low household consumption. There has always been attempts to undermine market-oriented reforms to reaffirm the power of the state, and it has proved one of their inefficiencies in the long-term.

India, on the other hand, has been an economy of varied methods and inputs. It is known for its diversity of economy – while the workforce is based around agriculture, it does not provide as much output as the growing service industry. India is gradually transforming into an open-market economy through economic liberalisation, deregulation and privatisation since the 1990s. Shocks of demonetisation and GST have recently slowed the economy, and demonstrate to a large degree why the Indian economy growth has not been as rapid as China's.

It is of note here that China is a one-party state and India a multi-party state. Further governmental reforms sought in India could not go through since the ruling party lacks a majority in their upper house of Parliament. On the other hand, the Chinese Communist Party can implement rapid development on a large scale with far fewer barriers. The authoritarian versus democracy debate is complicated by this – the inefficiencies inherent in cooperation. While it may be argued that the inclusivity provided is worth this, it is clear that the political system has a large part in creating such differences.

Another notable difference is the population. The population of China has a higher productivity of labour, producing more output with help from advanced infrastructure. Moreover, they are more urbanised. The urbanisation rate is approximately 58% in China and 37% in India for historical and cultural reasons. This adds to productivity in China, and increases economic growth.

A **poor applicant** would simply point out the difference in timeframes for reform and imply that both countries are on the same path but with different starting points. This would ignore the systemic differences between them.

Q57: Take a look at this graph. It shows the price of salt since 1800. You'll notice that it follows a recurring pattern. How can this have been sustained in the face of events like the Great War, the Great Depression, and The Second World War?

The answer to this is heavily dependent on what type of salt is being shown on the graph. Accurate graph analysis is therefore incredibly crucial.

Good Applicant: The demand for salt is split up into industrial, gritting, chemical and more. I will specifically talk about salt for consumption, an essential good. It is a nutrient, a preservative and a flavouring, and has been for many years.

Essentially, since salt is an essential good in terms of food consumption, it continually returns to its baseline through cyclical patterns. The demand for it continually increases as the population of the world increases dramatically. To match this, supply is able to continually increase. This is because salt is a very common commodity, found in abundance across the world. It is also renewable over relatively short period of time and therefore not at heavy risk of depletion.

Moreover, due to the heavy and cheap nature of salt, as well as its abundance, it is usually a regional good and not imported. This means inter-country conflicts such as wars are less likely to affect it. Depressions only affect demand and supply as far as economic growth is affected, and since it is forced to bounce back through monetary and economic policy, so too does the demand and supply of salt. Therefore, the market forces governing the prices of salt always return to a baseline, promoting a cyclical pattern.

A **poor applicant** may suggest that the cyclical pattern is coincidental.

Q58: How does the job of a manager differ from that of a director, executive, or leader?

Here, the question is going to rely on an intuitive understanding of how we use these words differently.

Good Applicant: I find that there's a Peter Drucker quote that explains this well: "Leadership is doing the right things; management is doing things right." Both are ways of organising groups with a common purpose – the difference comes, therefore, in what methods they use to do it.

It is worth pointing out that a leader and a manager have fundamentally different tasks. We expect leaders to build and define their group's objectives, values and methods from the ground up. Managers, on the other hand, are expected to be one link in a larger chain and may not be the ultimate deciding factor. Their role is more akin to successfully delegating workers and resources to achieve their objective efficiently. They may be the head of their group but more often, they have higher ups to report to. If so, they may manage their team but still have no personal influence over the team's overall objectives and methods.

A good example of this would be regional and local managers of a national company. If they are inventive, unique and perform with autonomy, they may well be leaders too, but they will most likely otherwise be managers only. Similarly, leaders can be unofficially chosen if they lead through example – in this case they will not have the official position of manager. They also need not be acting with the intention of others following: that can be an indirect effect of their charisma and force of personality.

Poor applicants may try to suggest there is no meaningful difference between them without thinking critically about the question. They may also begin with a statement about their differences but end up not directly comparing them.

Q59: How might we begin to work out the ROI from Christopher Columbus's expeditions?

Return on investment is a measurement of the profitability of an investment. It is the ratio of return relative to cost, used to evaluate stand-alone investments or compare them to other potential investments. Columbus' voyages can be evaluated individually to compare them and see their overall contribution to the economy.

Good Applicant: The first step in calculating return on investment, or ROI, is usually finding the net return on investment. This is done by subtracting the initial value of investment from the final value of investment. Then the resultant value will be divided by the total cost of investment and multiplied by 100 to produce a percentage ROI.

Hence, to calculate the ROI from Christopher Columbus' voyages we would need to consider first the different voyages. He made four voyages – their ROI can be calculated collectively or individually. To calculate the collective ROI, we ought to calculate the net return on investment. This would be the value of the goods and services imported from the countries they discovered, considering the cost that would have been incurred to get them from elsewhere. It would also include imputed costs of new slave ownership and other such economic conquests. Then the resultant value will be divided by the cost of investment, easily found in the size of donation from his funders such as the Catholic Monarchs of Spain. This value will then be multiplied by 100.

It is worth noting that cost here does not include the imputed cost to the destination countries, or environmental destruction, suggesting a flaw in the use of ROI.

A **poor applicant** would say that since the statistical values of some of the inputs and outputs may not be known, the process of calculation cannot be shown.

Q60: Is it possible to calculate ROI for exploratory organisations, like NASA?

Return on investment is a measurement of the profitability of an investment. It is the ratio of return relative to cost, used to evaluate stand-alone investments or compare them to other potential investments. NASA would use it to evaluate their different operations – and potentially to see whether terrestrial or extra-terrestrial investments are more profitable.

Good Applicant: The first step in calculating return on investment, or ROI, is usually finding the net return on investment. This is done by subtracting the initial value of investment from the final value of investment. Then the resultant value will be divided by the total cost of investment and multiplied by 100 to produce a percentage.

To calculate the ROI of a NASA operations, we begin by finding its tangible and non-tangible as well as fiscal and non-fiscal net gain. Then we divide this by the cost of production, debugging, testing and verification. This will usually be given as the development cost. This resultant value will then be multiplied by 100 to produce the ROI of the operation.

There are opportunity costs to NASA's operations that are not measured in the ROI, showing how it is not a perfect measure.

A **poor applicant** would say that since the statistical values of some of the inputs and outputs may not be known, the process of calculation cannot be shown.

Q61: A dramatic election leads to the formation of a new country in Central Africa, which promptly develops and introduces a new currency. How is this currency then valued on the international market?

The implication of letting the international market decide the value of a currency is that it is a 'free' floating currency. This can be shown diagrammatically with a demand and supply diagram of the currency.

Good Applicant: As with all goods and services, the value of a currency – here we can call it Currency X - is measured by its demand. In a floating currency, this will occur due to the market forces of demand and supply. The estimated value will be the value at which the demand and supply is equal.

This leads us on to the theory of value of currency. Historically, the amount of currency in circulation in a country was dependent on that country's reserves of valuable commodities. Now, the dollar is seen as fiat money – it is instead dependent on government policy indicating how much currency ought to be printed. That would be set by their monetary policy. Due to inflation and deflation, the stability of currency value is dependent on a set amount of money being printed – usually enough to trigger a small rate of inflation. This part of the process is internal and based on mechanics internal to the country.

Then comes the question of how value is determined between countries with different currencies. There are three ways this could be done. Firstly, it could be the measure of how much Currency X would buy in foreign currency. This is done by the exchange rate, determined by forex traders on the foreign exchange market. It takes into account supply and demand, as well as expectations.

The second method is the value of the country's Treasury notes. Through the secondary market for Treasurys, they can be converted into Currency X. When the demand for Treasurys is high, the value of the Currency X rises. This is dependent on a functional, independent monetary system within the country.

The third – and most realistic – way would be through foreign exchange reserves, or the amount of Currency X held by foreign governments. The more that is held, the lower the supply, and the more valuable the currency is – until none is left. In essence, this is forming a demand and supply equilibrium based on the amount of foreign exchange passing to and from the country.

A **poor applicant** may suggest a fixed exchange rate and unchanging exchange rate, though this is not what the question implies.

Q62: Why didn't the UK adopt the Euro?

For this question, there is a number of possible factors, most of which are interlinked. Make sure you acknowledge that and then try to do it justice.

Good Applicant: 19 of the 27 member states of the European Union use Euros as their primary currency and are therefore part of the Eurozone. This eases difficulty in exchange rates during trade. However, even before leaving the EU, the UK did not use the Euro, instead using the pound sterling. Though the UK is within the EU's trading bloc, this move was strategic. The UK is also not in the EU's Schengen area, showing their commitment to individual progress and pragmatism.

The euro was proposed as a single currency system for the EU in 1997. Gordon Brown, the England's Chancellor of the Exchequer at the time, proposed five economic tests for England to use the euro. The first of these tests is that business cycles and economic structures must be compatible such that the UK could manage with Eurozone interest rates. Secondly, the monetary system must have economic flexibility to solve local and aggregate issues. Thirdly, it must create a situation conducive to investment in the UK. Fourthly, it must allow England's financial services industry to be internationally competitive. Lastly, it must promote growth, stability and an increase in job opportunities. These benchmarks have been considered too high to ever feasibly pass, so many believe that standing by them means the UK will never adopt the euro.

There are also further practical reasons for this. It is considered by many a political move – many believe it would be crossing the rubicon of EU integration. Initial popular support of Brexit is the perfect indicator of why that would have been politically unpopular. Similar opinion polls in the UK have suggested that the majority of the British were against adopting the euro.

Finally and arguably most importantly, adopting the euro would force the UK to meet 'euro convergence criteria'. This includes a debt-to-GDP ratio which would limit their fiscal policy. It also includes controlled interest rates, limiting their monetary policy. Setting interest rates is currently a task by the Bank of England, and it is set to meet the UK economy's aims. This means that though the movement of the UK and EU's interest rates may align somewhat, they will not be the same because of differing priorities. Other losses of autonomy would include not being able to issue debt in the UK's own currency and losing the shock absorber having your own currency provides. Examples such as that of Greece can prove that.

Poor Applicant: A poor applicant may consider starting with an evaluative on whether we should be using Euros. This is not what the question is asking, though you might find that the answer fits well into what you've already said once you've given a clear answer.

PPE & HSPS

An economics applicant may be asked a question relating to political events or questions from a related subject, such as sociology. Even if you haven't stated any previous knowledge of philosophy on your application, you may be asked a question on any of these subject areas. However, you will not be expected to demonstrate specific detailed knowledge in an area not studied previously, you will simply be expected to apply your own point of view and understanding to the topics.

HSPS & PPE interviews generally consist of a large question with many smaller sub-questions to guide the answer from the start to a conclusion. The main question may seem difficult, impossible, or random at first, but take a breath and start discussing with your interviewer different ideas you have for breaking down the question into manageable pieces. Don't panic.

The questions are designed to be difficult to give you the chance to show your full intellectual potential. They will help guide you to the right idea if you provide ideas for them to guide. This is your chance to show your creativity, analytical skills, intellectual flexibility, problem-solving skills and your go-getter attitude. Don't waste it on nervousness or a fear of messing up or looking stupid.

The interviewer wants to see what you know and what you are capable of, not what you don't know.

When answering a question, you should be responsive to the interviewer and take on board their prompts and suggestions. If you are making an argument that is clearly wrong, then concede your mistake and try to revise your viewpoint – it is ok to say 'I didn't think of that' when taking on board a different viewpoint. Do not stubbornly carry on arguing a point that they are saying is wrong. **Making mistakes is not a bad thing** – if you can show that you have addressed a mistake and attempted to revise your argument upon the realisation of more information, you are showing a skill crucial to getting through essays and supervisions at an Oxbridge university.

There are no set patterns to the questions you can get asked. Most questions, however, will focus on a topic for which it is possible for any individual to have an opinion without previous knowledge of the area. This is to test the way you think about a topic and to test whether you are able to apply your own experiences and knowledge to an unknown subject area. These skills are important when studying Economics as the courses are largely essay-based and rely strongly upon the ability to construct an argument based on the information provided. Many questions are related to society today and may require the individual to be familiar with current affairs and big events in the news.

The questions will usually take one of a few possible forms based on highlighting skills necessary to 'think like a social scientist.' **Five main questions types** are:

- Why do we need... (borders, welfare state, international institutions, museums etc.)?

- Compare X to Y... (normally based on your essay or personal statement, so something you are familiar with)

- Distinguish between... (state and nation, race and ethnicity, liberalism and libertarianism etc.)

- What do you think about... (the current British school system, nature vs. nurture debate etc.)?

- Why is there... (gender inequality in the workplace, poverty etc.)? How would you solve it?

Questions also have recurring themes that appear because they are important for social sciences: legitimacy and role of government, human rights, poverty, feminism, international institutions, the purpose of education and different educational systems, voting systems, inequality and social classes.

GENERAL PPE & HSPS WORKED QUESTIONS

Below are a few examples of how to start breaking down an interview question, complete with model answers.

Q1: Do you feel that there is a logical cause for violent protest?

[Extremely clear-headed] **Applicant**: Well, I know that the law states that violence against other people or property is not acceptable, and yet I also know that violent protests still occur and this makes me wonder why. There must be a reason that people feel the need to turn to violence. This might be because of their personality or it may be something deeper such as the feeling of having no choice. If a point is important and the protest is for a serious reason, such as fighting for human rights, and all other forms of protest have been avoided, then maybe the only way to be heard is through violence. However, I don't think a violent protest can ever be justified. For example, take the 2011 UK Riots – violence didn't solve anything – it is a way of being seen and heard, but a horrific one. I don't think being heard for doing something that is wrong is the right way to be recognised.

This shows that **the question can be broken down into smaller-parts**, which can be dealt with in turn. At this point, the interviewer can give feedback if this seems like a good start and help make any necessary modifications. In this particular case, the applicant might be asked to expand on the reasons a person might resort to violence in protests and to give an example if possible. They may also be asked to provide a suggestion as to a better way to be heard than a violent protest. The details are unimportant, but the general idea of breaking down the question into manageable parts is important. The interviewer is not looking for an expert, but someone who can problem-solve in the face of new ideas.

173

A **poor applicant** may take a number of approaches unlikely to impress the interviewer. The first and most obvious of these is to simply answer 'yes' or 'no' with little justification or reference to an alternative point of view and with no attempt made to move forward. The applicants who have done this only make it worse for themselves by resisting prodding as the interviewer attempts to pull an answer from them, saying "fine, but I'm not going to be able to expand because I don't know anything about this", or equally unenthusiastic and uncooperative responses.

Another approach which is unhelpful in the interview is the '**brain dump'**, where instead of engaging with the question, the applicant attempts to impress or distract with an assortment of related facts or events: In this case, reeling off the law on violence or a list of historical riots and their outcomes. Having gotten off to this start isn't as impressive as a more reasoned response, but the interview can be salvaged by taking feedback from the interviewer.

Many of these facts could start a productive discussion which leads to the answer if the applicant listens and takes hints and suggestions from the interviewer.

Q2: How can you actually determine whether or not the moon is cheese?

[Extremely clear-headed] Applicant: What I am first going to think about is what needs to be considered when deciding whether or not something is true. This raises questions like "Is it patently absurd?", "Is it backed up by evidence?", and "What types of evidence do we require?". Next, I consider whether it is reasonably possible that this statement fits with other associated and established pieces of knowledge, e.g. the formation of the planets, stars, and satellites. If the claim is at odds with established knowledge, then I may be more inclined to believe it untrue. However, this does not necessarily prove anything. For example, in this case, what is meant by cheese? If we are talking poetically, or aesthetically then it may be considered reasonable to make the above claim.

Moreover, whose reality are we talking about, and indeed does the result vary depending on this? I mean, is it really possible to 'know' anything, or are we just making educated guesses based on a set of assumptions married with some data – and does this count as 'real'? Essentially, when I first looked at the statement I thought it was completely absurd and previously proven otherwise. However, after consideration of perspective, definition, reality, and knowledge, I am now not so convinced.

Just like the previous example questions, this is a step by step answer. The applicant has broken down their thoughts and provided the interviewer with a stream of their own workings of their mind. This allows the interviewer to understand how the individual is breaking down the question and gives an opportunity for the interviewer to intervene with further questions if required.

A **poor applicant** may state something like "Well because it obviously isn't" – without any further justification. The point of a question like this is to consider the many different ways in which we experience reality and develop our understanding therein. If the applicant fails to address more than the superficial, then they are unlikely to show an understanding for the point of the question.

Q3: Why do you think the British government continues to legalise smoking?

Good Applicant: I'd like to think about what other areas are considered by the **legislators of the UK** when they allocate legal status to things, as it can't just be health implications. With regards to smoking, there are a number of vested parties including tobacco companies and smokers themselves. Tobacco companies rely on smoking being legal in the UK for their income. If smoking were made illegal, then these companies would lose 100% of their UK revenue, which in turn, may impact the economy as a whole (these sales are far from insubstantial). Secondly, when thinking about smokers who are 20% of the UK's adult population (equating to around 10 million people), they represent a large fraction of the potential electorate.

Therefore, banning smoking would have significant implications for political intervention due to unpopularity, loss of freedom, etc.

As another point, smokers may claim that they have an addiction which is difficult to stop. They may also argue that smoking was legal when they first started to smoke. Thus, the government may face a legal battle if they were to suddenly make the product illegal. This may make a total ban on smoking impractical and a breach of an individual's right to choose. However, banning smoker on a more gradual basis may be feasible and is happening today; for example, it is now against the law to smoke in cars, in the workplace, and in public areas. Maybe **phasing out smoking** is more realistic, and is therefore what is being attempted in the UK. This would imply that it is not the case that legislators are unaware or uncaring of the health implications of smoking, but that they are attempting to reduce smoking in a less disruptive manner.

A **poor applicant** might fail to address the reasons why smoking has not been made illegal. It is not simply a case of saying "smoking is bad, therefore the government should ban it". The question of whether it should be banned impacts many people and showing an understanding of different perspectives and potential arguments is important for answering this question sufficiently.

Q4: If the nuclear balance of power was equalised globally, do you think there would still be war?

A **Good Applicant**: We all have learnt how dangerous nuclear weapons can be when **Hiroshima and Nagasaki** were destroyed at the end of World War 2. The threat to the environment, human lives, and even future generations is known, and the risk is too high. Nuclear weapons should not be used at all. On the other hand, it is true that there was no direct war between the USA and USSR during the Cold War and both had nuclear weapons. It seems possible that countries with nuclear weapons do not engage in war with one another as the high risk of a catastrophe deters them from using nuclear weapons, and hence the proliferation of nuclear weapons may prevent wars.

This shows that the candidate understands the question and is able to draw on some examples from A-level History. A **better candidate** would then engage in a discussion with the interviewer about the moral aspect of the topic or may choose to draw on a broader range of examples and realise that although proliferation of nuclear weapons may deter another world war, it could lead to more frequent small-scale wars. Examples of wars in Iraq, Vietnam, Afghanistan, and Korea during the Cold War demonstrate that there were, in fact, "real wars", and the USSR and USA backed smaller countries in war. So, the proliferation of nuclear weapons may have led to small-scale wars, yet prevented another world war. Making a moral case against any use of nuclear weapons, for instance, referring to the experience from Hiroshima and Nagasaki shows sensitivity about the topic.

A **poor applicant** may make a moral argument against the use of nuclear weapons before providing any insightful analysis and attempting an answer to the question. Another approach which is unhelpful is focusing too much on providing a yes/no answer to the question, and hence missing the point that the proliferation of nuclear weapons is a gradual process with various political, moral, and economic difficulties, and it is not plausible that all countries could get nuclear weapons overnight. The question is very broad and raises many interesting arguments for discussion, but 'brain dump' is not helpful here.

Q5: When we make contact with an extra-terrestrial civilisation, what should we tell them is humanity's greatest achievement?

[Extremely clear-headed] Applicant: The concept of humanity's greatest achievement is very subjective. It can either be measured in terms of effort needed to accomplish it, or in terms of impact. In the first case, humanity's greatest achievement could be the pyramids, since they required a tremendous amount of work with little technology, and are still standing today after thousands of years. In terms of impact, humanity's greatest achievement could be the discovery of penicillin for example. I think that it makes more sense to focus on a ground-breaking achievement from the past, rather than the most recent accomplishments of humanity.

177

If I were to tell an extra-terrestrial civilisation about penicillin, however, I would also have to provide an explanation on humanity's problems which it solved. Finally, I would have to take into account the aim of my message: am I trying to impress, intimidate, or simply inform?

A good applicant will understand the true aim of the question: creating an abstract situation in which he is encouraged to problematise the subjective concept of 'greatest achievement' and make an argument.

A poor applicant could misinterpret the question, and focus on the extra-terrestrial civilisation, talking about space technology and means of communication. Alternatively, he could choose an accomplishment and fail to justify his answer, or provide a lot of facts on the subject without problematising the concept of 'greatest achievement'.

Q6: In a democracy, can the majority impose its will on the minority?

[Extremely clear-headed] Applicant: First, I am going to think from the practical point of view: if by 'minority' we mean 'the ruling elites', does the majority have the actual ability to impose its will? The population only gets to make decisions on rare occasions: elections and referenda. Most of the time, decisions are made by a small group of people: the government. In 2002-2003, there were mass protests against the war in Iraq, but this did not stop Tony Blair from sending troops. It seems that once a government is in power, there is little that the majority of the population can do before the next elections. Secondly, we could think about the question from a normative point of view: should the majority be able to make most decisions in a democratic system? There is a difference between democracy and populism, where power is held by the masses. The latter could be problematic. If by minority we understand things such as small ethnic or religious groups, in a populist system they would have no say and could end up being oppressed. In a democratic system, minorities are protected by laws. However, we can see that the system is sometimes flawed. For example, in the US, there are only two major political parties: people with different agendas than Republicans or Democrats are pushed away from power.

This question can be answered in a number of ways, but a good candidate will show his capacity to deconstruct it, and think for a moment before replying. He will support his points with examples.

A poor applicant will rush into an answer without thinking and might end up getting confused between the different aspects of the question. He will either make generalisations without giving examples, or focus exclusively on a single real-life case, giving a lot of facts but without any argument or acknowledgment of a different point of view.

Q7: Why is there social inequality in the world? How would you resolve this issue?

[Extremely clear-headed] Applicant: I do not think that there is a single reason for social inequality in the world. Of course, it is not normal that 1% of the population controls almost 50% of its wealth. Greed and self-centeredness seem to be inherent flaws of humanity. However, I also think that there are other underlying factors behind social inequality. I cannot imagine a society in which everybody would have the same proportion of wealth and the same professional opportunities. People live in different places, speak different languages, and simply have different talents and skills. Thus, I do not think that social inequality can ever be fully resolved. Experiments such as communism in the USSR have attempted to artificially suppress inequality. This has not only entailed terrible crimes such as the extermination of entire groups in the society, but has also proved economically unsustainable in the long-term, with the Soviet economy eventually collapsing. Nevertheless, perhaps some form of **efficient taxation and governments granting more funds** to international organisations and NGOs could help reduce inequality.

A good applicant can have a different opinion on the subject, but will take into account other points of view, and will identify the difficulties associated with resolving such a complex problem, supporting his argument with solid A-level type factual knowledge.

A poor applicant could focus on only one of the two questions. He might give a 'trendy' answer such as "It's all because of the rich" or "Humans are bad so there is nothing you can do", without giving any real explanation or evidence, and refuse to engage fully with the questions.

Q8: To what extent is taxing the rich likely to lead to greater equality in society?

[Extremely clear-headed] Applicant: There is a big disproportion in terms of wealth between a small group of the 'rich' and the 'poor' majority. Therefore, it would seem logical to find a way of redistributing that wealth. As we can see, altruism does not suffice, since the problem persists despite a few notable examples of rich people giving big proportions of their fortune to charity, for instance, Bill Gates. Taxation does seem like a good solution. However, it needs to be designed efficiently. For instance, we must make sure that such a tax does not affect the economy negatively, for example, by dissuading the wealthy from opening new businesses and sources of income. Secondly, there have been cases where large funds were not used efficiently, but rather usurped by local warlords and criminal organisations, for instance in Somalia in the 1990s. It might be necessary to establish an international body of experts to design and monitor the implementation of projects funded by this tax.

A good applicant will be able to **identify both the positive and the negative sides of such a policy**. Regardless of whether he has any knowledge on the subject, he will provide a well-structured, logical answer.

A poor applicant might be intimidated by the question and refuse to answer by saying something like "I don't know anything about taxes". Alternatively, he might provide an answer which focuses only on one side of the coin, making it very vulnerable to counterarguments.

Q9: Is alcohol addiction always a result of the social environment, peer pressure, and negative role models?

[Extremely clear-headed] Applicant: Alcohol addiction is more widespread in certain social environments or countries: for instance, it is a much bigger problem in Russia than in the UK. I don't think that it would be appropriate to argue that nationality or ethnicity inherently determines the likelihood of alcohol addiction.

This is why explanations such as **peer pressure and negative role models** are very useful. Indeed, peer pressure can become integrated into culture. For example, drinking alcohol in large quantities on a teenage trip abroad or on an American Spring Break has become almost a ritual. In some cultures, drinking vast amounts of alcohol can be considered as a mark of virility, or politeness, which is conducive to alcohol addiction. However, we should not generalise. It is possible for someone to develop an alcohol addiction in an environment where drinking is frowned upon or rare, just as it is possible to remain abstinent while being surrounded by alcoholics. If an individual's parents and friends do not drink, and yet he becomes an alcohol addict citing a musician with questionable habits as his role model, it seems reasonable to assume that other factors, perhaps psychological, were at play. Thus, while the social environment is a very potent explanation for alcohol addiction, ignoring the possibility of other factors could have negative consequences, such as failing to properly address the issue.

A good applicant will **note the use of the word 'always'**, and attempt to come up with a counter-example.

A poor candidate might fall into the trap of agreeing with the statement without thinking of other points of view. He could refuse to reply stating his lack of knowledge on the topic, or give anecdotal evidence from his experience or environment without constructing an argument.

Q10: Imagine you are a historian a hundred years in the future, looking back on today. What aspects of society would you focus on?

[Extremely clear-headed] Applicant: I do not think that any aspect of history should be discarded as unimportant. However, I am most interested by politics and geopolitics. It is basically impossible to predict the future, and very hard to fully understand the present and its implications. A hundred years from now, we will have a much better understanding of some of today's unanswered questions. For instance, how successful are international organisations in fostering cooperation and preventing conflict? After all, the UN and the EU are relatively recent constructs, and did not fully exploit their potential until the end of the Cold War.

Determining whether international institutions have any real influence or whether they are just tools in the hands of self-centered states is one of the big debates in the study of international relations. Secondly, it would be interesting to see whether in the **age of mass information** and communication, humanity is able to learn from its previous mistakes. Parties of the extreme right are currently gaining a lot of votes in Europe, due among others to economic hardship. Will European countries suffer a fate similar to the Weimar Republic?

A good candidate will demonstrate a certain degree of knowledge on the current topic of his choice, and will be able to identify the way in which it might be perceived by a historian.

A poor candidate might avoid the question by saying something like "I think that humanity will destroy itself within a hundred years so there will be no historians left". He could also lose track of his argument by trying to impress the interviewer with his factual knowledge on a current topic, or attempt to make unjustified predictions of future developments.

Q11: What are the main reasons for persistent unemployment in the UK?

[Extremely clear-headed] Applicant: I think that people are often tempted to look for simple explanations behind complicated issues. This is why extreme political parties are so successful: they provide the population with easily identifiable scapegoats such as 'the current government', 'immigrants', or 'the EU', and blame them for every economic and social problem. In reality, issues such as unemployment have many reasons. One of them could be the discrepancy between supply and demand: what type of jobs people are prepared for at schools and universities, and what type of jobs are offered on the market. For instance, in Scandinavian countries, when an unemployed individual cannot find work for a certain period of time, he is offered courses which allow him to perform a different type of work, where there is more demand.

Another reason could indeed be **globalisation**, with the **international economic crisis**, and many companies moving abroad to reduce costs. However, this does not justify oversimplifying the issue by blaming solely external factors such as foreigners or international organisations. Instead, efforts should be made to better adapt the national system to the realities of the globalised world.

A good candidate will try to provide a balanced and well-argued answer, regardless of his political or moral stance. He will stay away from generalisations and normative statements based on little or no evidence.

A poor applicant might refuse to engage with a question on which he has little previous knowledge. Alternatively, he may make sweeping generalisations or provide an exhaustive list of factors without really explaining any of them.

Q12: Should prisoners have the right to vote?

[Extremely clear-headed] Applicant: I think that in a democracy, voting is one of the **citizen's basic rights**. The question is: should prisoners still be considered as citizens? It could be said that when they break the social contract of norms governing the society, their rights are also revoked. However, if a prisoner is deprived of all his rights, his eventual reintegration into society will be even harder. In my opinion, the right to vote should be granted to those prisoners who have not committed the gravest of crimes, such as murder or rape.

Moreover, in some countries, the issue of 'political prisoners' is still prominent, for instance, in China or Ukraine. If someone is imprisoned for disagreeing with the regime and has no right to vote for a different party or candidate, then there is little chance of change and the system moves one step further towards authoritarianism.

A poor applicant could focus too much on providing a yes/no answer based on personal beliefs or anecdotal evidence, without trying to engage with alternative perspectives on the question.

Q13: Is there such a thing as national identity in the world of globalisation?

[Extremely clear-headed] Applicant: In my opinion, while borders are becoming more and more permeable and people can communicate and travel from one part of the world to the other, national identity is not necessarily losing its potency. According to the Marxist theory, national identity was supposed to disappear, giving way to an international movement of workers. This was not really accomplished, and the communist countries which survived the longest such as the Soviet and Chinese systems, were those which mixed communism with nationalism. While from our 'Western' perspective it might seem that national identity is dying, this might be related to the fact that we live in relatively peaceful times: there has been no war on the current territory of the EU for decades.

However, in times of conflict, national identity becomes very powerful. We can see this on current examples such as Ukraine and Russia, but also in post 9/11 USA. I think that in times of external threat, people tend to unite under a symbol which differentiates them from the 'other'. Since the nation state remains the main actor in international relations, most conflicts are likely to oppose one nation against another, thus reinforcing the sense of national identity.

A **good candidate** can argue either way, but should be able to acknowledge both sides of the coin. He should be able to support his ideas with some factual A-level type knowledge.

A poor applicant might fail to engage properly with the question, instead of trying to impress the interviewer by dumping facts. Alternatively, he could make broad generalisations without supporting his argument with any real evidence.

Q14: What areas of Philosophy are you interested in?

[Extremely clear-headed] Applicant: I am interested in theories of the state. Many thinkers have attempted to tackle this issue throughout history, ranging from Plato, through Hobbes and Rousseau, to Marx. They all have very different visions of what an efficient political system should look like, whether the human being is inherently good or bad, and who should have the right to rule. What is interesting in this area of Philosophy is that the thinkers have often actually affected the reality.

The writings of Marx are the best example of this phenomenon since they have been used and abused by activists in many countries, leading to the October Revolution in 1917 and the establishment of the USSR, one of two systems dominating the international system for decades. I think that there are many interesting questions in this area of Philosophy. Is it possible to design a system which would be applicable to any setting and society? Do philosophers have a responsibility over how their writings are understood and used?

A good candidate will show both a certain degree of knowledge and of genuine interest in the topic of his choice. He will identify some of the big questions related to the field.

A poor candidate might give an exhaustive list of areas of Philosophy without going into depth on any of them. Alternatively, he could try to demonstrate his extensive factual knowledge of the writings of a single author, without engaging with the wider question on the area of Philosophy.

Q15: Tell me about some political texts that you have read.

[Extremely clear-headed] Applicant: I have looked at some political theory texts, such as Plato's Republic. In this text, the author is describing a perfect political system, an ideal city led by a philosopher-king. He also talks about other flawed political systems, such as tyranny or democracy. I think that this text is very interesting and useful for understanding political systems from the past, and has also inspired other, more recent authors. However, it is important to note that Plato writes from the perspective of Ancient Greece, and many of his concepts are outdated. I think that the term 'political text' could also apply to other types of documents, for example, party programmes, but even literary fiction. I recently read Bulgakov's Master and Margarita, a novel with fantasy themes such as the devil and witchcraft, written in the Soviet Union. Its focus on religion and the occult was also a hidden critique of the atheistic Soviet society. Similar things could be said about the Animal Farm or 1984.

A **good candidate** will try to go beyond simply giving factual knowledge on a text studied in class. He will try to come up with a critical approach towards the text showing a certain degree of independent thought, or problematize the term 'political texts'.

A poor candidate might panic if he has not studied texts of political theory in school, instead of making the best of it by trying to come up with different types of political texts. Alternatively, he might opt for dumping a lot of factual information on a text, instead of showing his understanding of it or demonstrating a critical perspective.

HSPS INTERVIEW QUESTIONS

Q1: How would you discretise the concepts of ethnicity and race?

Race and ethnicity are both highly complex topics. Your interviewer is not expecting you to be able dissect these or necessarily give a 'correct' answer. In society, definitions of 'race' and 'ethnicity' are not specifically discussed, because they are relatively nebulous concepts that are highly political. Therefore, the interview is interested in seeing how you think critically about this question, what experiences and knowledge that you draw upon, and how you can synthesise this into a coherent answer.

Because this question is highly political, you must be incredibly careful about the kind of language you are using. Interviewers will accept minor slip-ups in terms of terminology, but do not use racial stereotypes or discriminative language.

Good Applicant: Well, I'd like to first acknowledge that race and ethnicity are interrelated, and that I don't think it is possible for us talk about one without being aware of the other, because they are both so prevalent in discussions of identity. But, broadly speaking, I think the difference between race and ethnicity, is that race is mostly situated in physical aspects of who a person is, such as their skin colour, but also other biological aspects. In contrast, ethnicity is more closely tied to socio-cultural aspects of a person, where they were brought up, their language, nationality, and regional identities. I think there's also a difference in the histories of the two concepts. Whilst race has a deep past originating from colonial times and was often used to categorise, and thereby dehumanise, different people, as a concept, ethnicity is a more recent creation that is used to better understand the complexity of identity in the post-colonial and global era. I think ultimately both concepts are difficult to clearly define, and the boundaries between the differences are often blurred.

This response is structured well, it starts by stating the relationship that ethnicity and race, and how they both relate to identity. It then clearly cites two points contrasting how race and ethnicity are different, using broad examples to back up the points, without delving into potential slippery slopes that specific examples in talking about these topics might lead to. Finally, the answer makes it clear at the end that you don't have a firm opinion on what race and ethnicity are; it has critically engaged with the question whilst making it clear that you are open to further discussion.

A **poor applicant** could go one of two ways. Firstly, you might not be willing to engage in critical examination of the two concepts because you don't want to say something inappropriate, or you are unaware of exactly what the concepts might mean. Being cautious around these topics is important, but not answering the question asked at all also doesn't help. Secondly, a poor answer might rely upon stereotypes, or even use crude terms to discuss these two highly sensitive topics.

Q2: Would you argue that the society and the state are inseparable? If not, what separates them?

This question is a good opportunity to demonstrate your understanding of definitions of state, and how society fits into it, but also how a state is reliant upon society; they are different but often interconnected. As with many concepts in anthropology and political science, concepts and definitions are important for creating benchmarks for discussion, but are still nebulous and require open thinking combined with critical engagement.

Good Applicant: Fundamentally, I think that the difference between state and society relates to the way in which they are structured. The state is typically made up of formal structures and institutions to be maintained, and is reliant upon four key aspects: population, territory, government, and sovereignty. Now, each of these four aspects are themselves debatable in their definitions and parameters, but the key thing is they form the pillars upon which the state is established. In contrast, society is typically made of informal structures, and interpersonal and intergroup relationships. They are established and maintained through human behaviours, such as exchange of goods and ideas, and are typically highly flexible. With this in mind, state and society are also highly influential upon each other. The formal structures of the state can influence the way in which people in a society interact and their relationships, whilst the state is inherently dependent on the stability of society and the ability of people to cooperate and communicate.

This answer is structured well, making it clear that the applicant understands the question being asked, and that they are able to back up their argument with evidence and examples. Bearing in mind that these are difficult concepts to discuss in a single response, the answer does not go down a rabbit hole trying to wrestle with these ideas, but shows that they are able to engage with both concepts in the question, and draw contrasts between the two. The synthesis at the end also demonstrates that respondent is able to think beyond the basic question, challenge the assumption in the question, and demonstrate the relationships between the two concepts.

A **Poor Applicant** would become tied down with trying to define the two concepts and would run out of time before actually answering the question. Whilst it is important to demonstrate your understanding of the concepts, it is important to demonstrate that you are able to see the bigger picture and critically engage.

Q3: A Roman magistrate appears on your doorstep, and asks you to tell him about the United Nations – how would you compare it to his Empire?

This question is testing your ability to draw comparisons between two seemingly unrelated organisations. In order to answer this question, you need to be able to think creatively and accept that sometimes unconventional comparisons can sometimes change your perspective and are useful heuristics.

Good Response: Well, this is certainly interesting. I think one of the first points that I would compare is that both intentionally or unintentionally acted as peacekeeping bodies. In the case of the UN, this is through mediation, forums, and small peace-keeping forces, in the Roman empire, which I would argue did maintain a decent level of relative peace for 200 years at the outset of the empire (Romana Pax), 'peace' was achieved mostly through prosperity of the empire, fairly decent governance, and the violent crushing of any rebellions. Another point of similarity is the fact that power in the both the Roman empire and UN is actually held by a small number of stakeholders. In the empire this meant the emperor and a few others, and whilst the senate existed, their power was negligible. One could argue that a similar reality occurs in the UN; power is held by the Director General and the Security Council, much of the discourse carried out in the main house of the UN by its members do not carry with it much power, similarly to the senate. I think a third point of similarity are the UN's and the empire's goals around development. Both have or had missions of developing those areas under their influence, in the formers case through sustainable economic development and the latter through its building of grandiose architecture. A final point of similarity that I would draw would be between the multi-state nature of the two organisations; although the UN does not directly govern those states that make it up, unlike the empire, both had to deal with the complexities of multiple states.

At first glance, this is a challenging question, and indeed, as outlined in this answer, the similarities are not going to be perfect. One could argue that there are far more differences between the UN and the RE. Hence, this answer has done well here because it has found ways of drawing similarities between four different points of the UN and the RE through some creative thinking, which your interviewers will be impressed by.

A **Poor Answer** could very easily struggle to find similarities, and become bogged down by the fact that any similarities you can see aren't perfect. Equally, it would be very easy to begin by talking about the differences between the two as these are much easier to identify, and never really identify any points of similarity.

Q4: Some of us think that the poor live in poverty because they don't try hard enough – what would you say to people like that?

As with many Oxbridge interview questions, this question is intentionally challenging or jarring. Whilst it may be tempting to form a strong and subjective opinion one way or the other, you must endeavour to remain balanced, whilst still reaching a conclusion. Thus, you should present your arguments, and then conclude by making your opinion clear on the matter.

Good Answer: Well, to begin with, I can understand why this point of view may be so prevalent among neoliberals. I think that it is derived primarily from those in power and those who control big media outlets influencing the general public's thought. For instance, the fact that the Murdoch empire controls multiple media outlets allows it to hold great sway among the populace in the UK and other countries. Now, media moguls such as Murdoch have two primary objectives: manipulating people to agree with their way of thinking, and making money for themselves and those whose interests align with their own. One of the easiest ways for this money to be made is to push a neoliberal agenda, both in lobbying governments and convincing people through their outlets that this is good for them and their families.

In essence, this means creating the idea that people must be productive within the capitalist system, and that the amount you work will equate directly to your income. In reality, the neoliberal agenda is to deregulate markets and state involvement so that workers' rights and pay can be cut without repercussions. Alongside the propaganda that your worth is equal to how much you work, this creates an environment where the wealthy are able to monopolise the working and middle classes by making them believe that they can be successful, whilst using this as a front to extract wealth from them. In the end, the system crushes many people, especially when state safety nets have been removed, and become poor. Thus, the system is manipulated by neoliberals to make it seem like poor people are only poor because they don't work hard enough. In reality, I think that most of the time, poor people have been exploited by a system created by neoliberals who have simultaneously convinced people through media propaganda that it is the poor's fault for not working hard enough.

This is not an easy question to answer, and in part centres around unpacking what it means to be neoliberal. This answer is strong because it puts pressure from the start on the falsehood underpinning everyday neoliberals; that they are different from poor people. In fact, most neoliberals have been manipulated into their beliefs by moguls and the super rich, and their neoliberal belief system is actually perpetuating those falsehoods that are manipulating them. As well as demonstrating this issue, the answer logically works through the relationship between the political belief system of neoliberalism, the media, and the state. In the end, the answer draws together these lines of argument to answer the question and demonstrate that poverty is not a result of laziness, but instead a failure of state as result of the influence of money within politics.

A **Poor Answer** could react one of two ways. Someone who tacitly agrees with the notion of the question might argue positively, and agree with the question, whilst failing to challenge their own belief system, which would likely be picked up on the interviewer. On the other hand, it would be very easy to become personally offended by the question, as it is undoubtedly an insulting notion. Thus it is important to take the question apart and show that you are able to remain objective whilst still creating a forthright answer that takes a balanced approach.

Q5: What do you think lies behind the recent resurgence of Nationalism in Europe?

This question is testing several different aspects of your knowledge: your recent and deep historic understanding of nationalism within Europe, as well as how this plays out throughout the geography of Europe. In order to answer the question, it is important to highlight that nationalism is a broad idea that fluctuates over time and can mean different things to different people.

A **Good Answer:** I think first it is important to point a bit of an assumption within the question of whether nationalism ever really weakened in Europe. If we look at the history of Europe, really going back to the Roman conquests of Europe, when tribes of the different territories fought back to "protect their lands", we could argue that this is a kind of nationalism, or a kind of cultural or ethnic identity tied to the landscape. From there, throughout the history of Europe, I think that nationalism has always been bubbling under the surface in one form or another. Even when it may seem like nationalistic sentiment has diminished, there are always those factions within a state that advocate for nationalistic policies, and occasionally those with these sentiments achieve power and drive forward with those nationalistic attitudes.

With this in mind, it seems that we are in a time where people with nationalistic sentiments are gaining traction politically. I think there are a number of reasons for this. Firstly, nationalism in Europe is not isolated from the rest of the world, in the same way that nationalism within individual European countries is not isolated from other countries. To this extent, the election of Donald Trump, as well as other fascist leaders such as Jair Bolsanero, and Duterte to name just a couple, always have a knock-on effect elsewhere by emboldening other nationalists directly and indirectly (e.g., Trump's endorsement of Nigel Farage). Beyond just this, the migrant crisis, caused by the ongoing conflicts in the Middle East and North Africa, and exponentially exacerbated by Western and Russian interventions, has undoubtedly increased nationalistic sentiments in Europe as Europeans feel threatened by a sudden influx of people alongside some pretty incompetent policies and leaders unable to deal with this crisis. Finally, both of these issues are ultimately enflamed by the press, which is controlled by a small number of people who directly profit from the controversy that they drive especially around nationalistic sentiments in order to sell papers.

In summary, I think nationalism is an ever-present element of European sociopolitics, but that there are clearly events in the recent past and ongoing that continue to fuel nationalistic sentiments in areas of Europe.

This is a good answer because it shows that you are able to critically engage with the question, deconstruct and offer a foundational starting point by addressing the key assumption within the question. The answer is then structured well, outlining three key points that you feel has driven the strengthening of nationalism within Europe. Finally, it has provided a neat summary that synthesises everything you have tried to outline in your answer.

A **Poor Answer** might try to inherently question whether nationalism has strengthened at all in Europe. Whilst it is possible to play this as devil's advocate, it may inadvertently show that you have a poor grasp of current or recent historical events. Alternatively, it would be easy to become tied up in the deep history of nationalism in Europe, which whilst a useful point of comparison and grounding to your answer, would not address the idea of a recent development.

Q6. You're redesigning a map of the world, how would you go about deciding on national borders?

Whilst seemingly simple, in fact this question is seeking to have you draw upon your ability to synthesise several different disciplines, in reflection of the complexity of drawing of national borders, to answer the question. There is not necessarily a straightforward answer to this, thus you must instead draw upon your different subject knowledges, including history, geography, and politics, to demonstrate that you are able to bring together several different ways of thinking.

A **Good Answer**: At a basic level, national borders are drawn by the political or social bodies that control each side. However, the reality of the drawing of national borders is that there are often complex historical and geographical factors at play, alongside the political ones. For instance, geographical features such as mountain ranges or rivers, serve as physical boundaries that are used as straightforward and often practical borders, such as the Pyrenees separating France and Spain, or the Akagera river separating Rwanda and Tanzania. However, physical boundaries are not always a limiting factor to national borders and can even make the drawing of national borders more, not less complex. In the latter instance, take for example the occasionally conflicted border of India and China, which because of its size and location among the Himalayas, makes defining the border incredibly complicated.

Moreover, in historic terms, physical features have not always been a defining factor for drawing national borders. The invasion and colonisation of other countries, such as by the British or Mongolian empires, entirely betrayed the limitations of the English Channel and the Central Asian Steppe. Conveniently, this leads to consideration of the impact that historical events have on the drawing of national borders. In the post-colonial era, many of the national borders that still exist today are a direct result of colonial powers. Whilst these borders were still defined politically during their time between the colonial powers, it is interesting to examine how infrequently these borders are actually challenged by the modern nations that they affect. Overall, what I'm trying to elucidate, is that national borders are in fact incredibly complex and dynamic, and are affected by a whole array of factors on a case by case basis; almost no two borders are drawn in exactly the same way, and this is reflected in the way that they are drawn.

It would be very easy to write an entire thesis on this subject, as there are so many case studies that you could draw upon to provide examples and counter examples. Ultimately, this answer is strong because it is able to demonstrate that you have a wide understanding of the realities of the complexities of drawing national borders, and that it is perfectly fine, once you have outlined decent and varied evidence, as has been done here, to conclude that there is no finite answer to this question.

A **Poor Answer** would only rely upon examples that fit the narrative you create about how national borders are drawn. For example, it would be easy to argue that national borders are drawn as a result of conflict and upheaval, and then only illustrate this with one type of example, without considering the multitude of different realities involved.

Q7. Do you think that you have free will? Does free will as a concept relate to the notion of the state of nature?

This question is attempting to get you to think about what might normally be two unrelated concepts and understand how one can inform the other. This is a particularly pertinent question as it is a reflection of the kind of question that you might be asked to write an essay about during your time at the university. It should be noted that this question assumes your pre-understanding of the state of nature. If this is an unfamiliar concept to you, because you haven't studied a subject that considers it before, it is perfectly fine to say this to your interviewer, you will not be penalised. In many ways, it is better to acknowledge that you do not know everything, and ask for clarification, before attempting to answer it; interviewers are more interested in how you think than what you know.

A **Good Answer**: Well, thank you for clarifying for me what exactly the state of nature is. I think that the crux of this question centres around the idea that when the hypothetical state of nature existed, before the existence of societies, people would not have been constrained by social norms or rules, and whether or not this could potentially be defined as a time when we had true free will. In this context, I believe therefore, it is important to define free will as the ability to make decisions about your behaviour and life, unhindered by the actions of others or the rules of society. I think that this is a logical assumption to make, as so much of our modern behaviour is tied up in social contracts between people, and therefore free will in a true sense can rarely exist.

If this is case, then the issue becomes when do we consider that society actually started? If, for example, we look at other species that live in groups, such as chimpanzees, they still have social rules, ways of behaving in a group that are enforced by other members. Thus, in a sense, they cannot have complete 'free' will, because their behaviour doesn't exist in a vacuum; the things that they do have consequences for those around them. From this perspective, we could then analogously consider whether humans could achieve complete free will in a state where no groups, and therefore no social behaviours (i.e., societies) existed. However, there is an inherent problem in this assumption, and that is that the vast majority of humans do not exist in complete in isolation, nor would it be logical to assume that they ever have done, as we would have died out as a species. In reality, there will always be moments where people must interact - to have offspring etc. - and therefore, there will be moments where their free will is given up to the needs of the group.

Thus, to reiterate my original definition of free will, it is the ability to make decisions without anyone else's agency affecting or inhibiting those decisions. As I believe I've demonstrated, this kind of free-will can only exist in a hypothetical vacuum, because we as a species are never 100% isolated from the actions of others or from the effect of our actions on others. Based upon the reference I made to chimpanzees, even if there was a time before society when human behaviour was entirely 'natural', the reality is that living in any kind of group comes with implicit rules as a direct result of the agency of others. The relationship therefore between free will and the state of nature is only hypothetical, and whilst it might be easy to conclude that the state of nature was the only time when free will could have existed, as I have demonstrated here, I don't believe that even that would be possible due to our interdependent, group nature as a species.

This is by no means a straightforward question as it is dealing with two huge philosophical ideas. However, this answer is strong because whilst it would be impossible to fully elucidate the two ideas separately in an answer, it has achieved what the question is asking: for you to speculate about the relationship between the two concepts. As well as outlining generally the two ideas, it has used examples from primatology and made logical conclusions based upon your understanding of the two ideas. Ultimately, it synthesises the two ideas into a conclusion in order to answer the question.

A **Poor Answer** could become overwhelmed by the enormity of the two concepts that you are being asked to answer and get too caught up in trying to consider all the different interpretations of these ideas, without actually trying to draw a conclusion about their relationship. Equally, a poor answer might entirely focus on one or the other of these concepts, without paying heed to the other. In order to answer the question well, it is important to try to remain logical and bring each of your points back to how free will and the state of nature are related.

Q8. Do you think that primates, like chimpanzees, should be given the same rights as people?

This question hinges around two key points: how do we define 'human', and do chimpanzees sufficiently fulfil this definition. The easier option in this question is definitely to argue that chimpanzees are not human and therefore do not deserve human rights, however, there is definitely scope to make the argument that they do deserve rights. In some ways, the question can be considered: are humans unique in comparison to our closest relations, and how does this relate to rights?

A **Good Response**: Well, I think at a broad level, it is clear that whilst chimpanzees have a high level of intelligence, both social and emotional, that can be used to draw parallels with humans, that ultimately there is enough of a biological and cultural difference between humans and chimpanzees, that they probably shouldn't be afforded human rights. This being said, there is growing evidence that the 'uniqueness' of humans in comparison to chimpanzees and other animals is not as distinct as we first thought.

For instance, in the Great Ape family, humans are often touted as unique due to our bipedality, but there is plenty of evidence now that whilst chimps are not habitually bipedal, they certainly have the ability to do so for extended periods. Equally, the argument that humans in general are the only species to have cumulative culture (behaviours and technologies that are passed down through generations with increasing complexity) is also being challenged by evidence from chimpanzees, with suggestions that complex behaviours, such as termite fishing, are passed between generations. I think these two examples are excellent challenges to the notion of human uniqueness, and thereby a challenge to whether human rights should be exclusively human. Based upon this kind of evidence, maybe we need to re-evaluate how binary human : animal rights are, and consider whether animals that display higher levels of culture should have different levels of rights. This is of course a slippery slope, but as more and more evidence comes in to play about the complexity of animal (and especially chimpanzee and bonobo) behaviour, these are going to become more complex debates.

Whilst this question may at first seem like a straightforward question to answer, as outlined here, once you start dealing with *why* humans are considered unique and how this plays into our ideas of human rights, the answer becomes complicated very quickly. Thus, this is a good response because it tries to take a balanced approach, suggesting at the beginning that there are obvious differences between humans and chimpanzees, before going onto elaborate how this discussion is not as binary as it may at first appear, outlining the growing evidence for the complexity of chimp behaviour. Finally, it acknowledges that there is not necessarily an easy answer to this question, and that evidence in the future may cause us to re-evaluate our position.

A **Poor Response** could quite easily dismiss this question out of hand, stating that chimps clearly don't deserve human rights. Even if one was unaware of the evidence around chimp behaviour, a basic awareness of chimps will tell you that they are clearly highly intelligent and that it is worth considering how what you know about their biology or behaviour may play into arguments for giving chimps human rights.

Q9. What do you think is one of the most fascinating facts about where you come from, what makes that so interesting?

This question is an opportunity for you to be reflexive and demonstrate to your interviewers your interest in the world around you. In anthropology, the ability to be self-reflective, to understand how your background - including your culture, personal upbringing, and the environment in which these occurred - influences your study of other cultures and societies is fundamental to acknowledging that we all have our own set biases, or constructed lenses, through which we see the world. Here, you could discuss aspects of material culture, architecture, behaviour, or pretty much anything that you feel confident talking about. Be creative!

A **Good Applicant**: Something that has always interested me about teenagers and young people in Great Britain are attitudes and behaviours towards alcohol. It has always amazed me how willing people are to get inebriated to the point of passing out in the street, or causing themselves bodily harm, and then repeating this behaviour the following week. It is this self-destructive aspect that particularly fascinates me; people are aware of how much damage that level of alcohol can cause (both directly and indirectly) to their bodies, but they do it anyway. I suppose that ultimately it comes down to a combination of cultural acceptance - both tacitly through people accepting that this behaviour is the 'norm' and pragmatically through young people's ability to access alcohol.

It is particularly interesting when you compare these kinds of behaviours to other young people in other cultures. For instance, I know that in America, alcohol is very difficult to access as a young person, but marijuana isn't, and therefore the latter is far more prevalent. In France, people are often introduced to alcohol at a younger age, and the culture around drinking has less of a tendency towards binge drinking, but then, a huge majority of French young people smoke which is in contrast to young people in Britain. I think that these comparisons and experiences of other cultures can be incredibly interesting as points of comparison. This is because they both allow us draw way markers in other cultures to help our understanding as well as give us an alternative lens through which to reflect on our own culture.

This is a good answer because it has chosen an aspect of your culture that has interested you. It doesn't necessarily have to be a positive thing, indeed, often some of the most interesting behaviours are those that seem in some way counter-intuitive or deviant. Hence, not only does this answer outline why you're interested in this particular thing, but it also demonstrates how you've thought about this issue or thing in other cultural contexts. Moreover, it has shown how one cultural understanding can inform another.

A **Poor Answer** could choose something that you find interesting, but then fail to explain why you find it interesting. Whilst this question seems open ended, in the context of which interview you are in, it is important to demonstrate that you understand that this question is about society and/or culture, and show that your interested is derived from that context.

Q10. Take a look at these cave paintings, how might you analyse them for meaning?

This question will be accompanied by pictures of cave paintings (you may be given one or more to look at). There are a whole range of cave paintings that we now know about from across the world and across a whole range of time periods. The most famous cave paintings come from Europe (mostly France and Spain), but archaeologists are discovering new cave art globally all the time. Equally, this is the kind of question where an interviewer might throw a curve ball, and for instance, show you modern "cave art" in the form of graffiti inside an urban building, for instance. Regardless, you could cover a number of topics when deciphering them: content (is it a clear shape(s) or is it abstract), colours used, medium (e.g., paint, ochre, blood), location (e.g. ceiling, floor), and finally what is it symbolic or representative of; does it have a purpose? For the sake of this question, the following answer is in response to the image in this article, from Lascaux https://medium.com/@stevechatterton/what-the-lascaux-cave-paintings-tell-us-about-the-nature-of-human-desire-4c8d06deef83:

Good Answer: In this picture, there are a number of different animals clearly depicted. There are three distinct kinds of image, a bull-like animal with horns, what appear to be two brown and black horses, and two entirely black horses. The parsimonious explanation is simply that the artists here were depicting the animals around them. If this was the case, we could speculate about whether they simply drew these animals as a kind of appreciation of their beauty or whether they represented the animals that they were hunting. If this is a literal portrayal of the animals, it is also interesting to note that they appear to be demonstrating a level of depth perception that might imply a multitude of animals such that they overlap in the image.

Alternatively, we could interpret these animals in a symbolic way, with the animals being metaphorical for different groups in a society. Perhaps the horned bull represents a leader and the horses their followers. If this was the case, then the blurring of the animals may in some way represent levels of relationships, such that the brown and black horses have a closer relationship with the bull, than the black horses do. Perhaps the physical blurring of the animals here even represents a psychological blurring of people that is similarly observed in some contemporary cultures, with boundary between self and other being indistinct, with each person's identity and personhood melting into one another.

There is no correct answer here, the interviewers are more interested in your thought process and ability to make inferences rather than finding the 'right answer' (debates about what cave art actually 'means' are infinite). Thus, this answer shows your ability to think about the cave art from different perspectives, and offers different interpretations from these. It considers both a literal and a metaphorical interpretation and tries to link our understanding of these ancient people to modern cultures.

A **poor answer** might simply describe what is you see before you, without considering its wider implications or potential inferences. Whilst there is nothing inherently wrong with using a literal interpretation as a starting point, a literal interpretation must still be used to draw inferences about the people who created these artworks and suggest potential conclusions about these people from studying them.

Q11. What is love?

This question is an opportunity for you to demonstrate your ability to synthesise the scientific and the quantitative, with the qualitative and phenomenological. That is, what science has to say about love, versus what we find first- and second- hand through the human experience. As is so often the case, there is no right answer here, instead it is more important for you to construct a clear answer and try to draw a conclusion.

Good Response: I think that this question can be approached from two different perspectives. On the one hand, we have what science tell us, that is, that love is a particular set of chemicals, hormones, and impulses throughout your brain and body that lead you to be profoundly connected to another person. This makes sense from an evolutionary perspective because evidence shows that primate groups with stronger social bonds - including what we call 'love' - provide more support to one another, protect each other more, and in general work together better. Building upon this, in reproduction, love also makes sense as it draws people powerfully together, leading to copulation, and more often than not in heterosexual couples, offspring. Logically, it may also then play a role in keeping parents around. That is, love between the mother and the father may mean that offspring are raised together, reducing the workload for both parents. Even where love between the mother and the father doesn't occur long-term, the love between parent and child is, in the vast majority of cases, incredibly powerful, such that the parents are often willing to lay down their lives in order to protect their offspring. Thus, from this perspective what constitutes love is a set of evolutionary biological functions that serve a sociobiological function.

On the other hand, I think that there is a completely phenomenological element to love. That is, love is so much about the personal experience. To reduce love to a set of biological and evolutionary processes seems to do it an injustice. Indeed, when we look at all the things done in the name of love, whether it is war, poetry, sacrifice, or the construction of monumental architecture, there definitely is more to love than just chemicals. On that last point of monumental architecture, if you think about the construction of the Taj Mahal by Mughal emperor Shah Jahan as a tomb for his wife, then this is not something constitutes a biological or evolutionary process. That is, there was no way for him to produce offspring with his wife after her death. Yet, he still had built one of the most revered buildings in the world for love of her.

Hence, I think that there are definitely elements and viewpoints from biology that we can use to consider what constitutes love, but without an understanding of that qualitative, phenomenological, almost intangible element of the human experience that we call love, we would have only a small piece of all that constitutes love.

This is a strong answer because it is very structured. It first lays out the scientific evidence that is often quoted to comprise love, demonstrating your understanding of the different biological and evolutionary functions that love may comprise. The answer then goes on to demonstrate the sociological or social anthropological perspective, including an example that directly contradicts some of the reductionist arguments made from the scientific perspective. Ultimately, it concludes by synthesising these two perspectives and providing a clear answer to the question.

Q12. On the course we are introducing a new paper this year in which we can teach you about any part of the world you like – which part of the world do you think you will pick?

This is a question that allows you to show your wider interests in the world beyond your own nation and culture. This really is an opportunity for you to show a passion for studying cultures, political structures, and people.

A **Good Response**: I would love to learn more about Central Asia, especially the steppe, including the history, archaeology, and culture of, for instance, Mongolia. I think part of the reason that I would want to learn more about this area of the world is first and foremost is because so little is known or taught about its history or culture outside of the area. Studying history at school, even though my IB course was pretty international, we focussed on Europe, East Asia, and America. And then in discussions of international support for other countries outside of Europe, there is a lot of research done in Africa, South East Asia, and South America, but so often it seems to me that Central Asia is not nearly as talked about. In fact, I think the only time Western media covers the area is of 'flashy' aspects of the culture, such as eagle hunting. This has always somewhat surprised me as the Mongolian empire was the second largest in history stretching almost the entirety of Eurasia, Genghis Khan has 16 million direct male descendants, and in some ways it was the greatest overall influence on the world certainly in the first half of the 2nd millennium AD, with arguable influence throughout the entirety of the millennium. Beyond this, I'm aware that there is a deep past behind the Mongol empire, and the nomadic nature of those people really intrigues me, especially as so much of that behaviour continues to this day. And then finally, looking at the recent past of Central Asia and the culture there, I still know relatively little about it other than that China and Russia both have strong influence there, but I simply would love to learn more about the culture and people, and where they are from.

This answer is particularly strong because it not only shows a passion for learning about the archaeology, anthropology, and political science of the area, but it also outlines specific examples that you would be interested in knowing about. It shows that you have an awareness of many of the potential areas and ways that areas of the world could be studied, and it provides a clear justification and answer to the question.

A **Poor Answer** might fail to elucidate exactly why you're interested in a particular area effectively. In reality, you could choose almost any area of the world, but it is important to show (especially in the context of applying for HSPS or Arch. and Anth.) how relevant disciplines might approach these areas of the world. Equally, a poor answer might inadvertently exotically describe another culture, almost fetishising it rather than offering a more objective and intrigue-based approach.

Q13. Can you think of anything happening in the news at the moment which you feel is a particularly good example of a larger significant issue?

This is an opportunity to show your broader understanding of political events in the world. This question allows you to show your ability to draw connections between micro and macro events, and is asking you to demonstrate your ability to inform a broad understanding from a focussed perspective.

Good Response: With the inauguration of US President Joe Biden, we have seen the almost immediate reversal of the damaging climate change denial and policies of the Trump administration of the last four years. Whilst it is seems true that Trump did not have a clear understanding of climate change, it does not entirely explain his actions. Indeed, some of his ulterior motivation was clear; America has been incredibly reliant upon fossil fuels both in terms of directly powering its economy and indirectly providing jobs. This latter fact is still true, and whilst Biden's policies could create a shift away from a reliance on fossil fuels whilst providing many jobs in the long term through renewable energy projects, there are plenty of Americans who will feel pain in the short term as a result of job losses. This friction between a need for a radical change in policy and practice, whilst protecting people's livelihoods is particularly indicative of a world issue.

In America, fossil fuel companies who have wielded significant wealth and influence in the last 150 years in America, as elsewhere, constantly lobby governments to allow them to continue exploiting the planet and accruing wealth. The reason that this current affair is particularly indicative of a world issue is because almost every country on earth is wrestling with these same issues. They know that change is needed and needed now, but they are under pressure on two fronts, both from those large companies that want to continue making money and their own people who are either reliant directly or indirectly on jobs and income from fossil fuels, and for finding and building alternative sources of energy. This current affair is even more indicative of many countries' situations as it is indicative of how a change in democratic power can lead to rapid changes in policy one way or the other.

This is a good answer because it has identified a well-reported current affair that is an ongoing issue. Moreover, it is an issue that affects every person in the world and every country. Not only is the complexity of dealing with climate change a world issue, but the situation in America is particularly indicative of the balance that many governments are attempting to strike between multiple issues.

A **Poor Answer** might choose a current affair that does not relate to a world issue. That is, it might be particular to specific context and wouldn't be easy to draw parallels with a world issue, or alternatively it might be irrelevant at the world level e.g., dog kidnapping in the UK.

Q14. You are an archaeologist in the year 2500, excavating Oxford – what material culture might you expect to find from my present?

Material culture includes everything in human reality that does not relate to behaviours. Thus, this question is an excellent opportunity to be creative and really show your thought process in your answer, which is ultimately what your interviewers are most interested in. For ideas you could talk about: clothing, food, furniture, architecture, computers, cutlery, or lightbulbs.

Good Answer: Well, I think Smartphones are an interesting piece of material culture in contemporary society. In some ways, smartphones represent the pinnacle of modern technology. What once required an entire room of computer hardware, can now be carried around in our pockets. Moreover, it is remarkable to think about how far the technology in smartphones has come since their inception in the 2000s. I think this is the result of two key aspects of contemporary society: a thirst for connectivity and convenience that smartphones facilitate at an unprecedented scale, and the competition between large companies to create the best product. Particularly, if you think that one of the unique aspects of being human is our cumulative culture over time, then the smartphone is an excellent example of how this operates in contemporary society. Beyond just the developments of smartphones themselves, smartphones represent the accumulation of our communication and language abilities as a species. From when we first starting writing language, to postal and messenger services, to telegrams, to telephones, to emails, and now mobile phones. Not only this, but mobile phones in general and smartphones in particular are becoming more and more ubiquitous. Even in areas of the world where very little other technology exists, smartphones can be found, and they are more and more frequently being used in transformative ways for health and education purposes in contemporary society.

This is a strong answer because the object chosen is something that is highly indicative of contemporary society. Not only that, as illustrated in the answer, they have a clearly delineated history that is representative of how material culture changes over time and how it affects society. Moreover, it is a particularly nice example, because as demonstrated, not only are they a piece of material culture that are growing in prevalence throughout many societies, but they are also having a remarkable impact in peoples' lives.

A **Poor Answer** might choose an object that whilst a piece of material culture, fails to connect with the idea of contemporary society. For instance, if the answer had chosen a printing press, whilst this is undoubtedly a piece of material culture, it has almost no role in contemporary society other than as a historical object with very rare usage. It is important to be able to situate the object within that modern context.

Q15. Do you think that one's culture can shape one's perceptions? Is the way we see colour the same as someone from a different culture would?

The key to this question relies on understanding the difference between human perception and human categorisation. In order to answer this question appropriately, you need to first have a fundamental understanding that biologically and neurologically, humans are almost identical, and any differences occur within a relatively small standard deviation. This is particularly important, as any claims about the biological differences in humans, have in the past been used to oppress, dehumanise, enslave, and destroy other humans.

Good Answer: I think that the answer to this questions by how we define perception. Essentially, perception in relation to colour is the process by which light hits a surface, and different lengths of the colour spectrum are reflected into our eyes, which then pass information to the brain and are processed neurologically to identify certain colours. Now, irrespective of cultural influences, apart from people with conditions such as colour blindness, all humans process these colours in the same way. That is to say, that perception of colours is not culturally specific. That being said, what is culturally specific are the ways in which humans categorise colours. For instance, some languages have more than one word for slightly different shades of blue - in Russian, the word 'goluboy' is used to differentiate from the slightly darker 'siniy' - but if you showed these same colours to an English speaker, they would only use the word 'blue'. So in this instance, categorisations of colour are culturally specific, and the language that we use to talk about colours varies, whilst our actual perception is the same.

This is answer has a good structure, starting by breaking down the question to get to the heart of what is being asked, and demonstrating a clear understanding of this, before answering the question. This answer is particularly strong, because it then extends the response by showing how colour is categorised differently, whilst being perceptually the same, using a well-known example to back this up. It finally ties the extended part of the answer back to the original question.

A **Poor Answer** might fail to have understood the difference between perception and categorisation, and how these relate to one another.

211

PPE INTERVIEW QUESTIONS

Q1: You've been presented with an unknown symbol - how might you go about trying to decipher its meaning?

This is a question which looks at assessing how you reason in logical tasks. This is the kind of question which may throw a candidate in an interview, so it is important to have a few moments to gather your thoughts and think about how you would logically approach the question. It is also worth noting that the question does not just want you to discuss how you decipher symbols, but what you <u>first look for</u> when deciphering symbols. This means that it is unnecessary to give a full explanation of the full process you might go through to decipher a symbol.

Bad answer: I look to see if it looks like anything I am familiar with and then we can assume that the symbol will likely be this.

This is a bad answer because the candidate assumes that a symbol will be alike something you are familiar with. Just because a symbol might look like the letter d, does not mean it represents the letter d. The interviewer will also be unimpressed by the lack of creative thinking from this candidate, and the fact that they do not consider whether the symbol will be seeking to describe words, letters, or concepts.

Good answer: The main thing I first look for when deciphering a symbol is any contextual clue which may lead us in the direction of deciphering the symbol. For example, the date or location might help us. If the date that the symbol was written is from before writing as we know it existed, then it is unlikely to represent individual letters, but may instead represent concepts or words. As well as this, the location can help us to have an idea of what language it may be written in, which can be particularly useful if, for example, it is a symbol is a part of a broader sentence. This is because we can tell that, if it is written in English, single letter words will probably be either I or A, and a similar approach can be applied towards other languages. Another thing we should initially look for, which can be helped with this context, or by looking at other symbols around it, is whether the symbol does in fact seem to represent a letter, word, concept, or any other thing. This will significantly help us to decipher it.

This is a good answer because the candidate gives a very logical approach to how this question can be tackled. They also show that they can think creatively by considering how context will help to decipher a symbol.

Q2: What makes you human?

This is a very broad question which tests the candidate's ability to think about concepts that are often taken for granted. The candidate is not expected to reach a full definition of a human being, but should instead engage in a critical discussion about the difficulty of defining what it is that makes us human.

Bad answer: What makes us human is having an opposable thumb.

Or

What makes us human is the fact that we have a conscience.

These are both bad answers because they do not go into enough detail, as could easily be done by explaining why it is that these things make people human. Furthermore, they do not engage critically with those counterpoints which may be made against their definition of what makes us human. The first answer is bad because, though it is true that humans are unique in having opposable thumbs, it does not follow that this is the specific thing which makes us human. It seems that there is a lot more to being human than this. The second answer is bad because it does not address the fact that some people may argue that other animals have a conscience too.

Good answer: I'm not sure there can be one single thing that makes us human. Instead, I think it is probably a combination of a few things. The main one, I think, is our ability to reason. We seem to be unique as animals in our ability to reason. It is likely that other animals can reason to a degree, but nowhere near as much as humans can. Secondly, another thing that makes us human is the way we interact with other humans, and form societies. Humans are sociable animals, and therefore naturally form these communities. We would not be human if we lived in highly individualistic ways.

This is a good answer because the candidate goes into a lot more detail about some of the things which makes us human. Furthermore, they develop on this, explaining why it is that each of these things makes us human. They also consider arguments against their point, such as when they claim why reasoning makes us human despite the fact that other animals may be able to reason.

Q3: How would you go about assessing the number of people in here?

This is a philosophy question on the concept of personhood and identity. It is the type of question which might throw you so make sure that before you tackle it, you take a moment to sit back, and think about what it is the interviewer is really asking you. This type of question is one which you will not be able to give a definite answer for. Given this, it is important that you explain your thinking out loud, as you try to reach some kind of answer.

For the sake of the mock answers, I will assume that there are three people in the room: two interviewers and the interviewee.

Bad answer: There are three people. There cannot be more than 3 people, as I can only see three. There cannot be less than three, because I can see three. Anyone who thinks overwise is wrong.

This is bad because it fails to consider any other potential approach to the idea of personhood. It assumes that the way we tend to count people is inherently true, without questioning this at all. It also becomes argumentative in a way which can be tempting if faced with a difficult question like this, but is unhelpful in a philosophy interview. You should show that you are willing to be persuaded to consider other potential solutions to this question, rather than immediately shutting yourself off from different ideas.

Good answer: We would usually say that there are three people in this room. However, that assumes that the other people in this room are in fact people. We do not really know this. For example, you may both be philosophical zombies [*i.e. someone who looks and acts like a person, but doesn't really have a conscience or soul*]. I don't know that you have a conscience, so, assuming that being a person is in some ways defined by the existence of a conscience, I don't know whether either of you really are "people". If we think about what defines what it is to be a "person", we will find it hard to prove, in fact, that any of us have the features which make us by definition a person. For example, we might instead claim that a person is an entity that has free will. However, we don't really know that we have free will. We may be controlled by a God or something else to perform the actions we do, and be programmed to think that this is our own freewill. Therefore, we cannot truly know how many people are in this room.

This answer is good because it considers a range of approaches to the question of what it is to be a person. This candidate does not close themselves up to considering different philosophical arguments, as the weaker one does, and instead embraces a philosophical debate. They also demonstrate that they have a basic understanding of core philosophical ideas, such as free will, and the idea of philosophical zombies.

Q4: Do you think you know anything?

This is a philosophy question on epistemology, which is the branch of philosophy concerned with knowledge. It is fairly likely that you will get a question similar to this one, or which touches on some of the ideas you will consider for this question. There are a lot of ways you may consider answering this question. One thing which is important is to know that they will not be expecting you to have an in-depth knowledge of epistemology. They are just looking to see how you go about approaching questions like these.

Bad answer: No, it is not possible to know anything because, even though I think I know something, how do I know that I know it?

This answer is bad because, whilst the candidate begins to consider an interesting point in philosophy, they do not explain what they mean by "how do I know that I know it?". This is a commonly heard expression which has little meaning if you do not go onto explain what you actually mean. This makes their answer superficial.

Good answer: I'm sure we 'know' some things, but the problem comes in trying to prove that we know anything, and in trying to define what knowledge actually is. For example, I know that this is a chair, because I see it, and it looks like a chair. However, how do I know that chair-like things which are perceive are really chairs? Just because I see it, doesn't mean that it is really there, or that it is really a chair. I have no proof that what I perceive is knowledge. We might, instead, consider non-perceptual forms of knowledge, to see if we can 'know' anything. We can use deductive reasoning to argue that 2+2=4. I know that 2+2=4. However, these numbers are purely abstract, and are only assigned by humans. I therefore don't really have any proof that 2+2=4, beyond the fact that I have been taught that this is the case, and other people assume it to be so. However, this cannot be a satisfactory account of what it is to know something. Therefore, whilst I want to say that we do 'know' some things, I think it takes a lot to prove that we do.

This is a good answer because it really considers what the question asks. It is significantly less superficial than the bad answer, and considers different approaches to the problem of knowledge, especially how it can be possible to define knowledge. Although the candidate does not know overly-technical terms, this is not expected of them. They have noticed a difference between knowledge of things which we perceive (a kind of inductive knowledge) and deductive knowledge, which shows that they are thinking deeply about the problem.

Q5: You run a sweet shop next-door to a rival sweet shop - you've both been able to drum up considerable loyalty in your customers who will flat-out refuse to shop anywhere else, provided you keep your prices below a tenner per sweet. You each have 10 such loyal customers - but there are 100 potential customers on the street who don't care as much and will buy from whoever is cheapest. With this in mind, at what price point would you have to reach for it to be more valuable to sell everything for ten pounds?

This is an economics question which relies on you being able to do relatively simple maths. However, it uses a lot of words, which may throw you in the interview. However, for these kinds of wordy questions it is best to take a breath, and think about what you need to infer from the question in order to get the equation you need.

For the sake of this question, you should assume that there is 0 marginal cost associated with every additional unit sold. A **bad candidate** will assume this without stating, as it is always important to state your assumptions and first principles when answering a question. Whereas, a **good candidate** will state this assumption, and may discuss afterword how the answer would differ if marginal cost were greater than zero.

A **bad candidate** will state the answer without showing workings. You will be given paper to write on, so make sure you use this to show the interviewer.

Answer:

You will need to consider which numbers are useful from the question for working out your answer. Sometimes interviewers will throw some numbers in which are not useful. In this case, however, all numbers given are necessary to reach the solution. Note that the loyal customers will not buy **above** £10, but they will but at £10. As the business is seeking to maximise profits, if it opts for the price of the loyal customers, they should charge £10.

You should also discuss whether the non-loyal customers will also buy at £10. However, as you are in competition, once you reach the price at which it is no-longer profitable to undercut your competitor, if you raise your prices to £10, then the non-loyal customers will always go to your competitor.

Firstly, you want to show that it will be more profitable when 80 times the price is less than 10 times £10:

$$80p < 100$$

Next, solve for p:

$$p < \frac{100}{80}$$

Simplify this, and you will get the price:

$$p < £1.25$$

Remember, that you should use the less than sign, rather than the less than or equal to sign. This is because the question asks you to show when it will be more profitable to sell at £10, not when it will be more or equally profitable. This is an easy mistake to make.

It is worth also mentioning that £1.25 is a game theory equilibrium. Therefore, it is likely that both competitors, in the long run, will sell at this price.

Q6: You mentioned that you read [a philosophy book], tell me about it!

This is a broad philosophy question. You are likely to be asked a question along these lines, or asking you about a specific philosophical work you may have mentioned in your personal statement. The best way to tackle this question is to talk in as much detail as you can about the work. It is worth preparing some thoughts you have on a specific work beforehand, especially if you write about any philosophical texts in your personal statement.

The most important thing is to pick a work which isn't too easy, but also isn't too hard that you can't understand enough to engage in the argumentation. Be honest, and say when you didn't understand parts of the work. The interviewer isn't expecting you to have a perfect understanding of complicated philosophical works yet.

Bad answer: I read *An Introduction to Philosophy*, and I learnt that we cannot really know that we exist, or that we have free will. I enjoyed the book because it gave me a simple overview.

This is a bad answer, firstly, because it is short. The candidate gives some examples of philosophical issues, but does not expand upon them. It's not particularly necessary to say whether you enjoyed the book or not – the interviewer is more looking for you to engage in the particular arguments of the text. Finally, the main problem with this answer is that, whilst it is perfectly fine to read introductory philosophy books, these will not be the most impressive for interviewers. Furthermore, they do not provide philosophical argumentation to engage in.

Good answer: I read Plato's *Republic*, which I think gave a unique perspective on justice and political philosophy. I found particularly interesting his discussion in the first book about whether justice goes against your own interest. I think that this is an issue Plato preoccupies the rest of his work discussing, but I'm not sure if he ever really found a satisfactory answer. I struggled to understand some of the middle parts of the text, but I think he shows that justice is the same in a city and in an individual persona, and just as it is good for a city, so too is it good for a person. However, it seems like he doesn't fully explain why this means that justice doesn't go against your own interest as an individual.

This is a good answer because it shows that the candidate is aware of the arguments within the text, and they try to engage in them. It is an honest answer which does not try to be over-smart, or pretend to understand things that they don't know, and would not be expected to know.

Q7: What do you think would happen if inflation was impossible?

This is quite a tricky economics question which asks you to apply your basic concepts within economics towards an impossible theoretical situation. This question can be interpreted two different ways. Firstly, we can take this as 'inflation equals zero'; secondly, we can take it as 'inflation as a concept doesn't exist'. It is worth mentioning both of these potential interpretations, or asking the interviewer to clarify if they mean one in particular.

A **bad candidate** will not be able to see the difference between these two, or may conflate the two when answering the question.

A **good candidate** will consider both potential approaches.

Answer:

You will be given paper, make sure to show your workings, and to draw graphs to help you to explain.

If we consider that inflation is zero, we can potentially have, for example, both demand-side deflation, and supply-side inflation in a way which will lead to zero inflation, as shown on my graph:

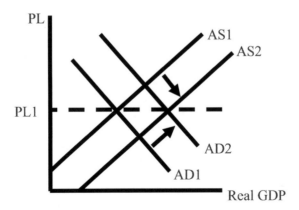

However, if inflation does not exist at all, as a concept, it will be impossible for these shifts to happen. This is because, if demand and supply shift non-simultaneously, then there will be inflation or deflation (which is a form negative of inflation). It is also theoretically impossible for both curves to shift simultaneously, due to the affect one curve shifting has on another.

Therefore, if inflation doesn't exist, it will be impossible for the aggregate demand or aggregate supply to shift at all. This means that it will not be possible for real GDP to be able to change in the short run. The same can be said of the long run, as any shift of the LRAS or SRAS curve will lead to inflation, unless done in a way, similar to our short run example, such that the price level does not change.

You can also, if we have time, consider the Phillips curve. This is probably not as important to discuss as the basic AD/AS graphs, but could give some useful insights.

Plotting the Phillips curve, which shows unemployment rate against inflation rate in the short run, you can show that it does not give a result for when inflation is zero – instead, as inflation tends towards zero, unemployment tends towards infinite. Practically, this does not make sense for an economy to have infinite unemployment. However, it may show us that, if inflation either does not exist or is zero, then, at least in the short run, unemployment will be very high.

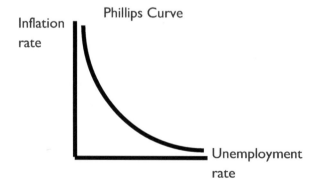

Q8: Do you feel that economists trust models too much?

This is a fairly broad economic question which will ask you to consider the merits of the way we usually approach economics, and to discuss behavioural economics, and the fairly recent academic move by behavioural economists away from relying on models.

Bad answer: No because economic models allow us to measure the economy, and therefore it is good that we have economic models.

This is a bad answer because the question does not ask the candidate to say whether economic models are good, but whether economists can rely too heavily on them. It is easy to argue that there are a huge amount of merit to economic models, and still discuss whether there are some cases in which economists rely too heavily on these models. Instead, this candidate fails to engage properly in the question.

Good answer: Models serve an important role in economics, both for helping us to try to measure the economy, and for predicting what may happen in the future. It helps to guide policy in order to aim towards good economic consequences, such as seeking high employment and economic growth. However, there are situations in which economic models will fail to properly predict what will happen in the economy, and thus, what policy makers should do. This usually happens, either because humans act in unexpected, irrational ways, or because some other thing happens which is unexpected. For example, even our most basic demand/supply models predict that the economy will follow certain rules to set the price and quantity of goods in an economic system.

However, just because there is an increase in supply, which, as the models would posit, means that there should be a decrease in the price of a good, doesn't mean that humans will automatically adhere to the new price. There may be delays in shifting to the price, or they may not change at all, due to consumer habit or other behavioural reasons. As well as this, surprise events may occur for which economists are unable to use models to prepare and plan policy. This happened with the coronavirus pandemic. Economic predictions which followed from models became invalidated by the sudden escalation of the coronavirus situation. Economists, in situations such as these, must be prepared to move away from the models and to adapt to new situations, as well as shifting focus towards examining the behaviour of how humans interact in new economic situations such as this.

This answer is good because it engages with the question. In doing so, the candidate doesn't jump to say that economic models are always either good or bad, but instead gives some examples of when they cannot be relied upon so heavily. This adds nuance to the argument, as well as showing knowledge of current affairs, and how recent events may affect the economy.

Q9: Do you think that sociology would make a valuable background for an Economist?

This question is a fairly general economics question which invites the candidate to consider economics in a cross-disciplinary way. Sociology is the study of human societies and how humans act in groups. It may be possible to link this discussion to the field of behavioural economics, but sociology specifically looks at how humans act together in society, rather than examining the behaviour of individual humans. The candidate should discuss how this can be used to enhance the study of economics.

Bad answer: Sociology is not useful for the study of economics because it studies different parts of society – sociology studies how people act in society, and economics studies money.

This is a bad answer because it is very simplistic and does not delph into the ways in which sociology may be useful for economics. Most good candidates will argue that there is at least some way in which sociology is useful, and there is a tendency in recent academia towards favouring cross-disciplinary approaches. Therefore, it is best to answer that yes, sociology is useful for studying economics. Furthermore, the definition the candidate gives is inaccurate, as economics is not only concerned with money.

Good answer: Sociology is useful for economics because there are ways in which the two disciplines can enhance one another. Economics looks into the production and consumption of goods as well as the allocation of resources, and sociology is concerned with the way in which humans interact with one another in society. Sociology can help us to study economics because no individual economic agent acts without influence from other individuals within society. For example, a study of culture can help economists to predict fashion trends which may affect the demand in an economic system for a specific type of good. On a more macro level, using sociology to look into issues such as race or gender discrimination in society can help us to find the courses of economic inequality, and to find ways to address this. This will enhance the study of economics because solving economic issues such as inequality – which may have a greater impact on the economy more broadly – relies on us being able to understand the courses, as sociology helps us to do.

This is a good answer because it explores the ways in which economics may be enhanced with the study of sociology, by using a clear discussion of the way in which the subjects interacts. Furthermore, it uses good definitions of the two subjects. It also considers the impact sociology can have on both micro and macroeconomics, which shows that the candidate is thinking about the question from multiple different angles.

Q10: What is GDP really? Do you think it can ever truly be measured?

This is an economics question which seeks for the candidate to be familiar with the concept of GDP, and how it is measured, and asks them to engage critically with this. This type of question is best tackled firstly by giving a definition for GDP is defined, then explaining how it is measured, before moving onto critiquing this. One of the most important aspect to consider will be goods that are sold in shadow markets, and therefore which aren't counted for in the calculation of GDP.

Bad answer: We can measure GDP by either working out the expenditure in an economy, by adding up the income in the economy, or by adding up the value added from output in the economy. All of these should add up to the same thing.

This candidate begins in a way which shows they have potential for a good answer. However, they miss the point of the question by only explaining how GDP is measured, and not engaging critically with this. The answer they give is also clearly knowledge that comes straight from an economic textbook, and the interviewer will not be impressed by the regurgitation of these facts without any unique analysis.

Good answer: GDP is the gross domestic product in an economy, that is, the total value of goods and services produced in a country in a year. The easiest way to measure this is by working out the expenditure in an economy by adding consumption, investment, government spending, exports minus imports. It can also be worked out by the sum of the incomes in the economy, or the sum of the value added from output in the economy.

However, these methods fail to capture every element of economic activity. This is because, some economic activity occurs in the form of shadow markets. These are underground and unregulated markets which are not recorded by the government owing to their nature. These include drug markets, which may make up some of the goods produced in the economy in a year, but which, for obvious reasons, will not be included in the government's sum for GDP. Therefore, the existence of shadow markets means that we cannot really measure GDP.

This is a good answer because the candidate explains what GDP is and how it is measured, and then engages with this critically. The candidate demonstrates good knowledge of GDP, but also good analysis skills in describing the issue which shadow markets cause for measuring GDP. They reach a clear and persuasive answer, which is stated clearly throughout.

Q11: What would you say are the major influence on the productive potential of a country?

This is an economics question which tests the candidate's knowledge of core economic theory. It requires knowledge of the productive possibility frontier (PPF), and the components which makes it shift. You will be given paper, which you may be able to draw a PPF on. However, this is not essential for the question. This is not a trick question so the best approach is to try not to overthink it.

Bad answer: If we increase investment through government spending then there will be an increase in the country's productive potential.

This is a bad answer because, whilst it is true that an increase in investment leads to an increase in productive potential, the candidate does not really engage in the question. They only give one way in which a country's productive potential can be influenced, which demonstrates a lack of knowledge on core economic principles. The candidate also does not go into detail or use real world, which would greatly enhance their answer.

Good answer: The productive potential in an economy can be modelled with a productive possibility frontier. This shows the potential output in an economy, which is also known as the productive potential. The PPF can shift either inwards or outwards by a change in a range of factors. These are the size of the workforce, the productivity of the workforce, the capital stock, the amount of raw materials, changes in innovation, political stability, and government spending or taxation. For example, the impact of coronavirus has meant that people have had to work from home. This is likely to have resulted in a decrease in productivity. If this is the case, then there will have been an inwards shift in the PPF in the UK.

This is a good answer because the candidate shows good awareness of core economic principles, and uses a current real life example to demonstrate their understanding of these on a deeper level. They also explain multiple ways in which productive potential can be influenced, making their argument significantly better than if they were to name just one.

Q12: Is there any particular value to the national debt?

This is an economic question which touches upon the core macroeconomic principle of government debt. This question asks the candidates to analyse the costs and benefits of having government debt, as well as to consider whether it is even possible not to.

Bad answer: A good thing about government debt is that the government can borrow to spend. This causes an increase in aggregate supply, which leads to economic growth. A bad thing about government debt is that the government has to pay interest on the debt which can be a waste of government resources. Therefore, whether it is good or bad to have debt depends.

This is a bad answer because the candidate does not choose one side of the argument to argue. They could also go into a lot more detail on both why it can be good to increase aggregate supply, and on why it can be bad to have interest to pay. Finally, the conclusion that the answer depends does not really seem to follow from the arguments which the candidate gives. This would need to be expanded upon to really make sense.

Good answer: I think that governments should have debt. This is because, even beyond the fact that most governments in the world at the moment have debts, and the fact that it is therefore questionable whether it is even possible not to have government debt, the overall benefits of debt outweigh the negatives, provided that the government uses the debt to fund things which will lead to economic growth. For example, the government may borrow to spend on investment. This can be used to increase productivity within the economy, which will lead to an outwards shift in aggregate supply. This causes an increase in the output of the economy, which causes an increase in real GDP. This will also have a multiplier effect. It is true that there are some disadvantages to having government debt, such as the fact that the government will have to pay back interest on their loans, and that having large debts may decrease confidence in the government. However, the fact that many countries have large amounts of government debts, and have a track record of being able to cope with these, means that, as long as debt doesn't get too large, there is unlikely to be a decrease in confidence. Furthermore, the multiplier effect is likely to cancel out some of the costs to the government associated with paying interest. And, those whom the government pay interest to, through government bonds, are likely to spend this money they gain, causing further economic growth. Thus, governments should have debts.

This is a good answer because the candidate goes into a lot of detail, showing knowledge of core economic principles, and an ability to apply them to more complicated problems. They go beyond the basic pros and cons which the bad candidate gives, to examine the affects of government debt in more detail.

Q13: Should you or I care about inequality?

This is an economic question which asks the candidate to think more about the good and bad effects of inequality. Often economics is concerned with things such as profit maximising, and being economically efficient, and in the process, forgets about inequality. This question therefore invites the candidate to discuss this in more detail, and to make the case for or against inequality. The candidate, however, does not need to focus purely on the economic effects of inequality, and can also bring in moral arguments to make their case.

Bad answer: Inequality is bad because it is unfair for some people to have less than others when it is through no fault of their own.

Or

Inequality is good because it is the result of the market deciding where to allocate resources, which benefits the economy overall.

Both of these answers are bad because they do not consider the other side of the argument. This is a very contentious debate which will lead candidates to have a strong conviction in favour of one side of the argument, but a good candidate will still consider the other side, and give reasons for why the other argument is wrong. Furthermore, the first answer fails to consider economic arguments, and the second answer fails to consider moral arguments. Both could be strengthened by exploring equality in a greater depth.

Good answer: I strongly believe that inequality should matter to economists. This is on two grounds. Firstly, inequality is morally wrong. Inequality means that a huge amount of people are born in situations where they are unable to improve their lives, due to being unable to access the same resources as those who are lucky enough to be born comparatively better off. If people were more equal, then everyone would be on a more equal level when it came to accessing opportunities, such as being able to study at Oxford. It is unfair that some humans are predestined not to have these opportunities due to the situation which they are born into. There is no way we can morally justify this, and those who argue that inequality is fine tend to overlook the moral arguments to make this case. However, there is also an economic argument in favour of reducing inequality. A small amount of inequality may be both economically and morally justifiable, however, at the moment, inequality is so large that many of the millionaires and billionaires hoard a lot of their wealth. Poorer people have a significantly higher marginal propensity to spend, and, therefore it is more economically sensible for this money to be distributed to less well off people. This would lead to an increase in aggregate demand, with a multiplier effect as more money circulates in the economy. This would lead to an increase in real GDP, and therefore economic growth. This therefore makes more economic sense than allowing the market to allocate resources, which turns out in this case to be less efficient. Therefore, inequality should matter to economists.

This is a good answer because the candidate goes into a lot of details to explain why their answer, both on an economic justification, and a deeper, moral one. They demonstrate a good knowledge of the concept of marginal propensity to spend, which is important for this question.

Q14: You're a politician in charge of the country, and you've accumulated a considerable deficit in the national balance of trade - is this an issue?

This is an economics question which asks you to analyse one of the core concepts in macroeconomics. It expects you to have a familiarity with the idea of the balance of trade, and to critically engage with the assumption that it is bad to have a trade deficit.

Bad answer: Trade deficits are bad because it leads to a devaluing of the pound and that makes the economy weak. Also, it means that people become unemployed as jobs go to those who create goods in foreign markets instead.

This is a bad answer because, whilst the candidate shows some awareness of some of the consequences of a trade deficit, they do not discuss why these consequences happen. Furthermore, it is not true that the pound being devalued makes the economy weak. A weak pound may be a sign of a weak economy, but the candidate is confusing cause and effect. It is likely that the economy was weak first, and that this caused a trade deficit, which caused the pound to devalue, rather than the other way round. Thus, the candidate shows a lack of economic understanding.

Good answer: A trade deficit isn't inherently a bad thing. It may be a sign that there is a problem with the economy, and in such a case, we shouldn't view the trade deficit as the problem, but the underlying causes of this. For example, if the economy is suffering from a lack of productivity, there may be a trade deficit as the UK will be unable to provide all the goods and services in home markets to satisfy demand, and thus may import more goods than they export. This causes a trade deficit.

However, it is not the trade deficit which is inherently bad, but the productivity. In fact, a trade deficit can be thought of as good because it naturally fixes itself. For example, when there is a trade deficit, the pound gets devalued as there is less demand for the pound owing to the fact that consumers are not buying goods from the UK. However, when the pound is devalued, it is lower in price compared to other currencies, and therefore, it becomes comparatively cheaper to buy UK goods using pounds. This means that there becomes an increase in demand for the pound. Therefore, the trade deficit should in some way fix itself, and the value of the pound should return to normal. This means the trade deficit doesn't matter as much as some might argue.

This is a good answer because the candidate demonstrates clear knowledge of the ways in which the balance of trade works. They give a clear and detailed explanation of the consequence of a trade deficit, as well as persuasively argument.

Q15: Do you believe that the market should be completely free, or should government intervene?

This is an economics question which seeks for you to discuss the problem of market failure in macroeconomics. The interviewer will be looking for the candidate to demonstrate knowledge of the ways in which the market can fail, and governments can intervene to solve this. With this type of question, it is impossible to talk about every possible way in which the government should intervene, and so a stronger candidate will try to stick to one or two examples, and go into significant detail on this.

Bad answer: The government should not intervene because the market allocates resources much more efficiently than governments will ever be able to.

This is a bad answer because, whilst the candidate is right to discuss the allocative efficient which markets may have over the government, they assume that allocative efficiency in markets is <u>always</u> higher, and in doing so, they do not consider cases when there is market failure. It is unlikely that a candidate will perform well by claiming that there is never any way a government needs to intervene, even if they are in favour of less governmental intervention more generally. They should instead opt to explain cases of market failure and how the government can fix this.

Good answer: Yes, there are cases when the government should intervene in the market. This should happen when there is market failure, as is the case with public goods and merit or demerit goods. For example, public goods are goods which are non-rivalrous and non-excludible. This means that there is no profit to be gained by providing the good, and thus the market is not incentivised to provide it. This occurs in street lighting, which local governments fund, to make up for the failure of markets to provide it. If the government did not intervene in this case no street lighting will be provided. Merit goods can also benefit from government intervention because, in the case of merit goods, the market fails to provide the good at the level which is socially desirable. These goods, such as education, have positive externalities. The government should therefore subsidise merit goods to increase the production and consumption of the merit good to the socially desirable level. Therefore, there are some cases when the government should intervene in the market.

This is a good answer because the candidate focuses on a few cases of market failure, and explains why the government should intervene in these cases. The candidate demonstrates good understanding of market failure, and gives a very good answer, especially, of why public goods need to be provided by the government.

Q16: What would you say to someone who argued that 2008's Credit Crunch can only be blamed on regulators?

This is an economics question which expects the candidate to have an awareness of current affairs, and of economics in the real world. The interviewer will be looking for the candidate to apply core economic ideas to this real life situation, and to show a strong ability for critical analysis. These kind of questions are very common, and so candidates should prepare themselves by researching some of the largest events in current affairs and the economic impact these will have, prior to the interview.

Bad answer: Yes, it was a failure of regulation because if the government told banks to stop lending to those who couldn't pay it back, there wouldn't have been a crash.

This is a bad answer because, whilst it shows that the candidate is broadly aware of the reason for the financial crisis, they clearly do not show a deep understanding of it. They also do not explain how regulation could have helped the situation. In general, this answer is far too brief, which will give the interviewer the impression that the candidate cannot think of anything to say.

Good answer: Yes, it was a failure of regulation. This is because the financial crisis happened when banks lent out large high-risk loans for mortgages in America to people who would be unable to pay them. This led to a housing market bubble which then crashed when people found themselves unable to pay back the loans with interest, and therefore had to default on the loans. This meant that many financial institutions failed in America. As a consequence, banks around the world, including in the UK, found themselves in crisis, as there became a shortage in funds to cover day to day costs, causing a liquidity crisis.

There are two ways in which financial regulation may have helped. Firstly, if the markets had been more regulated in America, then American banks would not have been able to lend out such high risk loans, which were very likely to be defaulted on. Secondly, If the financial market in the UK had been more regulated, UK banks may not have been so reliant on American banks for their own stability, and thus, they would have been more resistant to the spread of the financial crisis from America. Therefore, the financial crisis of 2008 was a failure of regulation.

This is a good answer because the candidate demonstrates an in depth knowledge of the financial crisis, and its causes. They discuss how regulation may have prevented the crisis, and therefore persuasively argue that the financial crisis was a from a failure of regulation.

Q17: Let's say that the value of the Yen and the Dollar exchange places overnight, what do you think the impacts of this would be on the global market?

This is an economics question which expects the candidate to have a good grasp of the way that currencies work. This is a very hard question, so make it is important to take a few minutes to think about it, and not to become too stuck on the question. Work through the question bit by bit to make it more manageable.

Bad answer: The Japanese Yen in America would eventually become equivalent to what the US Dollar is currently, as the currency adapts itself to the economy. The same thing will happen the other way round, with the US Dollar in Japan becoming equivalent to how what the Japanese Yen currently is. The two will therefore swap value.

This is a bad answer because, whilst it shows that the candidate shows an awareness of the fact that currencies reflect the economy they belong to, and therefore should in the long run settle down to the usual rate that the relative countries would expect their currency to be at, the candidate shows no understanding of the short run consequences. It is not enough to say that the two will simply swap value, which may well happen in the long term, but after a very tumultuous short term in which the respective countries will see huge changes in their balance of trade. Furthermore, the explanation which the candidate does give is confusing.

Good answer: If the values of the US Dollar and Japanese Yen were swapped overnight, there would be a huge swing in the economy of both America and Japan, as well as of other countries. In America, the US Dollar would very suddenly be worth considerably less. This would mean that there would be a surge to buy the US Dollar, as it becomes a comparatively more price-competitive option on the global financial market. This will cause it to suddenly increase in price. In contrast, Japan will have the opposite effect, where people will rush to sell their Yens, due to them being worth a lot of money. This will lead to a devaluation of the Yen. In the process, in America, as US Dollars are so cheap, there will be a huge increase in demand for US goods from foreign markets, leading to an increase in exports from America. This means that there will be a sudden trade surplus. The opposite will happen in Japan, where Japanese goods will become comparatively expensive, and foreign goods comparatively cheaper, and so there will be an increase in imports for Japan. This means there will be a sudden trade deficit. In the long term, the currencies will therefore return to normal. However, not without economic chaos which will result in the short term from such sudden and drastic changes. As well as this, so many other currencies linked to US Dollars, and so many countries' reserves are held in US dollars, as the currency usually considered the strongest in the world. Therefore, these countries would lose a lot of money overnight as the US Dollar suddenly became worth less. This would cause these countries to suffer from further economic problems, including the potential to enter a recession as a result.

This is a good answer because the candidate demonstrates an awareness of exchange rates, the trade balance, and the ways in which foreign markets interact. They also do well to bring in how it would affect other countries than America and Japan.

Q18: Do you think that property tycoons should pay more attention to how you win in monopoly? Why?

This is an economics question which is the type of unusual and unexpected interview question that is typical of an Oxbridge interview. The interviewer will be looking for the candidate to demonstrate that they can think creatively, and to apply some of the tactics they would use in monopoly in real life. The question also requires for the candidate to have an awareness of the problems economists face with applying economic principles to reality.

Bad answer: In monopoly I buy the properties which are most likely to be landed on. In real life, you should also produce goods and services which are most likely to be demanded by consumers.

This is a bad answer because the candidate fails to discuss the difficulties involved in applying monopoly tactics to real life. They also do not give that creative a discussion of their monopoly tactics, and only discuss demand and supply in a very simplistic way.

Good answer: In monopoly, the best way to win is to buy up properties which are most likely to be landed on, of the same colour, and then develop these as quickly as possible. In real life, there obviously doesn't exist the same colour scheme which incentivises buying one colour property in monopoly, but we can compare this to buying similar businesses in real life, which would give a company greater market share. Therefore, this it is a good tactic to purchase more businesses in the same market in order to increase your market share as much as possible, so that you have more power over price setting in order to profit maximise.

As well as this, you should, just as in monopoly, develop the business as quickly as possible in order to become more efficient, as happens with business expansion, and therefore to be more able to cover costs and profit maximise. This happens because the marginal cost per additional unit produced is often diminishing, and, thus, the business will make marginally increasing amounts of profit through expansion, until they reach economies of scale. However, such expansion is not always possible in real life, due to limited resources, other competitors who may make it significantly harder to expand than is the case in monopoly, and market regulations which prevent monopolisation and strong concentration of markets.

This is a good answer because the candidate considers creatively the ways in which monopoly tactics can be applied to microeconomics. They demonstrate a good knowledge of core business principles. They also go on to show an awareness of the difficulties that businesses face in expanding, and trying to increase market share.

Q19: What makes diamonds so much more valuable than raw steel?

This is an economics question which looks for the candidate to assess their knowledge of how goods end up having their particular level of demand, and why demand doesn't always match usefulness of the good. It also invites the candidate to discuss how supply affects price of goods.

Bad answer: Diamonds are expensive because there are less diamonds and so there is small level of supply. This means that the place on a demand/supply diagram at which the two lines cross is at a very high price. Because there are so few, there are a small amount of people who will be willing to pay lots for diamonds. In contrast, there is a large supply of steel, and so the supply curve crosses the demand curve at a significantly lower level. Therefore, steel is cheap.

This is a bad answer because, although the candidate does explain the supply side reasons for the price, they do not discuss any demand side reasons at all. This misses the point of the question, as interviewers will be looking for candidates to explain why there is such demand for diamonds, which have significantly less functionality than steel, which has a large amount of uses.

Good answer: Diamonds are so expensive for two reasons. Firstly, because the supply is very limited of diamonds in comparison to steel, the market price for diamond is very high, as the market allocates the few diamonds to those who are willing and able to pay for them. In contrast, the high quantity of steel that can be supplied means that the market price for steel is significantly lower. However, this does not really explain why demand for diamonds is so high, given the limited function we have for diamond in comparison to steel. This can only be explained by the fact that fashion has caused demand to be higher for diamond than the amount of uses we have for them would suggest. This is an irrational human behaviour which has made the relatively useless good desirable because it acts as a symbol for wealth – the lack of availability of diamond is therefore what makes them fashionable, which drives them to have such high demand.

This is a good answer because the candidate explains both the supply side reasons and the demand side reasons for why diamonds are so expensive and steel is so cheap. The candidate does well in seeing that the lack of supply for diamonds is what may actually drive demand for them.

Q20: Many industries are outsourcing less and less as it is disincentivised by government policy, do you think this is a bad thing?

This is an economics question which allows the candidate to talk about outsourcing, both from the point of view of businesses and of governments. This is a fairly simple question, so you should make sure not to overcomplicate your answer

Bad answer: Outsourcing is a bad thing because outsourced companies only look for their own profits, and therefore do not offer the best service to consumers, which the government can do better.

This is a bad answer because the candidate seems to think that the only type of outsourcing is governmental outsourcing. The candidate is right to explain that outsourcing business tasks from the government to the business introduces a profit motive which was previously not there, and therefore may mean they don't act in the interest of the consumer. However, this candidate does not realise that private companies may outsource business processes to other companies. Therefore, it cannot be the case that in <u>every</u> example of outsourcing, a profit motive is introduced which was not previously there.

Good answer: Outsourcing can be good in some situations, and bad in others. Many private companies outsource business processes to other private companies in quite simple ways which help to create efficiency. This can happen when, for example, a café outsources a painting business to decorate their café. This is quite a simple example of outsourcing and one which is non-controversial. In this case, no new profit motive is introduced where there wasn't one before. However, when the government outsources business processes to private companies, this becomes more controversial.

In these cases, I believe that outsourcing is a bad thing. This is because, the government has the responsibility and the electoral motive to act in the interest of the public. When they outsource business processes to private companies, they do so under the argument that they are more efficient due to the fact that they have a profit motive which the government didn't. However, quite often the reason they are more efficient is because they strip the costs of the businesses down in order to increase profit margins. In the process, the consumer or the general public who they are paid to provide for, are likely to lose out on some of the services the government would have provided. Private companies will seek to act for the sake of profit, instead of in the interest of the people they are supplying the good or service to.

This is a good answer because the candidate does not simply talk about government outsourcing, but considers outsourcing more generally. They also provide a clear and persuasive justification for their argument, and consider the argument from the other side.

242

Q21: How do you go about valuing a unique commodity? Let's say you're setting prices for a unique air-route, how would you decide how much to charge to make as much money as possible?

This is an economics question which expects the candidate to demonstrate knowledge of microeconomic principles, and specifically with how a company should profit maximise. The interviewer will expect the candidate to demonstrate knowledge of market concentration and monopolisation, as well as being able to work out how costs effect profits.

Bad answer: You should look around to see what other airlines are charging. Then you should charge less than them to undercut those airlines.

This is a bad answer because, whilst the candidate demonstrates some knowledge of competition theory, they do not consider other important factors such as cost of flying and the fact that , as the new airline flies a unique route, there are some ways in which the new airline is a monopoly. Therefore, the airline does not need to undercut other airlines.

Good answer: The first thing which should be considered is the cost involved in flying from London to Tokyo. Tickets must at least cover costs. The second thing to consider is the competition for pricing. If the company is a monopoly, then they will have complete market power to set prices as they please. The new company does fly a unique route, and for this reason it is in some ways a monopoly. However, it does not truly have 100% of the market share due to the fact that there will be some indirect ways to get between London and Tokyo.

Nevertheless, the company will be able to charge a very high price as their large amount of market power means they have a lot of freedom to set their own prices. The next thing to consider is at which specific price they should pick for maximum profit. It usually will be the profit maximising solution to charge the highest price that enough people will be willing and able to pay to completely fill the plane. However, if some are willing to pay such a high price that they make up for some people being priced out of plane tickets, then it may not be profit maximising. This is unlikely is unlikely as it would require for these people to be willing and able to pay a significantly higher amount. Therefore, the price the airline should set is that which is the maximum that enough people are willing and able to pay in order to sell a ticket for every seat.

This is a good answer because the candidate discusses core economic concepts in a good amount of detail. They especially do well in analysing what kind of market share the business has, and therefore what kind of freedom they will have to set their own prices. They do not make the mistake that the bad candidate does in presuming that the company will have to act very competitively.

Q22: Why do you think financiers and financial institutions are so preoccupied with the golden ratio??

This is an economics question which requires the candidate to have some knowledge of banks and investment, as well as how the stock market works specifically. Don't worry if you struggle to get the answer to this in an interview. It is a very difficult question. Start by thinking about what the golden ratio is in maths, and seeing if you can apply this to banks and investment firms.

Bad answer: The golden ratio is considered the mathematically perfect number, and therefore markets stock markets will naturally increase or decrease in proportion to the golden ratio.

This is a bad answer because, whilst the candidate demonstrates that they have some knowledge of the way in which the golden ration comes into the stock market, they do not really explain this in a non-confusing and clear way. Furthermore, they don't really explain what the golden ratio is.

Good answer: The golden ratio is a special number in mathematics, symbolised by the Greek letter phi, which is the ratio between consecutive Fibonacci numbers that the Fibonacci sequence tends towards. This is considered in many ways the mathematically perfect number, as it is a number which occurs frequently in nature. The number also occurs, so the theory holds, in the stock market. For example, when an individual stock market sees an increase in stock price, the amount it increases and then the amount it retrospectively decreases, is propionate to the golden ratio. Therefore, banks and investment firms obsess over this number because it allows them to help predict how much stock prices will rise and fall, and therefore, at which points they should sell stocks, and at which points this should buy stock. This helps them to maximise profit.

This is a good answer because the candidate shows knowledge on a complex theory. The candidate will not be expected to have perfect knowledge of this, but it is good to show knowledge of the ways in which banks and investment firms seek to predict the rise and fall of stock markets. This candidate also does well in explaining the benefit of predicting this.

Q23: How would you go about trying to identify the warning signs of an economic recession - if you could spot it soon enough, can you think of a way to avoid depressions?

This is an economics question which requires the candidate to explain some of their core macroeconomic concepts in order to show how they might predict recessions and depressions. However, the candidate must also show awareness of how economic shocks may unexpectedly happen.

Bad answer: We can predict an economic recession by seeing if GDP is about to slow down. A depression can be avoided by the government investing in the economy to encourage spending, and therefore to encourage growth.

This is a bad answer because the candidate does not really show how an economic recession can be predicted. A recession does happen following a slow down of growth in GDP, which is followed by a decrease in the rate of growth of GDP, but in waiting for the economy to slow down, we are not really predicting a recession, but seeing it happen in real time. The candidate does not acknowledge that it is actually very difficult to predict a recession. As well as this, the candidate fails to fully explain why their solution for preventing a depression would in fact prevent it.

Good answer: A recession occurs when the rate of growth of GDP is negative for two consecutive quarters. A depression occurs when there is a decrease in real GDP over a significant period of time. It is quite difficult to predict a recession as it is hard to know when the upturn of the business cycle will change (i.e. how long a boom will last).

However, there are some warning signs which may show that we are leading towards a recession. These may be things like a decrease in consumer confidence, which leads to decreased expenditure, or an increase in unemployment. However, often, when these things are significant enough to be noticeable, it is too late to avoid a recession. There may be earlier sign that the economy may later suffer a recession, such as the existence of market bubbles, which may crash and cause a recession. However, it is very difficult, again, to see which markets are bubbles, and when they will crash. Once there is a recession, there are some things which the government can do to prevent it being prolonged, and becoming a depression. These include investment to create jobs. This helps to tackle unemployment, and therefore to increase the disposable income available to economic agents. This mean they will increase expenditure, leading to an increase in growth of GDP, thus helping to prevent a depression. This will serve as an injection into the economy, will would also have a multiplier effect, leading to even more economic growth.

This is a good answer because the candidate shows awareness of the causes of recessions and depressions, as well as how to prevent a depression. They also demonstrate a good level of understanding of how difficult it can be to predict an economic recession.

Q24: Do you think that India, which has a substantial space programme, should still be getting aid payments from other countries?

This is an economics question which requires the candidate to discuss the controversial topic of aid, and to critically analyse whether aid should be given to countries who choose to allocate their own resources to things such as international space programmes, which do not help those in poverty. The candidates which perform best will be prepared to pick one side of the argument, rather than remaining on the fence. They must also, however, consider the arguments against their viewpoint

Bad answer: Aid should not go to countries that have international space programmes because they have enough resources to allocate to space programmes, and, therefore, they should allocate these resources instead to helping to fight poverty in the country.

This answer shows potential insofar as they begin to make a compelling argument for why aid should be given to countries that have international space programmes. However, the candidate fails to use much of an economic justification for this, and therefore gives a fairly superficial answer.

Good answer: I can see why we would want to avoid giving aid to countries which have international space programmes, on the grounds that these countries should allocate their resources to higher priority areas, such as tackling poverty. However, the fact that the countries have international space programmes does not mean that they would reallocate these funds towards helping to solve poverty in the country if aid is removed. It is true that it should be the government of India's responsibility to tackle these problems in their country if they are able to.

However, this doesn't mean that we shouldn't give aid if they do not opt to do so, as this would mean taking away financial support in the form of aid for those who may not get the support from the government instead. Furthermore, there are reasons beyond helping these people which make aid a good thing to do, such as maintaining good relations with other countries. Giving aid which is well targeted may help lift these people out of poverty, which means that they have more disposable income, and so can increasing spending, which will lead to economic growth. However, at a certain point, once the country is developed enough, the UK may be able to stop giving aid and instead increase trade with these countries, which has economic benefits for both countries involved. This is, however, most efficient once countries have a large enough level of development that consumers have disposable income to be able to increase spending. Therefore, we should not look towards whether a country has a space programme to see whether we should continue to give aid, but whether the poorest are at a level in which they will be able to survive, and the economy is strong enough to be able to benefit more from trade instead.

This is a good answer because the candidate shows a clear knowledge of the benefit of aid, ad the reasons why aid might be stopped in a country. The candidate evaluates the arguments against their position, and arrives at a nuanced answer.

Q25: How would you judge the extent of the differences between a capitalist and a communist system?

This is a question which could be asked for both economics and politics. It invites the candidate to demonstrate their understanding of the different political and economic systems, as well as to critically analyse the difference between the two. The candidate should seek to utilise real world examples where possible.

Bad answer: Capitalism is an economic system in which goods, property, and businesses are owned privately, whereas communism is an economic system in which they are owned by the state. Therefore, the two are different.

This is a bad answer because the candidate demonstrates a lack of critical analysis about the difference between the two economic systems. It is perfectly fine to argue that they are different, but the candidate fails to engage in the alternate argument. They could also benefit from stating more clearly why the two are different.

Good answer: Capitalism, it is standardly claimed, is an economic system in which goods, property, and businesses are privately owned, and resources are therefore distributed through market mechanisms. Communism is an economic system in which these are owned by the state instead, and so resources are distributed by the government. The main difference between these, therefore, is the fact that, in communism, private property doesn't exist, and so the allocation of resources does not depend upon the free market.

However, this picture is complicated by the existence of mixed economies. These exist when some things are owned and distributed by the government, and some by the free market. Most countries which have a mixed economy are considered capitalist countries, on account of the fact that they have private markets. The standard definition is in fact not that suitable for capitalism because it is impossible for nothing to be owned and distributed by the government, if a country has a government. Therefore, there is at least some way in which all capitalist countries allocate resources through the government, unless they are an anarchist country, which is an oxymoron. Therefore, a line must be drawn in order to determine at which point a mixed economy is a capitalist country, and at which point it is communist. This is what causes people to argue that they are not so different. However, I believe that the existence of any private market at all makes a country capitalist, and, therefore, capitalism does maintain a fundamental difference to communism.

This is a good answer because the candidate is able to engage with the arguments on the other side of their argument, because reaching a persuasive conclusion. They also engage critically with the standard definitions of capitalism and communism, in a way which enhances their argument.

Q26: Your friend is running a struggling corner shop, she knows you've done some work on economics and asks for your advice - they have £25 they'd like to spend on developing their sales, what three things would you recommend that they do, with or without that money?

This is an economics question in which the candidate needs to show their knowledge of core microeconomic concepts, as well as their understanding of businesses. With this kind of question, it is important that the candidate does not over think the answer.

Bad answer: The business should spend money on expanding, on marketing, and on innovation to create new and unique products.

This is a bad answer because, whilst the candidate demonstrates awareness on the ways in which businesses can increase their sales, they are overoptimistic with how far the £25 will go. As well as this, the candidate fails to explain why these things will increase sales, or give any kind of discussion on how much each measure will cost them. Furthermore, the answer is far too brief and vague.

Good answer: One thing to consider is that £25 is not that much money, and will only stretch so far. Therefore, businesses should be smart with how they utilise this money. The best way to increase sales would probably be to spend the majority of the money on advertising. Facebook provides a useful and free platform to promote the business. Some of their advertisement may come at no cost, such as by posting about the business in local Facebook pages. They can also use Facebook to target ads at people who will most likely use the goods and services they produce, and who are local to the business. Some money may also be used on making the front of the business, such as the store if it is a shop, appealing for customers.

Some cleaning products and a bit of paint can go a long way in encouraging customers to visit their store, without involving a large expenditure. Finally, the business owner can spend time teaching employees how to be approachable, and to cultivate an atmosphere of good customer relations. This again can help make the business appealing to customers, and encourage local people to see the business in a good light. These collectively will increase the number of customers and therefore increase sales.

This is a good answer because the candidate explains their three recommendations, and explains in detail why these will help increase sales. They also give a vague idea of how much each of their recommendations would cost, which helps to show the interviewer that they know what they're talking about.

Q27: Do you think the separator between a global company and a failed company is innovation, or are there other factors at play?

This is an economics question in which the candidate needs to show their knowledge of core microeconomic concepts, as well as their understanding of businesses. It also requires the candidate to have some knowledge of the difference between international markets and home markets.

Bad answer: Some brands go global because they sell highly desirable goods or services at a good price, whereas others fail because people in different countries do not want to buy their goods or services.

This is a bad answer because the candidate shows a lack of awareness about the reasons some brands are able to go global. They do not explain specifically what it is which may make a product desirable in a global market, and why some brands will fail to appeal them. This answer could also benefit from a discussion of the ways in which exchange rate mays affect which brands go global, and the ways in which marketing of a brand may affect this.

Good answer: Some brands may go global because they have a good understanding of the new markets which they are entering. As demand for a good or service may be affected by the culture of the country they look to trade in, it is important for the brand to have properly researched this, in order to cater their product towards this market. It is also important, for the same reason to cater their advertising and marketing towards the new market they seek to enter.

One of the most common reason that a brand may fail to break into a global market is because they fail to understand the cultural differences which affect demand for certain products. As well as this a brand which is based in one country may have an advantage over another, when it comes to breaking into a foreign market, on the grounds that the goods are cheaper to produce in that country, and the exchange rate is favourable to them exporting the good. This means that government policy on trade may affect whether a brand is able to go global.

This is a good answer because the candidate shows an understanding of both the microeconomic and the macroeconomic reasons why a brand may be able to go global. The candidate gives an insightful analysis on the ways in which culture affects demand in a country, and therefore shows that business should cater their goods and marketing towards the markets they wish to enter into.

Q28: What do you think were the main factors driving the American Great Depression - do you think that understanding its causes could teach us valuable lessons?

This is an economics question which invites the candidate to discuss the history of economics, and the kind of real life consequences which economics can have. It is very important that candidates should have an awareness of the cause of the great depression before the interview, as a question on this kind of topic, or related to it, has a high chance of coming up.

Bad answer: The great depression happened in America as a result of the Wall Street crash which led to millions of Americans becoming unemployed. We should avoid this in order to ensure that unemployment doesn't increase as it did them.

This is a bad answer because, whilst everything the candidate explains is true, they fail to really explain what caused the great depression, the reasons for the Wall Street crash, and how this effected markets other than the financial market. Furthermore, they do not explain why this led to unemployment, and they do not go into much detail on what we can learn from it.

Good answer: The great depression happened in America because, following a large expansion in the stock market in the 1920s, there was a sudden crash. This became known as the Wall Street crash. This led to a panic, with investors pulling out of the stock market, leading to many investment businesses going bankrupt. It sent shockwaves through the economy, and drastically reduced consumer and producer confidence, which led to a decrease in expenditure on consumption and investment, and therefore, a decrease in productive output. This meant that there was a drastic decrease in growth. One of the most significant consequences of this was that individuals got laid off, and unemployment reached a record high. As unemployment became so high, people were unable to spend, and the depression therefore continued to worsen. One lesson that can be learnt from this is for the government to regulate the financial sector to help avoid crashes in the stock market, and to temper the damages when these crashes do happen. As well as this, we can learn that, when a crisis begins to unfold, an increase in unemployment can make matters worse, and allow the crisis to dig itself even deeper. The government should therefor act early to save as many jobs as possible, by investing to create new jobs.

This is a good answer because the candidate shows a good awareness of what happened in the great depression. Furthermore, they very effectively apply their knowledge of economics to this event, and come up with some good and detailed recommendations for what can be learnt from this event in history.

MATHEMATICS

A mathematician may be called for a **General Interview** or several maths **Subject Interviews, including Economics** which can be difficult to prepare for. Unlike other subjects where an ability to think critically about the subject may be enough, maths interviews will require technical knowledge of all of the mathematics you have studied as well as an extensive complement of mathematical abilities and techniques.

Mathematics interviews will almost always take the form of questions outright testing if you are familiar with mathematical concepts and techniques. While there are several topics more likely to come up, **any topic covered in school until the day of your interview could come up** and you would be expected to show that you can solve these problems. This section will give some pointers on which questions may appear and which techniques any applicant should be familiar with, but the only real way to succeed is by being incredibly skilled and intuitive in solving mathematical problems. These are perhaps not the most encouraging words for an applicant, but Oxbridge has an exceptionally high bar for mathematicians, and the reality is that only gifted mathematicians will be accepted. Given that you have gotten as far as the interview, Oxbridge believes that you have the necessary technical knowledge of mathematics to interview successfully. So, at this point, you need only practice how to best present your answers and deal with the strange questions which may be asked (as well as revise all your school material!).

The form the interview takes can vary from college to college. You may or may not be asked to sit a test first, and if you are, this test is often used as a foundation for the interview, so the expectation is usually that the applicant will answer a few questions fully rather than all the questions on the test. The interview may build on the problems in the test or discuss techniques, etc. Try to view these tests positively – they are letting you choose your strongest topics for the interview. Test or not, the interviewers (usually) try to make the interview less frightening by **starting slowly with some easier questions and working up to some harder problems**.

The most popular topics that appear in subject interview questions are:

- Integration and Differentiation (e.g. differentiate $y = x^x$)
- Imaginary Numbers
- Trigonometry (e.g. Euler's Formula)
- Probability
- Combinatorics and Series

Any technically difficult question is almost certain to be about integration, differentiation, trigonometry, and complex numbers in some combination.

The interview is much less likely to thoroughly test topics from earlier years in school such as logarithms, solving lower polynomial equations or geometry. However, knowledge of these is assumed to be basal to higher topics, so you may be asked questions which assume knowledge of these or an 'easy' starter question about one of these topics. Double-check you are still familiar with these topics; as you revise you can use them to make your own practice questions for some of the techniques discussed later, such as practice proofs (e.g. prove the Pythagorean Theorem is true or why $10^0=1$).

The advanced topics listed above would be used to test the ability of the applicant to solve problems of a high technical level, but mastery of important mathematical techniques and reasoning may also be tested. An applicant may be asked to demonstrate techniques on either advanced or rudimentary topics.

For instance, **proofs will almost never be required for advanced topics**. Interviewers will usually be testing how you think about concepts and present mathematical solutions, so **often ask deceptively simple questions**. Prove that there is an infinity of primes, prove that some given value is the sum of two squares, or prove than 4n-1 is a multiple of three, are examples of this type of question. This is not about demonstrating advanced knowledge, but about showing that you can use an appropriate method to approach a problem and present your solution in a logical way with proper use of mathematical language. You may be asked to prove something specifically by contradiction, so be prepared.

You may also be asked a similar style of question (e.g. "Why is the product of four consecutive integers always divisible by 24?"), but even when not asked to give a formal proof, present your answer well, laying it out in an attractive and logical way. The companion to proof questions, but for more advanced topics, are the 'Show that'/'Derive' questions. You could, for example, be asked to show that a trigonometric identity is valid or to derive an expression for differentiation from first principles.

The most common technique you will be asked to demonstrate is **graph sketching**. It is likely that you will first be given functions you are expected to be familiar with [e.g. e^x and $\sin(x)$], and then some function combining these (e.g. $e^{\sin(x)}$), or a new function (e.g. x^x). You would be expected to find the intercepts, stationary points, asymptotes, and maybe inflection points. Sketching is almost certain to come up, so check that you still remember how to sketch graphs for all the main types of functions and that you know how to combine functions when sketching graphs. It is probably safest to revise this from the basics, not just rely on the memory of how each function looks.

It is not uncommon to be asked a question which tests your ability to interpret word problems as equations. These may be physics-type questions of the 'Two trains leave two stations heading for each other at...'-type, or probability or geometric questions, or any number of other problems which are simple to solve once the equations are set up right. Rarely, you might also be asked a question where you need to 'brain dump' in a constructive way. An example is 'Tell me what you know about triangles', where you need to think through your approach carefully in order to lay out what you know in an **appropriate order and a way which emphasises the most important points**.

In general, the best preparation is to **revise all the topics you have studied at school**, taking particular note of the ones listed above. Make sure you understand how all these topics are constructed, both the specific derivations of concepts you have studied and how mathematicians systematically added these ideas to the body of mathematical knowledge through methodical work and proofs.

WORKED QUESTIONS

Below are a few examples of how to start breaking down an interview question, complete with answer outlines and model answers.

Q1 (i): Do you know why $\det(AB) = \det(A)\det(B)$*?*

The Fibonacci numbers are defined as $F_{n+1} = F_n + F_{n-1}$ *with* $F_0 = 0$ *and* $F_1 = 1$*. Can you show that* $\begin{pmatrix} F_{n+1} & F_n \\ F_n & F_{n-1} \end{pmatrix} = \begin{pmatrix} 1 & 1 \\ 1 & 0 \end{pmatrix}\begin{pmatrix} F_n & F_{n-1} \\ F_{n-1} & F_{n-2} \end{pmatrix}$*?*

The determinant can be thought of as the scale factor of the transformation. So when we write down det(AB), we can think of it as doing the transformation A and then the transformation B. The scale factor of a composition of transformation is the same as the product.

One can also achieve this by doing the algebra on two general 2x2 matrices.

The first part follows directly from the definition of matrix multiplication and then using the definition of the Fibonacci numbers.

The question seems to be guiding us to the fact that:

$$\det\begin{pmatrix} F_{n+1} & F_n \\ F_n & F_{n-1} \end{pmatrix} = \det\begin{pmatrix} 1 & 1 \\ 1 & 0 \end{pmatrix}\det\begin{pmatrix} F_n & F_{n-1} \\ F_{n-1} & F_{n-2} \end{pmatrix}$$

Q1 (ii): Hence show that $F_{n+1}F_{n-1} - F_n^2 = (-1)^n$

We know that the determinant of the first matrix is -1 so iteratively apply this identity and use the fact that for $n = 1$ the determinant is -1 to get $(-1)^n$.

Q1 (iii): Can you think of an alternative way of showing this?

Alternatively, induction works here, $F_{k+2}F_k - F_{k+1}^2 = (F_{k+1} + F_k)F_k - (F_k + F_{k-1})^2 = -(F_{k-1}F_{k+1} - F_k^2)$, as required.

Q2: A rectangle's four corners touch the edge of a circle. What is its largest possible area?

There are two ways to do this. Taking a **geometric approach**, consider the diagonals of the rectangle. We know that the diagonals of the rectangles pass through the centre of the circle. The diagonals form two angles, ϑ and $\pi-\vartheta$. The area of the inscribed rectangle is, therefore, $\sin \vartheta + \sin (\pi-\vartheta) = 2 \sin\vartheta$, either from the angle addition formulae or just knowing that $\sin (\pi-\vartheta) = \sin\vartheta$. Thus this area is maximized when $\vartheta = \pi/2$, and this is a square. This area will then be 2.

Alternatively, you can **approach it computationally**. If we look at the circle $x^2 + y^2 = 1$ we know that the rectangle has vertices (a, b), $(a, -b)$, $(-a, b)$, $(-a, -b)$. Consider the *square* with vertices $(\pm(a + b)/2, \pm (a + b)/2)$. This has area $(a+b)^2$. Compare the area of this circle to the area of the rectangle, it has area *4ab*. But, $(a + b)^2 \geq 4ab$ (as $(a + b)^2 - 4ab = (a-b)^2 \geq 0$). Thus the square is bigger and it only gets larger when we consider the square projected out onto the circle.

Q3: What is integration?

Integration is two possible things: a good candidate will discuss both of them. Integration can be considered *the inverse of differentiation* or it can be considered a process to *find area*.

For the first, we know the fundamental theorem of calculus that states $\int f'(x)dx = f(x) + C$ where $\int$ is considered the indefinite integral (or $\frac{d}{dx}\int_a^x f(t)dt = f(x)$). Such a definition makes sense whenever what we are integrating has a closed form anti-derivative. However, a candidate who has done S1 should be aware that there is no anti-derivative for $\exp(-x^2)$, and thus an approach to integration should be more flexible than simply computing the function that differentiates to it. Throughout such an explanation, a candidate may be asked to prove one variant of the fundamental theorem of calculus (they would probably be encouraged towards the second of these) and proof should be given.

For the second, we have some notion of 'area' under a curve, typified by the area under rectangle, or the area under a straight line. Such an approach leads to the definition of definite integration, e.g., $\int_a^b f(x)\,dx$ is the 'area' under a curve. This may be made more precise, eg, a candidate may be expected to recall the trapezium rule (or lower/upper Riemann sums if these have been seen before), e.g., we can *approximate* the integral by taking sums of this form.

Q4: What is differentiation? Can you explain why $\frac{d}{dx}x^n = nx^{n-1}$?

Differentiation is the act of finding the gradient of a curve at a point, e.g., taking a curve and then considering its tangents. We then map x to the gradient of the tangent at this point.

More formally, we consider $\frac{f(x+h)-f(x)}{h}$ where we think of h as very small. This gives a *secant* of the curve. We then take h closer and closer to zero and come up with some notion of the limit. This is then defined to be the derivative.

$$\frac{(x+h)^n-x^n}{h} = \frac{hnx^{n-1}+\frac{h^2n(n-1)}{2}x^{n-2}+\cdots}{h} = nx^{n-1} + q(x) \qquad \text{where } q \text{ is some}$$

polynomial in x (and h). So, on taking h to be extremely small, the second term vanishes.

Note that for both of the above questions, attempting to define differentiation or integration in terms of its **action on polynomials**, e.g., in terms of what $\int x^n dx$ and $\frac{d}{dx}x^n$ is possible. However, one needs to be a lot more careful than one thinks one would have to be. It is possible that such a situation would not end well, e.g., it is probably a poor candidate who attempts to define integration and differentiation in terms of x^n. Such an issue may also arise with questions of the type 'differentiate x^x', another staple interview question.

The response xx^{x-1} is very incorrect and implies a misunderstanding of what differentiation is. (Bonus: $\frac{d}{dx}x^x = \frac{d}{dx}e^{x\log x}$ apply the chain rule with $u = x\log x$ to get $x^x(\log x + 1)$. Since $xx^{x-1} = x^x$ we (in fact) get a bonus, the 'wrong' answer is right if and only if $\log x = 0$, eg, $x = 1$. Thus it's incorrect everywhere, which is pretty bad).

Q5: Which is harder, differentiation or integration?

Both. You can think of either as harder (and successfully argue it!) but the general rule is, for A-level students, integration is harder. For undergraduates, differentiation is harder.

Differentiation is harder: The issue is that one can integrate a function such as *f(x) = 1* for *x > 0* and 0 for *x > 0*. What you get is $\int_{-\infty}^{x} f(t)dt = t$ for $t > 0$ and 0 for $t < 0$ (and *t = 0* at *x = 0*). This shows that we can integrate functions that have 'jumps' in them. We note that for both of the definitions of integration we have given above (including the one based on differentiation) this works, e.g., the integral of $f(x)$ legitimately is this thing. So, there are functions you can integrate but not differentiate, e.g., differentiation is harder.

Integration is harder: The issue here is that whenever you have a nice explicit function, e.g., $\tan[e^{-x^2}\log(\sin x)]$ we could instantly write the derivative of this down. It's not a pleasant thing to do; however, it reduces to repeated applications of the chain rule and the product rule. So, any function with an explicit 'formula' (whatever that means) can easily be differentiated. This is different for integration: $\int e^{-x^2}dx$ is the most commonly known example. There is no expression of this integral in terms of elementary functions. This is because (ultimately) integration is not as algorithmic. Substitution and by parts are *rules* that may simplify the integral, or may not.

A good candidate will pick one and argue it well (following the rough outline here, these are two most sensible interpretations of the question). The interviewer may prod the candidate in the other direction, e.g., by drawing the function $f(x)$, or writing down e^{-x^2} and encouraging through.

261

Q6: What is the area of a circle? Prove it.

As to be expected, the area of a circle is πr^2, where r is the radius of the circle. At this point, the interviewer would ask the candidate for a definition of π. One has various retorts: however, there are two sensible ones. The first is that it is the ratio of the circumference of a circle to its diameter. The second is that it is the smallest non-zero root of $\sin x$ (in essence, every other definition in terms of a trigonometric function is the same).

Again, various proofs exist of which two are now shown: If $x^2 + y^2 = r^2$ we have that $y = \sqrt{r^2 \text{-} x^2}$, where $\sqrt{}$ can take positive or negative signs. We take the positive sign, eg, we get the semi-circle. Then the area of the circle $= 2\int_{-r}^{r}\sqrt{r^2\text{-}x^2}\ dx$. We set $x = r\cos\theta$ and then $\frac{dx}{d\theta} = \text{-}r\sin(\theta)$, and the integral equals $2\int_{0}^{\pi}r\sin(\theta)\sqrt{r^2(1\text{-}\cos^2\theta)}\ d\theta$. Then, since $\sqrt{(1\text{-}\cos^2\theta)} = |\sin\theta|$ we get that the integral $= r^2\int_{0}^{\pi}\sin^2\theta\ d\theta$. Integrating $\sin^2\theta$ is a tricky business: however, nothing that $1\text{-}2\sin^2\theta = \cos(2\theta)$ allows us to conclude that the area of the circle $= r^2\int_{0}^{\pi}(1\text{-}\cos(2\theta))d\theta = \pi r^2$. (Here we are using that π is the smallest root of the sin function).

Another **integration-based proof** is called the onion proof: you can consider the circle as a union of rings going outwards. Each ring has an area equal to the diameter x a little bit, so when we integrate we get that area $= \int_{0}^{r}2\pi t\ dt = \pi r^2$. This proof uses that fact that π is the ratio of the circle's circumference to its diameter. Although technically correct, it is not a particularly good proof as making all the intermediary steps precise is a gargantuan task.

Q7: *If* f(x + y) = f(x) + f(y) *and* f *is differentiable, what is* f(x)?

If g(xy) = g(x) + g(y) *and* g *is differentiable, what is* g?

If h(x + y) = h(x)h(y) *and* h *is differentiable what is* h?

If f(x) is differentiable, consider:

$$f'(x) = \lim \frac{f(x+h)-f(x)}{h} = \lim \frac{f(x)+f(h)-f(x)}{h} = \lim \frac{f(h)}{h} = f'(0).$$

So f has a constant derivative, e.g., $f(x) = Ax + B$ where $A = f'(0)$. Note that $f(x + 0) = f(x) + f(0)$, eg, $f(0) = 0$, and therefore $B = 0$.

For $g(xy) = g(x) + g(y)$, consider $g(e^u e^v) = g(e^{u+v}) = g(e^u) + g(e^v)$ e.g., the function $G(y) = g(e^y)$ satisfies the first part. We thus have that $g(e^y) = Ay$, e.g., $g(x) = A \log x$.

The same trick works for *h*, except consider $\log(h(x))$. This is of the form Ax, eg, the solution e^{ax}.

This question is straight forward, however, each stage requires somewhat of a jump. The candidate would be expected to *know* the answers and then be guided. The first step of using the derivative is not obvious, and there are various false starts a candidate could make (and various not so false starts). Obtaining that *f(0)* is good, using the fact that *f* is differentiable is good, writing down the Taylor Series works. Using the fact that *f* is differentiable is good, writing down the Taylor Series works. Using that $f(n) = nf(1)$, and $f(\frac{1}{n}) = \frac{1}{n}f(1)$ can be helpful too. The issue of "are there any functions other than the ones listed" is an interesting one. For such a function to exist, it would have a lot of bad properties.

Questions 8-16 are fairly straightforward questions that might be asked at the start of the interview and wouldn't take longer than 2-5 minutes.

Q8: If x is odd, show that $x^2 - 1$ is divisible by 8.

$x^2-1 = (x-1)(x + 1)$. If x is odd, $x - 1$ and $x + 1$ are both even. Since the difference between $x - 1$ and $x + 1 = 2$ and they are both even, one of them must be divisible by 4. Any multiple of 4 multiplied by another even number will result in a number that is divisible by 8.

Q9: If x is a prime number > 3 show that $x^2 - 1$ is divisible by 24.

$x^2 - 1 = (x - 1)(x + 1)$. Since x has to be odd, $x^2 - 1$ must be divisible by 8 (see *Q8* above). We now look at the remainder when we divide by 3, it is clear that we can't write x as $3n$, so either $x = 3n + 1$ or $x = 3n + 2$. Thus, either $x + 1$ or $x - 1$ is divisible by 3.

Q10: Can you define a prime number? Can you show every number is either prime or a product of prime numbers?

We proceed (surprisingly) by induction. We claim that every number above 1 is either prime, or is a product of primes. Suppose it is true for all $m < n$. Then either n is prime, in which case we are done, or there is some prime number p that divides n. So, consider $\frac{n}{p}$, which is strictly smaller than n. But then, by induction, we are done.

Q11: How many zeroes are there in 10? What about 100?

The number of zeroes is determined by the number of 5's, 10's, and 25's in the factorial. Thus, 5 has one zero, 10 has two zeros etc...

25 can be expressed as 5 x 5 so contributes two zeroes. Similarly, all multiples of 25 contribute two zeroes. This can be extrapolated to give:

Number	Zeros	Number	Zeros
100	2	95	1
90	1	85	1
80	1	75	2
70	1	65	1
60	1	55	1
50	2	45	1
40	1	35	1
30	1	25	2
20	1	15	1
10	1	5	1
Total	12	**Total**	12

Thus, there are 24 zeroes in total.

Q12: If I have a square of paper that is 10cm by 10cm, I cut out squares from the corners and fold up the result to form a cuboid. What is the largest cuboid by volume I can form?

Denote the length that has been cut out by a. When we fold it up, we get a cuboid of base length and width $10 - 2a$. It has height a. So the volume is $a(10 - 2a)^2$. Expand and differentiate, the volume is $4a^3 - 4a^2 + 100a$. Differentiating with respect to a, and setting equal to zero to find the maximum, we get $12a^2 - 80a + 100 = 0$, which we can factorize as $4(a - 5)(3a - 5) = 0$. $a = \frac{5}{3}$ is the solution we want, and thus the volume is $\frac{5}{3}\frac{400}{9} = \frac{2000}{27}$.

Q13: Suppose Alice, Bob and Charlie work together, digging standard-sized holes. It is assumed that Alice, Bob and Charlie do not affect each other when they work. It is known that Alice and Bob can dig a hole in 10 minutes, Bob and Charlie can dig a hole in 15 minutes, and Alice and Charlie take 20 minutes to dig a hole. How long does it take Alice, Bob and Charlie to dig a standard-sized hole?

Suppose that digging a hole involves doing 60 units of work. Alice and Bob thus work at a rate of 6 units per minute, Bob and Charlie work at a rate of 4 units per minute, and Alice and Charlie work at a rate of 3 units per minute. So, if we denote the rate of work that someone does by the first letter of their name, $A + B = 6, B + C = 4$ and $A + C = 3$. Adding all of these together and dividing by 2 gives that $A + B + C = \frac{13}{2}$. So, it takes Alice Bob and Charlie $60/(13/2) = 120/13 \approx 9$ minutes 20 seconds.

Q14: Integrate $\cos^2 x, \cos^3 x, \cos^4 x$

$2\cos^2 x - 1 = \cos(2x)$, e.g., $\cos^2 x = \frac{1}{2}(1 + \cos 2x)$. Thus, $\int \cos^2 x = \frac{1}{2}\left(x + \frac{1}{2}\sin(2x)\right) + C$. We have that $\cos^3 x = \cos^2 x \cos x = \frac{1}{2}(\cos x + \cos x \cos 2x)$. Then by the product to sum formula, $\cos x \cos 2x = \frac{1}{2}(\cos x + \cos 3x)$. Putting this in and integrating gives $\frac{1}{12}(9\sin x + \sin 3x)$. At this point, it is quite likely that the interviewer would stop you as the principle is seemingly obvious at this point, $\int \cos^4 x\, dx = \int \frac{1}{4}(1 + \cos 2x)^2 = \frac{1}{4}\int 1 + 2\cos 2x + \cos^2(2x)\, dx$. Expanding (again) gives $\frac{1}{4}\int(1 + 2\cos(2x) + \frac{1}{2}(1 + \cos 4x))dx$. Integrating we get $\frac{1}{32}(12x + 8\sin 2x + \sin 4x)$. There are a couple of other approaches to this question; De Moivre's theorem springs to mind, and we could also split and integrate by parts if we were looking for a general $\cos^n x$.

Q15: Integrate and differentiate x log x.

$\frac{d}{dx}(x\log x) = 1 + \log x$. For $\int x\log x\, dx$ we integrate by parts, $\int x\log x\, dx = \frac{x^2 \log x}{2} - \int \frac{x}{2}\, dx = \frac{x^2}{2}\left(\log x - \frac{1}{2}\right) + C$.

Q16: Integrate sin²x

The first key point to notice is that you cannot integrate this straight away and will need to manipulate sin²x in order to integrate this. A poor candidate will not notice this and will proceed to say that the answer is -1/3cos³x. When asked to differentiate this, they would hopefully realise that this is incorrect.

Knowledge of the trigonometric Identity $\sin^2 x + \cos^2 x = 1$ would be a good starting point. You could then use the double angular formula [$\cos(a + b) = \cos a \cos b - \sin a \sin b$] as this can be used to remove cos²x.

As with all of these type of questions, it is essential that you talk through your working as much as possible. If the candidate seems stuck, then suggest formula you might get reminded of the trigonometric identities.

Once you've identified the identities, you can then substitute back in and solve by the following:

$$\int \sin^2 x dx = \int \frac{1}{2}(1\text{-}cos2x)dx$$

$$= \frac{1}{2}\int 1\text{-}cos2x)dx$$

$$= \frac{1}{2}\left(x\text{-}\frac{1}{2}sin2x\right) + C$$

$$= \frac{x}{2}\text{-}\frac{1}{4}sin2x + C$$

Whilst it is not mandatory to know how to do this straight away, the interviewer would expect you to be able to complete this once you're given the two identities.

Q17: As you may or may not know, $\sum_{i=1}^{k} i = \frac{i(i+1)}{2}$. As you may not know, $\sum_{i=1}^{k} i^2 = \frac{1}{6}i(i+1)(2i+1)$. As you may or may not know, $\sum_{i=1}^{k} i^3 = \frac{i^2(i+1)^2}{4}$. As one may guess, there is a general rule lurking here, $\sum_{i=1}^{k} i^n$ is an $n+1$ degree polynomial in k. Can you prove this?

(Hint: Consider $\sum_{i=1}^{k}[(i+1)^{n+1}\text{-}i^{n+1}]$

We proceed by induction and use the hint. The question tells us that the answer is true in the case $n = 1$ (and 2 and 3) so we only need to show that the truth for all $n < p$ implies the truth for $n = p$. To see this $\sum_{i=1}^{k}[(i+1)^{p+1}\text{-}i^{p+1}] = (k+1)^{p+1}$, as every term apart from the last cancels identically. However, it also equals $\sum_{i=1}^{k}\sum_{j=1}^{p}\binom{p+1}{j}i^j$ (by expanding the binomial series $(i+1)^{p+1}$. If we write $S_j = \sum_{i=1}^{k} i^j$ we get that this equals $\sum_{j=1}^{p}\binom{p+1}{j}S_j = (k+1)^{p+1}$. So, $S_p = (k+1)^{p+1}\text{-}\sum_{j=1}^{p-1}\binom{p+1}{j}$. But now we're done, the right-hand side is a polynomial of degree $p+1$. This, in fact, gives an explicit expression for the polynomial, which was not required.

MATHS INTERVIEW QUESTIONS

Q18: It is estimated that 5% of the population in a country have a contagious disease, so everyone is tested. You test positive. Based on your test result, there is a 50% chance that you actually have the infection. How accurate is the test?

This question is attempting to test your attention to detail and introduce a key skill for all good scientific researchers and mathematicians: the ability to understand into the true significance of statistics, even if it is contradictory.

A **poor student** would rush through to an answer, or fail to understand the distinction between P(+ve test | illness) and P(illness | +ve test) and as a result get no further than making a statement to the effect of 'not very accurate'. Certainly, if 50% of people receiving a positive test result aren't actually infected, it seems as though something has gone wrong – but it's important to consider this mathematically and make sure you arrange your thinking in a logical and thorough fashion.

This is a conditional probability question, so to start, you will need to consider the range of possible outcomes for any one person: they have the disease and test positive, they have the disease and test negative, they don't have the disease but test positive, and they don't have the disease and test negative.

You would also be given information by the interviewer on any assumptions you needed to make, and in this case for simplicity we will assume that 'accuracy' is the percentage of correct tests (ie. P(+ve|infected) or P(-ve|not infected)) which can be called 'x'. It's also worthwhile to let population be 'P' to simplify later.

The key to this question is in spending some time understanding the probabilities and information you've been given, as well as being able to make some reasonable estimations or guesses. Drawing a diagram is a good way to summarise the information given – and while not essential, many candidates find it difficult to give a **good answer** if they don't start here (work alphabetically):

		Has the disease?		
		Yes	No	**TOTAL**
Test result?	Positive	(C) x % of (A)	(D) 1-x % of (B)	(C) + (D)
	Negative			
	TOTAL	(A) 5% population	(B) 95% population	

A **very good candidate** may then incorporate the remaining information from the question, or they may simplify this for themselves, by realising that rather than continuing to work with percentages of percentages, they could simply put a total number on the population (e.g. 100 million) to allow them to get more of a feel for what's going on in the question.

This approximation results in the following equation (setting C and D equal to each other due to the 50% from the question):

$$x(0.5P) = (1\text{-}x)(0.95P)$$

And therefore $x = 0.95$, so the test is 95% accurate.

A **good candidate** would, without further prompting, make a comment on whether this seems like an answer they would have expected, which it almost certainly won't. They may then begin to try and explain how it can be that a 95% accurate test results in a situation where only 50% of positive tested people are actually unwell.

The key here is that a small percentage of a large number (the incorrect positives) can often equal or exceed a large percentage of a small number (the true positives). What is the implication of this for mass testing issues in situations such as the covid-19 pandemic?

For further reading on this topic and apparent statistical anomaly, you may be interested in searching for 'Bayes' Theorem' online.

Q19: Plot $\dfrac{x^2}{1-x}$

Curve sketching questions are really common in at least one of the maths interviews which you may complete. This is because they're really easy to understand, so the interviewers know that everyone understands what they need to do – and there's no room for ambiguity!

In this question a **poor candidate** might sketch a quadratic graph and then fail to link the denominator in any way. Alternatively they may simplify to give x^2-x – which happens to even the best candidates under pressure. So do always double check your working with fractions!

A **good candidate** will attempt to break the question down into more manageable steps, as shown below, and will talk the interviewer through the steps as they go. They may begin by stating a few of the things they're going to do, for example, *"There are quite a few things which come to mind for this question – I think it would help to draw a few sketches of curves like a quadratic or a reciprocal, and maybe differentiating will help at some point. I'm going to start by sketching some simpler curves, just so I can get a feel for what's going on"*. Steps to consider are generally shared across all curve sketching questions, so you should try and apply these to the other relevant questions in this book and see if they help. Some common steps are:

<u>Breaking the graph into smaller components</u> (e.g. $y = x^2$, $y = \dfrac{1}{1-x}$) before compiling them into the curve asked about in the question. If you only take one piece of advice from your interview practice 'break problems down into more manageable pieces' will help you in your interview, your A levels, and at university and beyond.

<u>Substituting in points</u>. It's important not to do this too much, because it's shows a 'brute force' approach, which isn't particularly effective the more complicated the questions you're being asked are. (There are also issues with errors when dealing with sinusoidal plots depending on how big the gaps between the points you substitute are – look up 'aliasing' for more information). That being said, you need to 'get a feel' for what's going on – and substituting in some points can be very helpful for this.

Linked to the step above, <u>find the points where the curve crosses the co-ordinate axes</u>. In this case there's only one point of intersection at $(0,0)$.

Find, by calculation or logical deduction, any <u>areas where the curve has asymptotes or is undefined</u>. For this curve $x \neq 1$

<u>Differentiate</u> to find turning points. This is often one of the first ideas that candidates have, and is in many cases a very good idea. In this question, it may be slightly challenging, and you can probably work out all the information you'd get from differentiating without needing to (e.g. the turning point at the origin). This means that differentiating may actually hinder rather than help, and it's important you show you've considered whether the methods you're employing are going to help before you power through them! Making a comment to show you've considered and dismissed this as an idea, rather than not considered it, is always a good idea.

It's important to bear in mind here that you could spot what the curve would looks like very quickly, and do a poor interview, or fail to get through to a solution and still get your offer – so don't worry about how the solution is going as you're doing it! These problem solving questions should be a discussion.

Q20: Plot $\ln(x^x)$

We've included a couple of examples of curve sketching questions given they are so common, and so 'easy to ask' to test your maths ability (and you might find some in subjects for other sections too). The good thing is that unlike a lot of Oxbridge interview questions you can actually create your own 'method' for these, and work through the steps to get towards your answer. So, once you can do one of them, you can have a good go at any of them!

A **poor candidate** may be unfamiliar with the logarithm function, or may interpret the x^x as a similar (but incorrect) function such as x^2 or 2^x. It's important that even if you simplify to one of these to get an idea of what's happening, that that's intentional (and you tell the interviewers what you're doing).

A **good candidate** would work through a number of the steps below to gradually get towards their answer, and the **best candidates** would do so in a clearly structured and logical way. For example, starting with a statement such as, *"There are quite a few things which come to mind for this question – I think it would help to draw a few sketches of curves like a log graph, and also x^x, and maybe differentiating will help at some point. I'm going to start by sketching some simpler curves, just so I can get a feel for what's going on"*.

From this, the following pieces of information may be found:

Using log laws you can rearrange to give $x\log(x)$ – you may or may not find this useful, but it can be a helpful place to start (and is helpful if you intend to differentiate).

The point of intersection is $(1,0)$, as in a standard log curve, and $x = 0$ remains an asymptote.

Following this curve, follow up questions could include more complex functions, such as $\log{(x^3 \text{-} 2x^2)}$ – you would need to link what you found above to these specific values to build your answer.

Q21: Prove $\sqrt{3}$ is irrational.

Proofs are relatively common at interview, though this particular proof is unlikely to arise. That's because most mathematics applicants will have worked on developing proofs, including the proof that $\sqrt{2}$ is irrational as part of the specification – and the interviews intend to test how you apply knowledge, rather than what you know.

Nonetheless, there are a number of really important steps in developing any proof and generalising, which you should bear in mind regardless of the specifics of the question. For this particular example, we're going to demonstrate using proof by contradiction. In other words, we're going to assume that it is rational, and then show that the maths we get out of this just doesn't work.

A **poor candidate** may be uncertain as to what is meant by irrational, or may show a poor understanding of the intention of mathematical proof. The key point here, is that regardless of the question, proving by demonstrating something works with an example isn't a convincing proof. You need to prove that it works for *all* possible values, not just some of them – and for that you will normally need algebra.

A **good candidate** would, with prompting, give a solution including many of the steps below:

Assume that $\sqrt{3}$ is rational, this means there exist numbers a and b such that $\sqrt{3} = \frac{a}{b}$.

Importantly, a and b must *by definition* share no prime factors, otherwise this fraction could be simplified by dividing by the shared factor(s).

This can be rearranged to give $a^2 = 3b^2$.

If a^2 is divisible by 3 (which it must be given than a and b are both integers) then a must also be divisible by 3.

This means, you could set some constant, k, equal to the value when a is divided by 3, to give $(3k)^2 = 3b^2$ or $3k^2 = b^2$. This means that b^2 must be divisible by 3.

As our definition above was that a and b must be coprime (share no prime factors), we've found a contradiction. We've now proved that both a and b would have to be divisible by 3, and so our original statement cannot be correct.

Q22: Find the roots of the curve $y = \sin(x^2) - x$

This is a fairly standard rearrangement question, at least at first glance. The best thing that you can do when answering these questions is to persevere, even if you feel you've hit a wall. Ultimately, if you're going completely wrong the interviewers are likely to give you prompts and discussion points to highlight other areas to think about. So, don't worry about whether you're going in the right direction too much, as long as you're going somewhere.

A **poor candidate** may be able to identify that the roots will be when $y = 0$, but then get stuck at $\sin(x^2) = x$.

A **good candidate** may get stuck with the equation in $\sin(x^2) = x$ or $x^2 = \sin^{-1}(x)$ form. They would then refocus, to attempt to get some kind of understanding of what is going on graphically. Figuring out how many roots there would be, and approximately where they would be, is a great start to this question. In order to do this they would need to sketch $y = \sin(x^2)$ and $y = x$ and find the point of intersection. (Take a look at some of the other curve sketching questions in the book if you get stuck with this).

The **best candidates** may instead simplify to $\sin(x) = x$. This is a common 'small angle approximation' but how true is it? The crux of this question is in whether there are multiple points of intersection (if the 'x' line falls below the sine curve), or if there is only one at the origin. Once you can find whether a standard sinusoid is above or below the line $y = x$, how would the $\sin(x^2)$ curve differ?

The final answer, is that there is only one root, at $(0,0)$.

Q23: What is your favourite number?

This is one of those questions which you may have seen if you've ever googled 'oxbridge interview questions' or something similar. A lot of the articles will be full of slightly bizarre questions, which all seem like they have some kind of catch or trick to them. Hopefully you're gradually beginning to see that your interview will actually be a lot more technical than that! That being said, these sorts of questions can arise, and the most important thing you can do is keep calm and not try and find the right answer – because there isn't one!

This would very likely be one of the very first questions in an interview, and it aims to get you talking so that when you get onto the more technical questions you don't just sit in silence. So talk!

A **poor candidate** might be overly concerned with trying to seem well read or overly complicated, and as a result give an answer that they can't really have a discussion about, or which doesn't seem genuine. Very few people will actually think that 'Graham's number' is there favourite number and it's much better to give an answer you could talk about than one you couldn't.

Aside from this, there really is no wrong answer, so you could say something like:

I really like π. It's the very first number you learn about which is represented by the Greek alphabet, and I remember finding it completely bewildering at first. It's also really simple, despite being irrational and therefore infinite, and I think that there's something really magical about that.

24 is my favourite number. It's an abundant number because it's factors exceed the number, and I just find it incredibly useful because it's divisible by 2,3, and 4 – so there are lots of situations in which you'll find that if one of the numbers is a multiple of 24 everything simplifies really nicely.

'i' is my favourite number. We've only very recently learnt about imaginary numbers at school, but I just find the whole concept fascinating, and the applications in physics and engineering, for example if you're looking at electricity are really interesting. I think the idea that theory about physically observable systems would give us imaginary numbers is so surprising!

Q24: Why do we approximate many functions in maths to be sine and cosine?

This question challenges your understanding of *why* we arrange mathematical models the way we do, rather than simply *how* you go about conducting calculations and making rearrangements. The interviewers could ask similar questions about the use of exponentials and logarithms to model growth and decay, or ask specifically about applications in partial differential equations, for example, if you're applying to pure maths or a subject where the majority of applicants have studies Further Maths at A-level.

A **poor candidate** would give an answer which fails to recognise that when modelling scenarios, the use of sine, cosine, or any other model is a *choice*. Many oscillations aren't inherently sinusoidal, but are close enough that modelling in this way is the choice that we make. Therefore, an answer such as 'lots of things are just sine or cosine curves with a small amount of offset' would be largely missing the point of the question.

A **good candidate** would recognise two key features of sinusoids which make them incredibly useful for modelling:

We can do calculations and analysis on them *analytically* rather than numerically.

We can often simplify other functions into a number of sinusoids added together.

This is beneficial for a number of reasons, and you would be able to choose which scenarios you might use to illustrate this answer. But the key is that we can simplify significantly using sinusoids without a large impact on accuracy. Numerical solutions to equations are difficult to code and similarly difficult to calculate by hand, and are also limited in their accuracy anyway.

We can also use composite functions which is more straightforward with sinusoids. If this is of particular interest, this is the basis of Fourier Analysis, which you may wish to research further. It will be a constituent part of your first or second year if you are studying maths, computer science, physics, or engineering, and can be an interesting topic to look into further as part of an EPQ or further study you're carrying out as part of your application.

Q25: Given that $y = \cos(t)$ *and* $x = t^{2t}$ *Find* $\frac{dy}{dx}$

This question is not unlikely at interview, but does require you to have a knowledge beyond that which you're expected to have for admissions tests or at the beginning of your application. In general, the interviewers will expect that even if you haven't studied differentiating trigonometry or exponentials, or more advanced differentiation rules such as the chain rule, product rule, or quotient rule at the point that you first apply – you may have studied them by your interview. It is therefore particularly important to make sure that you are *at least* up-to-date on your mathematics A-level by the time of your interview, and if you're applying for maths, computer science, physics, or engineering that you have read ahead on calculus topics if you haven't studied them formally yet. Alternatively, if you attend a college where you complete all of A-level maths in the first year, make sure you revise!

With that in mind, this question requires the use of the chain rule:

Most candidates will be able to find that $\frac{dy}{dt} = -\sin(t)$.

But then the difficulty arises in attempts to find the differential of t^{2t}. The distinguishing factor between **poor candidates** and **good candidates** in this question is, primarily, in the resilience shown in tackling this second part of the question. **Poor candidates** will generally operate on the assumption that there is some piece of knowledge which they are missing which is preventing them being able to complete the question. However, it's important to bear in mind that the main purpose of interviews is to challenge your problem solving skills, so you should always work with the understanding that you can do it *if* you can find the way through!

Differentiating t^{2t} can then be completed as follows:

$x = t^{2t}$ so $\log_t x = 2t$, or alternatively $t = \frac{1}{2}\log_t x$

It is then necessary to change the base of the logarithm using the change of base formula $\log_a b = \frac{\log_n b}{\log_n a}$:

$\frac{\ln x}{\ln t} = 2t$ so $\ln x = 2t \ln t$

This can be differentiated with respect to t using implicit differentiation on the left, and the product rule on the right, to give:

$$\frac{1}{x}\left(\frac{dx}{dt}\right) = 2\ln t + 2t\left(\frac{1}{t}\right)$$

Which rearranges to give: $\frac{dx}{dt} = 2x(\ln t + 1) = 2t^{2t}(\ln t + 1)$

Finally, use the chain rule to give $\frac{dy}{dx} = \frac{dy}{dt} \times \frac{dt}{dx}$ and the final answer is:

$$\frac{dy}{dx} = -\frac{\sin(t)}{2t^{2t}(\ln t + 1)}$$

Remember, you needn't get to the final answer to give a good answer. You also would expect on a question like this to receive prompts from the interviewer, or perhaps an explanation of techniques you haven't come across (such as implicit differentiation), so that the interviewers can test your ability to assimilate and apply information quickly and accurately.

Q26: $e^x = yx$. *Does this curve have roots? If it does, find them.*

This question could ask about solutions or roots, and you should be familiar enough with the meaning of the word 'root' to be able to solve this question regardless of the language used by the interviewer.

A **poor candidate** would struggle with the form that the equation was given in, and give an answer based on the premise that 'to find roots you set one side equal to 0'. This is generally true for equations of the form $y = f(x)$ but is a common error that even strong mathematicians make when faced with an equation in another form in a high-stress situation such as their interview.

The key, therefore, is to remind yourself of how you find solutions – when the curve crosses the x-axis $y = 0$.

This then leads to a series of logical steps which most **good candidates** would be able to work quickly through. This question would, most likely, be a starting point for a more involved examination of what the curve looked like, or what the curve could be used to model.

$y = \frac{1}{x}e^x$ has roots when $\frac{e^x}{x} = 0$

The **best candidates** will be able to quickly recognise that as this curve tends to infinity the numerator will increase more quickly than the denominator, and therefore the value of $\frac{e^x}{x}$ will increase as x increases, and so will not tend towards an asymptote of zero in either direction.

This means that the curve could only have roots where the numerator equalled zero, which e^x cannot, and therefore the equation has no roots.

As a follow up exercise, you may wish to practice sketching this curve, or finding a value of x for which there is only one solution (hint: sketch e^x and $y = \frac{1}{x}$ first).

Q27: How would you prove that e is irrational?

This question is challenging for most students, as it can lead them to believe that either they *know* the proof based on their previous knowledge, or they don't and therefore won't be able to answer the question. And, it is true, that if you haven't previously seen a proof that e is irrational, you are incredibly unlikely to be able to create a proof on the spot in your interview – it took the entire mathematical community around 50 years to generate a proof in the first place, with Euler being the first to find a proof. Certainly, you're unlikely to be able to find such a proof in 20 minutes in an Oxford interview – so the question to ask yourself is why would the interviewers ask this question?

A **poor candidate** would perhaps struggle to see a way to begin the proof, and therefore may sit silently, or simply state that 'irrational means that it is a non-repeating decimal, or it can't be written as a fraction' but say little more than that.

Good candidates will give an answer which confidently displays their knowledge of *what proofs are*, even though they are unlikely to get to an answer without significant direction or prompting from the interviewers. Comments such as 'obviously you can't prove by example, as if e is irrational then it is infinite and non-repeating and so you will never be able to check all the digits' may seem obvious, but play an important part in beginning your conversation with your interviewers. Following this, you may give examples of types of proofs you're familiar with, for example 'I think you would have to do a proof by contradiction, assume that it can be written as $\frac{a}{b}$, and then find an error in the logic'.

You can find details of the proof itself in numerous resources on the internet (Fourier's proof is generally more accessible and easy to follow than Euler's if you do research this independently).

Importantly, you must return to the question of *why* from the beginning of this question. If you aren't going to find your way to a proof, why would the interviewers ask? And the reasoning is that questions such as this one give an excellent opportunity for your interview to become more of a conversation than an 'interrogation' or questioning. The interviews aim to replicate the tutorials or supervisions which you will have at university, and therefore the best way to test your ability to persevere, take on board new information, and communicate with the tutors confidently (yet politely) is by posing questions which necessitate that conversational or discursive aspect to your answer. This is how the interviewers will find the **best candidates**.

Q28: How would you derive π?

This question seeks to understand your ability to propose both practical and analytical methods for problem solving. Most candidates will be expected to have a good understanding of what π is 'the ratio of the circumference of a circle to its diameter' – and therefore to give a strong answer to this question you will need to go deeper into *how* you would be able to calculate this increasingly accurately.

A **very poor** candidate wouldn't be able to give an explanation of π such as the one above, and would therefore struggle to propose any method.

Most candidates would be expected to propose a method such as 'measure the length of the circumference and the length of the diameter of a circle, and divide to find π'.

Average candidates may propose methods which could be used to find an increasingly accurate value based on the practical method above, for example 'use the biggest circle possible, measure the lengths multiple times'.

Once this discussion had reached a lull, it is likely that the interviewers would prompt candidates to consider analytical (theoretical) methods which could be used to find the value of π. This is the area where most candidates struggle, and so you should expect this to be discussion based.

Good candidates would, with prompting, consider ways that you could find the perimeter of a shape, similar to a circle by calculation rather than measurement. They may discuss fitting a shape such as a hexagon inside a circle (with vertices intersecting the circumference), and then propose that increasing the number of sides the shape had would give increasingly similar values for the perimeter as compared to the circumference.

The **best candidates** may consider a way to find a threshold, rather than a lower bound for the values of π. For example, creating one shape with vertices intersecting the circumference gives a lower bound, and creating another with the centre of the sides intersecting the circumference (so the shape is larger than the circle) gives an upper bound. This is the basis of Archimedes' method.

Where there was time remaining, the interviewers may ask you to calculate how many sides the regular polygon would need to have to calculate π accurately to a certain number of decimal places, for example – and you should consider if you can calculate the maximum possible percentage error without needing to use your pre-existing knowledge of the accurate value of π.

Q29: How would you prove that any integer can be expressed as prime factors or is itself a prime number?

The statement that every integer can be expressed as prime factors (or is itself a prime number) is commonly called the *Fundamental Theorem of Arithmetic* (or the *Unique Factorisation Theorem*). As with the majority of proofs which your interviewers could ask about, it has (by necessity) already been proven, though it did take a number of mathematicians much longer than your interview to construct the proof. As a result, you must make sure to show your thinking and make logical, common-sense proposals for how you would structure the proof, rather than expecting to silently think your way through to a method. The majority of students <u>will not</u> construct a proof in response to this question even though the logic is quite simple once you've been shown how it works, so you need to make sure you are fully out of the 'exam' mindset in which the answer is the goal. For your interview, you must focus on explaining the method.

A **poor student** might simply attempt to prove by example for the first 5 or 10 integers. While it is useful to demonstrate your understanding of the question using an example it is important that you clearly state that you are not attempting to *prove* based on this. After all, there are an infinite number of integers, and you have a finite amount of time.

A **good student** would therefore begin by stating a few examples, with a clear comment showing that this was for their own context or to structure their own thinking. For example, $1 = 1^1$, $2 = 2^1$, $3 = 3^1$, $4 = 2^2$, $5 = 5^1$, $6 = 2 \times 3$ and so on. They may then propose types of proof which they're aware of, for example, could you use proof by contradiction, and assume that there is a number which can only be written as a product of non-prime factors before finding an error in the logic. You should expect to receive prompts and hints from the interviewers, but only if you give them something which demonstrates your own ideas for them to comment on.

The **best candidates** would form a logical argument based on this, for example:

"Assume there is a number, n, which is the smallest non-prime (and therefore can be written as a × b) *which also has non-prime factors.*

Based on our definition, 'a' and 'b' must be non-prime.

However, as 'n' is the smallest non-prime, 'a' and 'b' must, themselves, be able to be written as prime-factors.

If 'a' and 'b' could be written as prime factors, then 'n' must also be able to be written iu terms of the same primes. And therefore our original premise fails."

Following this the interviewers may ask you to prove that each integer can only be written one way (for example, there is no way to write 48's prime factorisation other than $2^4 \times 3$, excluding simply rearranging the numbers such as 3×2^4).

Q30: I drove to this interview with speed, v, and will drive the same route back. How quickly would I have to drive home for my average speed over both journeys to   be   2v?

This question is a great example of times in which your 'gut instinct' can lead mathematical calculations astray. It is also incredibly accessible, as it relies solely on knowledge of $\text{speed} = \frac{\text{distance}}{\text{time}}$, and nothing more advanced.

Poor candidates would focus on their gut instinct (perhaps the answer is '3v' so that you average 2v overall?) and fail to form coherent mathematical statements.

Most candidates would be expected to, as a minimum, define a distance 'd' which is the length of the journey, for example, even though this may not actually be used.

Good candidates may then focus on calculations, for example forming an equation such as:

Average speed $= \frac{\text{total distance}}{\text{total time}}$ where total distance can be calculated as $vt_1 + v_2 t_2$.

This then gives:

$2v = \frac{vt_1 + v_2 t_2}{t_1 + t_2}$ with the candidate aiming to calculate v_2 in terms of v.

This equation can be rearranged accordingly, which results in an expression for v_2 of:

$v_2 = \frac{vt_1 + 2vt_2}{t_2} = v\left[\frac{t_1}{t_2} + 2\right]$

This is where the majority of candidates will get stuck, because you know very little about t_1, t_2 or their ratio. However, **good candidates** will return to the question to consider any information they may have that they haven't used yet – namely, the distance for each of the journeys is the same. Using $d = vt_1 = v_2 t_2$ gives a ratio for $\frac{t_1}{t_2} = \frac{v_2}{v}$. This therefore gives:

$v_2 = v\left[\frac{v_2}{v} + 2\right] = v_2 + 2$ which is clearly contradictory.

In other words there is no possible solution for v_2.

The **best candidates** will then attempt to put this into context (particularly given that this is counterintuitive at first glance for most people). A statement such as 'to have twice the average speed overall, you would need to travel twice the distance in the same time' – in other words the return journey would have to take no time at all' would be excellent here.

Moving on from this, you may have a discussion of the differences between time-averaged, and distance-averaged speed and the implications of the different averages on calculations such as this one.

Q31: What's the sum of all the positive integers?

This question, perhaps surprisingly, tests your understanding of sequences and series, as well as your ability to discuss difficult mathematical concepts such as 'infinity' intelligently.

A **poor candidate** might make a statement such as 'you can't get a sum' or 'it's infinite' and then fail to engage with further discussion. While it is natural to give an initial answer such as this, you should make sure to leave the door open to discussion, a simple adjustment to 'well, my initial instinct is that you're adding ever increasing infinities on, so it's going to be infinite' makes it clear that you're open to discussing this further.

You should expect the interviewers to prompt you in a question such as this one, and so you may begin by considering a few simpler sums, for example, could you find the sums of the following:

$$S_1 = 1\text{-}1 + 1\text{-}1 + 1\text{-}1 + \cdots$$

$$S_2 = 1\text{-}2 + 3\text{-}4 + 5\text{-}6 + \cdots$$

A **good candidate** would make logical and clear statements when finding the sums above, for example, S_1 could equal 0 or 1 depending on where in the sequence you stopped it. Therefore, you could say that the sum to infinity was either of these numbers or, perhaps, $\frac{1}{2}$ (as an average of the two). They would also make clear links between the initial steps that they've been given and the later ones. For example, the interviewers have likely asked you to find the sum to infinity of S_1 either because it is directly useful for the later calculations, or because the skills you used are applicable – so you should use this to your advantage when considering a method for later questions.

The **best candidates** would identify that $2S_2 = S_1$ (consider the following):

$$S_2 = \quad 1 \quad -2 \quad +3 \quad -4 \quad +5\ldots$$

$$S_2 = \qquad 1 \quad -2 \quad +3 \quad -4\ldots$$

$$1 \quad -1 \quad +1 \quad -1 \quad +1 = S_1$$

From this, a similar rearrangement can be undertaken to write the original sequence $S = 1 + 2 + 3 + 4 + \cdots$ such that $S\text{-}S_2 = 4S$, from which the conclusion that the sum of all the integers is $-\frac{1}{12}$th follows.

While you should expect prompting and direction in order to find your way through the proof, you would need to demonstrate your ability to comment on this result (does it match your expectations?) and its implications clearly.

Q32: What is the probability that two people in a lecture hall containing 30 people share a birthday?

This is a classic mathematical brain-teaser (look up the 'Birthday Problem' if you're interested in reading more), and is such is relatively unlikely to arise in an interview because there's just too much risk you'll have seen it before! However, it does demonstrate a number of very important points about the somewhat counterintuitive nature of probability, which are transferrable to a wide range of questions.

The first thing in this question is to break it down into a smaller question. What's the probability that a person's birthday is on a given day of the year? This is fairly straightforward to approximate as $(\frac{1}{365})$ and all candidates would be expected to make it at least to this value. **Good candidates** may recognise that this is actually based on a significant assumption, that birthdays are evenly distributed throughout the year, which isn't actually the case in reality. An **excellent candidate** may consider this and attempt to draw a conclusion about the effect of the assumption on the final calculation. In fact, if people are considerably more likely to be born on certain days, and less likely to be born on others, then the chance of two people being born on the same day would be higher than we will calculate with the value above. This is therefore a calculation of the 'worst-case' (which is always the best way for your mathematical model to be!).

Following this, it quickly becomes very difficult to figure out how to calculate the probability that two people are on the same day. It is much quicker to instead ask, what is the probability that none of the people share a birthday? To be a **good candidate** in your maths interview, you must be comfortable adjusting and adapting the question if the first attempts you make aren't going anywhere, and this is a prime example.

The solution then follows:

Let person 1 have any birthday (probability = 1, it is certain that their birthday is on one of the days of the year). In order to not share a birthday, person 2 would have a choice of the remaining 364 days of the year (364/365), with person 3 having a choice of 363/365, and so on.

These can be collected to calculate the probability that no one shares a birthday, and then the answer found as 1 minus the value calculated above. If you're attempting the solution here, the answer you should arrive at is that there is a **70.6%** chance that 2 people in the group of 30 share a birthday, though of course do remember that reaching the answer is of significantly less importance in the interview than being able to make logical conclusions as you work.

Follow up questions may ask whether this value surprises you, or what the minimum number of people you would need to have in a group is for it to be more likely that two people share a birthday, than that no one does (p>50%). Alternatively, how many people do you have to have in your group for it to be pretty much certain (99%+) that two people share a birthday? Could you plot a graph of how the probability is varying?

Q33: Find $\frac{d}{dx}[y\sin(y)]$

This question will be fairly run of the mill if you've completed 'implicit differentiation' in your studies before your interview. This is why it's worth reading ahead on differentiation and integration from second year maths prior to your interview to familiarise yourself with some of the key techniques. If you haven't previously seen implicit differentiation it should still be solvable, based on your understanding of differentiation using the chain rule and a bit of algebraic rearrangement.

A **poor candidate** would, as a result of the unfamiliar way in which the question is posed, attempt to answer a different question. Common errors include rearranging '$y\sin y$' by equating it to '1' to give $y = \frac{1}{\sin y}$ or even $y = \frac{1}{\sin x}$ to be differentiated.

An **average candidate** may differentiate with respect to 'y' rather than x. In which case the standard chain rule can be used, with $u = y, v = \sin y$, and $u' = 1, v' = \cos y$ to give $\frac{d}{dy}(y\sin y) = \sin y + y\cos y$. However, they wouldn't be able to adapt this to consider how to differentiate with respect to x.

A **good candidate** would likely require prompting to consider the chain rule, but then may be able to create a generalised result such as:

$$\frac{d}{dx} = \frac{d}{dy} \times \frac{dy}{dx}$$

In other words, the differential with respect to x can be found by doing the differential with respect to y, multiplied by $\frac{dy}{dx}$.

The **best candidates** would then revisit the chain rule results from earlier, in order to ensure that the $\frac{dy}{dx}$ terms were multiplied in appropriately (avoiding the temptation to simplify multiply the entire expression without certainty or justification).

The calculation is therefore:

$$u = y, v = \sin y, \frac{du}{dx} = 1 . \frac{dy}{dx}, \frac{dv}{dx} = \cos y \left(\frac{dy}{dx}\right)$$

This gives:

$$\frac{d}{dx}[y \sin y] = \frac{dy}{dx} \sin y + y \cos y \left(\frac{dy}{dx}\right)$$

Q34: What can you tell me about Fermat's Last Theorem?

While questions about your personal statement are less likely to arise in Oxbridge interviews than at other universities, it is essential that you prepare for them and prepare for them well. Many students who apply for maths will talk about a mathematical or scientific concept such as Fermat's Last Theorem as one of the areas of maths which inspired them or led to their interest. You should prepare for the "What can you tell me about...?" questions that may come up based on your interests.

A **poor answer** to a question such as the one above would demonstrate little to know understanding of the actual concept which had been discussed in the personal statement. Or would focus on passive activities which you had carried out such as 'I read a really interesting book about it'. While showing evidence of wider reading is important, the act of reading itself is not something which will make you stand out from the crowd! So you should take this as an assumption, rather than something for you to discuss.

A **good answer** to a question such as this one, would show that you understood the concept you had chosen to discuss, and also have an awareness of the areas you don't understand. Many candidates give poor answers because they want to avoid talking about areas they don't understand in their interview (understandably) and the result is that they seem as though they have failed to grasp the complexity of the topic they're discussing. It took world leading mathematicians hundreds of years and entire new branches of mathematics to prove Fermat's Last Theorem, for example, so there are going to be bits which you don't understand!

The resulting answer might therefore include some of the following comments or discussion points as a start:

"Fundamentally, Fermat's Last Theorem states that Pythagoras's equation doesn't work for any integer power which is greater than 2 and which was only publicly proved very recently. The thing that I found really interesting about that was just how simple it was, but because it's proving a negative it's so much more challenging than finding a single example that works if you were proving a positive"

If you're applying for mathematics at Oxford, then it is worth bearing in mind that the Mathematical Institute (where you will attend your lectures) is in the Andrew Wiles building, named after the Oxford Mathematician who finally provided the proof.

Q35: Derive the equation for the volume of a sphere. ($V = \frac{4}{3}\pi r^3$)

This question tests your understanding of integration, and your ability to adapt techniques you may have previously learnt in school (such as 'volumes of revolution' to increasingly challenging situations.

A **poor candidate** would struggle to find a starting point to the question, and *importantly* fail to aid their own collection of information to develop a method. Even if you didn't know how to approach a question like this one, the very best thing you can do is draw a diagram. You will struggle to draw too many diagrams in an interview, but it is easy to draw too few!

A **good candidate** may begin by simplifying the question, or asking a separate question which they think they are more likely to be able to answer as a 'way in' to the method. For example, many candidates begin by attempting to derive the equation for the area of a circle (πr^2) first. To do this, you would have to first create an equation for a circle, such as $r^2 = x^2 + y^2$. If you intend to integrate to find the area with respect to x, this then gives you $x = \sqrt{r^2 \text{-} y^2}$. You would then have to develop limits, and decide whether you need to differentiate solely with respect to x, or also with respect to y.

The **best candidates** may begin to transition (using prompting) to polar co-ordinates. If integration with respect to x is 'summing' infinitesimally small rectangles, than could you integrate in a circle (with respect to θ) and sum infinitesimally small segments of the circle instead?

Importantly, you must also show an understanding of where your volume of revolution formula comes from, rather than just using it as a quotable result, in order to be able to adapt it appropriately for this question.

Q36: Sketch the graph of $y = e^{(x^x)}$

In this question a **poor candidate** might sketch an exponential graph, and then simply make it steeper in order to account for the additional power of x.

A **good candidate** will attempt to break the question down into more manageable steps, which is important to ensure that no points are missed. The most common error students make on this question is in point testing with positive values (e.g. e^{2^2}, e^{3^3}) and simply drawing a steeper exponential curve. However, if you consider $e^{-1^{-1}}$, $e^{-2^{-2}}$ and $e^{-3^{-3}}$ then you will see that there is something slightly unusual which happens in the negative quadrant. It's also important to try and outline the areas which you're going to look at, so that you show a clear and logical approach. *"There are quite a few things which come to mind for this question – I think it would help to draw a few sketches of curves like an x^x curve and an exponential, and maybe differentiating will help at some point. I'm going to start by sketching some simpler curves, just so I can get a feel for what's going on".*

Key points for this curve are:

It crosses the y-axis at $(0, e)$ and there are no roots on the x-axis.

Differentiating gives $x^x e^{(x^x)}(\ln|x| + 1)$ - this could equal zero if any of the three terms follow the rules: $x^x = 0$, $e^{(x^x)} = 0$, $\ln|x| = -1$. As a result there's a local minimum at $x = \frac{1}{e}$ – the **best candidates** would begin to explore why other maxima or minima don't appear this way?

It's important to bear in mind here that you could spot what the curve would looks like very quickly, and do a poor interview, or fail to get through to a solution and still get your offer – so don't worry about how the solution is going as you're doing it!

Q37: Sketch the graph of $y = x^{e^e}$

Based on the discussion and information gleaned in the previous question, the interviewers may then move on to a related question, to test your ability to extrapolate and work more quickly through the second question.

The important thing in questions such as these is that you don't get too focused on the similarities at the expense of checking your working in context or keeping your eye on the big picture.

In this question, a **poor candidate** will immediately jump to the previous equation – or perhaps the differentiation result they found previously. Common errors include stating that $\frac{d}{dx}e^{(x^x)} = x^x e^{(x^x)}(\ln|x| + 1)$, and therefore $\frac{d}{dx}\left(x^{e^e}\right) = e^e x^{(e^e)}(\ln|e| + 1)$. While this is tempting, you should make sure that you correctly identify where the variables and constants are (for example x^{e^e} is essentially simply a polynomial to be differentiated.

Good candidates would ensure both attention to detail and a thorough consideration of the areas of importance. In this case, for example, your differential would be $e^e x^{e^e - 1}$, which will therefore equal 0 when x is 0. Similarly, recognising that this is simply a polynomial with order e^e (very approximately 4) can simplify your thinking significantly.

You need to ensure that the final curve has (as a minimum) the point of intersection with the axes at the origin. You also *must* consider which quadrant (above or below the axis) the negative x values would fall within. For practice, it is worth plotting polynomials with non-integer order, in order to check your understanding. For example, plots of $x^{1.5}, x^{2.5}, x^{3.5}$ would all be illustrative of the wider pattern or trend which you would want to be able to spot here.

Q38: What is the value of studying mathematics to everyday life?

This question would most likely be a warm up or 'ice-breaker' question. The primary aim of questions like this is slightly different from the other questions you'd be asked in your interview. Whereas the majority of an Oxbridge interview in maths and related subjects will be technical, subject specific, or problem solving based, these questions aren't. The purpose of these, then, is two-fold. Firstly, they generally check your motivation for the subject by asking about your experience, personal statement, or understanding of the course and university you're applying to. Secondly, and perhaps more importantly, they get you talking! It's important to remember that there isn't a 'right answer' here, so you shouldn't second-guess yourself trying to find one. Instead, use these ice-breakers as an opportunity to start your conversation with the interviewers, and you'll be a lot more likely to talk through your methods in later questions too!

A **poor answer** to this question might suggest that mathematics has little value to everyday life, or conversely make a sweeping (but unsubstantiated) statement that it's the only thing of value, *"everything is maths"* but without qualification.

A **good answer** would draw on your own personal areas of interest – because how you determine value is uniquely personal. You may, for instance, attempt to show that it has economic value, or social value, in facilitating the creation of new or innovative technologies. Alternatively, you might focus on the value of knowledge exploration and creation for its own sake. Importantly, as there is no right answer, the one you can give with the most conviction would be the one which reflects the reasons you've applied for your subject – not what you think they might want to hear.

Q39: How would you calculate the total number of possible moves in a game of chess?

This question may seem as though it unfairly disadvantages you if you're unfamiliar with the game of chess! However, it is important to note that in questions such as this one, you are asked 'how would you calculate' rather than 'calculate' and so you need only lay out a method (e.g. "I would need to know this piece of information, and this piece of information, from which I could calculate...") rather than needing to be able to give or substitute in numbers.

A **poor answer** in this question would get too involved with what can be done in a game of chess. Some students will attempt to work out the number of possible board states after the first move: "*In the first move there are 8 pawns which can move either 1 or 2 spaces forward, which is 16 moves. Plus the two knights could move, and there are 4 possible spaces in total they could go to. So after the first move there's 20 board states.... Then the second move happens and there are...*". While this is a good start to an answer, it does risk getting so caught up in finding a number that it doesn't show an understanding of the bigger picture.

A **better answer** would begin with more of an overview, for example "*I think there are two key pieces of information you'd need, one would be an idea of how many more possible board states there are on average after each turn, and the other would be an idea of the number of turns*".

The **best answers** would show an appreciation of the limitations of using averages in each of these cases, and may begin to fill in some of the numbers if they could (for example, after the first turn there are already 400 possible board states).

The numerical answer to this question is generally accepted to be around 10^{123}, which is named Shannon's number after one of the founders of modern information theory. Although no one ever calculates the number in their interview – there isn't time!

Q40: Is there a difference between ∞ and 2∞?

Infinity is an exciting concept for most mathematicians! Importantly though, its one which is easy to get lost in, or, without having studied number or set theory, one which is very difficult to fully grasp. This question would therefore be less about your initial gut reaction and focus more on your ability to interact with the interviewers as they probed your thinking or gave you additional information which may support or contradict your previous arguments. It is very important to give yourself time to think in these discussion heavy questions, as it can be easy to get muddled up in what you've previously said when trying to answer quickly. There is, however, a balance between answering quickly, and answering thoughtfully. So while you don't want to sit in quiet contemplation for too long, you should always take a couple of deep breaths to buy yourself time to think.

What constituted a poor or strong answer would therefore depend more on how you responded to interviewer prompts than any substance of your original argument (given you're unlikely to have previously considered the implications of set theory in detail). However some key points are:

A **poor answer** would include a definitive statement of 'yes' or 'no' with little by way of justification. If you're unsure how to answer, or can't think of a justification it's okay to say something like "*I know from some reading I've done that there isn't really a difference, because there aren't bigger or smaller infinities, but it is something which seems contradictory and hard to justify*". Remember, they're not expecting you to know *everything* or what would they have to teach you once you arrived!

A **good answer** may argue either that there is a difference, or that there isn't. It has been proven that there are only two kinds of infinity, and that infinity is better thought of as a state of many values or a set, rather than being a number which you could write as '2 x infinity' – but this isn't something they're expecting you to know. Importantly, the answer would be good if it responded to examiner hints thoughtfully, *"surely 1+ a number is bigger than the original number"* might be met with a statement that *"infinity isn't a number you find on any number line, so while 1+ a number is bigger, that doesn't apply to a concept of infiniteness"*, for example.

Q41: How would you prove that 3^n-1 is even for any integer value of n?

Proof questions are relatively common in Oxbridge interviews, so you should ensure that part of your preparation at least covers the basics of what proof is. Importantly, in a mathematical proof you must show that something will be true for all relevant values, which generally can't be done by example. The most relevant kinds of proof are proof by contradiction and proof by induction, whereas to disprove something you need only find a counterexample.

In this question a **poor answer** wouldn't progress beyond substituting a few values of 'n' in and showing it works for those. Likewise, candidates can sometimes make statements such as *"obviously with 3^n you're just multiplying by 3 each time and if you keep multiplying by odd numbers it must be odd"*. While this statement is correct (and is a helpful observation to build on), you can't use a statement such as this as part of a convincing proof, it's a bit like saying *"it just is"* as part of a 'show that' style exam question!

A **good answer** would, either based on personal experience or under prompting by the interviewers take a 'proof by induction' approach to this question. Can you prove that if it is true for any value $n = k$ then it must be true for the next integer $n = k + 1$? If it is, then all you need to do is show that it works for the first value of n and you have a proof for all real numbers.

This results in working such as:

1. Show for n=1. 3^1-1 = 2. This is even.

2. Assume for $n = k$. 3^k-1 = 2a where a is some constant.

3. Calculate for $n = k + 1$. 3^{k+1}-1 = 3^k(3)-1 = $3(3^k$-1$)$ + 2

We can then substitute in the previously assumed result to get:

3^{k+1}-1 = 3(2a) + 2 = 6a + 2 = 2[3a + 1]. This is even (can be written as a multiple of 2)

Therefore if this is true for any value of n (e.g. n=1) then it's true for the next (n=2) and the next, and so on.

Q42: If you have 120cm² of cardboard to make a (cuboid) box – what's the maximum volume the box could have? Prove this is the maximum.

This question, and similar optimisation questions, can commonly arise in mathematics or maths and computer science interviews in particular, as well as in tangentially related subjects such as economics. Optimisation questions are often incredibly easy to ask 'how would you make the biggest box?' or 'how would you find the shortest route?' and as a result fit the Oxbridge interview style very well – being easy to ask yet difficult to answer.

For this question a **poor answer** would attempt to make an educated guess, or several, taking a 'brute force' approach to this calculation. While substituting in numbers is never a bad idea to get an idea of the scale of the problem you're dealing with, it certainly won't form a conclusive or persuasive proof. Other common mistakes in this question are in failing to use the value of '120' correctly. Many students will decide that the most efficient shape is likely to be cubic, and then will divide the 100 by 3 for each of the dimensions. However, if you had a 40 x 40 cm box the surface area of a single face would exceed the total amount you have – so be careful.

A **good answer** would attempt to form an equation, and would start by drawing a diagram! If you have a cuboid with dimensions x, y, and z. Then you can form the following equations:

$$xyz = V$$

$2xy + 2xz + 2yz \leq 120$ and therefore $xy + xz + yz \leq 60$

In this case you have 2 equations and 3 unknowns, so it isn't immediately solvable at this point. The key however is in differentiating – and the **best answers** will recognise that you can differentiate to find the change in volume with respect to x, y, or z.

Using the assumption that the shape will be cubic will get most students to their answer - $V = 40\sqrt{5}$. However, the key here is proving it – and so the **best candidates** will use their differential equations in order to verify that their answer is a maximum.

READING LISTS

The obvious way to prepare for any Oxbridge interview is to read widely. This is important so that you can mention books and interests in your personal statement. It is also important because it means that you will be able to draw upon a greater number and variety of ideas for your interview.

Make a record of the book, who wrote it, when they wrote it, and summarise the argument. This means that you have some details about your research in the days before the interview.

Reading is a passive exercise. To make it genuinely meaningful, you should **engage with the text**. Summarise the argument. Ask yourself questions like how is the writer arguing? Is it a compelling viewpoint?

Quality over quantity. This is not a race as to how many books you can read in a short period of time. It is instead a test of your ability to critically analyse and synthesise information from a text – something you'll be doing on a daily basis at university.

ECONOMICS:

- The Economist / The Financial Times
- Steven Levitt: *Freakonomics*
- Partha Dasgupta Economics: *A Very Short Introduction*
- Paul Krugman: *End this Depression Now!*
- Robert L Heilbroner: *The Worldly Philosophers*
- Dan Ariely: *Predictably Irrational*

PPE:

- J.S. Mill: *On Liberty*
- Jeremy Bentham: *Defence of Usury*
- Niall Ferguson: *The Ascent of Money*

HSPS

- Karl Marx: Communist Manifesto
- Hogg & Vaughn: *Social Psychology*
- Schaffer: *Introducing Child Psychology*
- Durkin Blackwell: *Introducing Child Psychology*
- Schaffer: *Making Decisions About Children*
- Manfred Steger Globalisation: *A Very Short Introduction*
- Jan Art Scholte Globalization: *A Critical Introduction*
- Colin Hay: *Why we Hate Politics*
- Andrew Gamble: *Politics and Fate*
- Bernard Crick Democracy: *A Very Short Introduction*
- Joy Hendry: *An Introduction to Social Anthropology*
- Chris Browne & Kirsten Ainley *Understanding International Relations*
- Nicholas Abercrombie: Sociology: *A Short Introduction*

MATHS:

- *The Man Who Knew Infinity*: Robert Kanigel
- *A Mathematician's Apology*: GH Hardy
- *Fermat's Last Theorem*: Simon Singh
- *Game, Set and Math*: Ian Stewart

FINAL ADVICE

Before Your Interview

Make sure you understand your curriculum; your interview will most likely use material from your school courses as a starting point.

Remind yourself of the selection criteria for your subject.

Read around your subject in scientific articles and books, visit museums, watch documentaries, anything which broadens your knowledge of your favourite topics while demonstrating your passion for your subject. They may ask you at the interview which articles you've read recently to check you are engaged with the subject. Scientists should try New Scientist's online articles to start you off; TED talks are also a great way to be quickly briefed on cutting-edge research, and it's more likely you will remember the name of the researcher, etc.

Practice common questions or sample questions – this is better done with a teacher or someone you are less familiar with or who is an experienced interviewer.

Make up your own questions throughout your day: Why is that flower shaped like that? Why is that bird red-breasted? Why does my dog like to fetch sticks? What did I mean when I said that man wasn't 'normal', and is this the criteria everyone uses? How do I know I see the same colours as others?

Re-read your personal statement and any coursework you are providing. Anticipate questions that may arise from these and prepare them in advance.

Read and do anything you've said you've done in your application – they may ask you about it at the interview!

Check your interview specifications – what type of interviews you will have for which subjects, how many there will be, where, when, and with whom they will be so there are no surprises.

ON THE DAY OF YOUR INTERVIEW

Get a good night's sleep before the big day.

If you are travelling from far away, try to arrive the night before so that you're fresh in the morning. Getting up early in the morning and travelling far could tire you out and you might be less focused whilst being interviewed. Many colleges will provide you accommodation if you're travelling from a certain distance away.

Take a shower in the morning and dress to your comfort, though you don't want to give a sloppy first impression – most opt for smart/casual

Get there early so you aren't late or stressed out before it even starts.

Smile at everyone and be polite.

Don't worry about other candidates; be nice of course, but you are there for you, and their impressions of how their interviews went have nothing to do with what the interviewers thought or how yours will go.

It's OK to be nervous – they know you're nervous and understand, but try to move past it and be in the moment to get the most out of the experience.

Don't be discouraged if it feels like one interview didn't go well – you may have shown the interviewers exactly what they wanted to see, even if it wasn't what you wanted to see.

Have a cuppa and relax, there's nothing you can do now but be yourself.

The Most Important Advice...

❖ Explain your thought processes as much as possible – it doesn't matter if you're wrong. *It really is the journey; not the destination that matters.*

❖ Interviewers aren't interested in *what you know*. Instead, they are more interested in *what you can do* with what you already know.

DON'T be quiet – even if you can't answer a question. How you approach the question could show the interviewer what they want to see.

DON'T rely on the interviewer to guide you every step of the way.

DON'T ever, ever, ever give up.

DON'T be arrogant or rigid –you are bound to get things wrong, just accept them and move on.

DON'T expect to know all the answers; this is different than school, you aren't expected to know the answer to everything – you are using your knowledge as a foundation for original thoughts and applications under the guidance of your interviewer.

DON'T think you will remember everything you did/wrote without revising.

DON'T be afraid to point out flaws in your own ideas – scientists need to be self-critical, and the interviewer has already noticed your mistakes!

DON'T be defensive, especially if the interviewer is hinting that your idea may be on the wrong path – the interviewer is the expert!

DON'T get hung up on a question for too long.

DON'T rehearse scripted answers to be regurgitated.

DON'T answer the question you wanted them to ask.

DON'T lie about things you have read/done (and if you already lied in your personal statement, then read/do them before the interview!).

DO speak freely about what you are thinking and ask for clarifications.

DO take suggestions and listen for pointers from your interviewer.

DO try your best to get to the answer.

DO have confidence in yourself and the abilities that got you this far

DO be prepared to discuss the ideas and problems in your work.

DO make many suggestions and have many ideas.

DO show intellectual flexibility by taking suggestions from the interviewer.

DO take your time in answering to ensure your words come out right.

DO research your interviewers so that you know their basic research interests. Then ensure you understand the basics of their work (no need to go into detail with this).

DO prepare your answers to common questions.

DO answer the question that the interviewer has asked – not the one you want them to!

DO practice interviews with family or teachers – even easy questions may be harder to articulate out loud and on the spot to a stranger.

DO think about strengths/experiences you may wish to highlight.

DO visit www.uniadmissions.co.uk/example-interviews to see mock interviews in your subject. This will allow you to understand the differences between good and bad candidates.

Afterword

Remember that the route to success is your approach and practice. Don't fall into the trap that *"you can't prepare for Oxbridge interviews"*– this could not be further from the truth. With targeted preparation and focused reading, you can dramatically boost your chances of getting that dream offer.

Work hard, never give up, and do yourself justice.

Good luck!

This book is dedicated to my grandparents – thank you for your wisdom, kindness, and endless amounts of love.

Acknowledgements

I would like to express my gratitude to the many people who helped make this book possible. I would like to thank *Dr. Ranjna Garg* for suggesting that I take on this mammoth task and providing invaluable feedback. I am also grateful for the 30 Oxbridge tutors for their specialist input and advice. Last, but by no means least; I am thankful to *David Salt* for his practical advice and willingness to discuss my ideas- regardless of whether it was 4 AM or PM.

About Us

We currently publish over 85 titles across a range of subject areas – covering specialised admissions tests, examination techniques, personal statement guides, plus everything else you need to improve your chances of getting on to competitive courses such as medicine and law, as well as into universities such as Oxford and Cambridge.

Outside of publishing we also operate a highly successful tuition division, called UniAdmissions. This company was founded in 2013 by Dr Rohan Agarwal and Dr David Salt, both Cambridge Medical graduates with several years of tutoring experience. Since then, every year, hundreds of applicants and schools work with us on our programmes. Through the programmes we offer, we deliver expert tuition, exclusive course places, online courses, best-selling textbooks and much more.

With a team of over 1,000 Oxbridge tutors and a proven track record, UniAdmissions have quickly become the UK's number one admissions company.

Visit and engage with us at:

Website (UniAdmissions): www.uniadmissions.co.uk

Facebook: www.facebook.com/uniadmissionsuk